MW01259715

IT RAINS FISHES

Legends,
Traditions
and the Joys
of Thai Cooking

KASMA LOHA-UNCHIT

WATERCOLORS BY
Toby Goodenough

DRAWINGS BY
Margaret DeJong

Pomegranate Artbooks
SAN FRANCISCO

Published by Pomegranate Artbooks
P.O. Box 6099, Rohnert Park, California 94927

Text © 1994 Kasma Loha-unchit
Watercolors © 1994 Toby Goodenough
Pencil drawings © 1994 Margaret DeJong

Library of Congress Cataloging-in-Publication Data

Loha-unchit, Kasma.
      It rains fishes : legends, traditions and joys of Thai cooking / Kasma
Loha-unchit : watercolors by Toby Goodenough : drawings by Margaret
DeJong. — 1st ed.
          p.   cm.
      Includes index.
      ISBN 0-87654-356-5 (pb)
        1. Cookery. Thai. 2. Thailand—Social life and customs.
I. Title.
TX724.5.T5L64   1995
641.59593—dc20   94-49451
                                               CIP

Designed by Bonnie Smetts Design

First Edition

Printed in Korea

To Mother,

who taught me how to cook;
and to the heartful country folk
of Thailand, whose way of life
in harmony with the land is
threatened by the encroachment
of modern development

CONTENTS

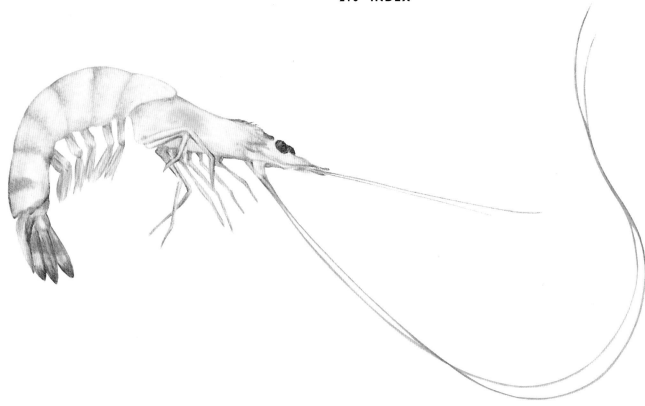

IT
RAINS
FISHES

Legends,
Traditions
and the Joys
of Thai Cooking

KASMA LOHA-UNCHIT

Pomegranate Artbooks
SAN FRANCISCO

Growing up in Thailand is a most wondrous gift! The land is lusciously endowed with natural abundance, and the waters teem with the fullness of life. Amid thick, lush jungles and nature's wild groves, a mosaic of cultivated rice fields and orchards graces the land. With the nurturance of such natural resources, it is no wonder that the faces of the people shine bright with happiness. It is also little wonder that one of the joys of the Thai people centers around food and the sharing of food.

A cherished saying, *Nai näm mee bplah, Nai nah mee kao,* dates back to the dawn of the kingdom's history some seven hundred years ago in the Sukotai era (Sukotai means "Dawn of Happiness"). The saying literally translates as: "In the water there is fish, in the fields there is rice." It reminds the Thai people of the roots of their prosperity and is taken from a larger inscription on stone tablet, the oldest discovered evidence of the Thai alphabet. The inscription is attributed to the Great King Ramkamhaeng, the beloved father of the nation:

This Sukotai is good:
In the water, there is fish
In the fields, there is rice
Whoever wishes to trade
may trade
The king does not take advantage
of his subjects
The faces of the people shine
bright with happiness
This is prosperity.

Thailand is still rich with rice and fish, and both are the main staples of the Thai diet today, as much as they were during the days of Sukotai. Recent statistics show the average Thai consumes 350 pounds of rice per year. This translates to almost a pound a day of the nutritious grain consumed in various forms, from basic steamed rice to almost endless varieties of rice noodles, crackers and cakes.

The central heartland of the country, fed by several large rivers, is much like the fertile Nile River Valley. During the months of the monsoons, the rivers flood their banks with rich nutrients and life-giving waters, and the main crop of rice is cultivated. With a well-established system of irrigation, a second crop is grown and harvested, making Thailand one of the world's premier producers of the grain. Travelers who drive cross-country find themselves surrounded by vast expanses of rice fields in a changing array of colors, from thick patches of vibrant green, tender shoots to the warm embracing glow of golden stalks.

During my childhood, it seemed that wherever there was a puddle of water, there were fishes swimming in it: small ones, big ones, silvery ones, black ones, ones with whiskers, ones without whiskers, some with dots, some without dots, some swimming in schools and some alone. All were very intriguing to a curious little girl who loved getting her hands and feet wet. It didn't take much convincing for me to believe that it rains fishes!

When it rains during the monsoon season, it really pours, by the bucketfuls and tubfuls, and one can get soaked in a matter of seconds. I remember that whenever dark, ominous clouds suddenly moved in uninvited to crowd out an otherwise sunny afternoon, frightening flashes of lightning and roaring thunder often followed, along with pelting rain. With a pillow over my head, I would endure. Just as quickly as they came in, the thunderstorms passed after

IT RAINS FISHES

lasting an hour or two, the sun returned and the birds were out singing again. I would waste no time in grabbing my little red pail and shovel and rushing out to the front lawn, where my brothers and I picked up fishes flipping and flopping around on the grass!

Some were tough little guys, like the *bplah maw* (or "doctor" fish) wiggling at a quick pace to get across the garden to the pond on the other end of our property. They are small, but their sharp, spiny back fins protect them from being easily caught. Of course, I got stabbed a few times before I smartened up and learned to throw my bucket over them and shovel them in. Their meat is deliciously sweet and tasty; after all, as is common knowledge among gourmet cooks, the muscle that moves the most is the tastiest part of any animal, and these little "doctor" fish really know how to wiggle their entire weight around. So, after risking painful jabs to catch them, it seemed particularly satisfying to devour them that same evening at the dinner table.

Thailand's heavy downpours often cause temporary flooding, especially on the flat lowlands of the central region. A torrent of water splashing down into a pond is sure to stir up the fishes and disorient them. Or, perhaps the fishes get excited by the big dose of negative ions from the refreshing water from the heavens and start to jump. Some jump too far or are carried by the current onto land, and when the flooding subsides quickly after the storm, they are caught in little puddles or are stranded on the grass flopping around, hoping sooner or later to find their way back into the pond. Another possibility that I cannot disallow is that a lot of fishes, much like their distant human relatives, get bored living in the confines of the same pond, day in and day out, and welcome the first opportunity to travel and experience the world beyond. Indeed, there are some fishes that possess strong instincts to migrate, from pond to pond and canal to canal, until they reach the big river and maybe even the ocean, much like the self-directed and intent little "doctor" fish.

When my cooking students and I travel around Thailand, we usually see young men and boys catching fishes in the flooded rice fields while their relatives are busy planting rice. My students are often amused by the scantily clad young men with nets or woven baskets in hand, squatting perfectly still on rocks in the middle of muddy puddles, exhibiting great patience and alertness, ready to jump at the first fish that strays within reach. Watching them reminds us of cats stalking birds or crickets in a field.

There are several varieties of fish that are able to thrive in mud during the dry season, and with the return of water during the monsoons, they can be found swimming around in the pools again. The central lowlands of Thailand are a vast alluvial plain, at sea level and below. Some parts remain marshy and boggy a large part of the year, providing a rich breeding ground for all kinds of water life. Whenever I am in Thailand, I still marvel at the abundance of fish everywhere there is water, from the smallest, most unlikely puddles and mud holes to the larger ponds and streams. And then I think of the myth I grew up with, that it rains fishes, and see that it does ring with truth. After all, if it didn't rain, there would be no water. Without water, there would be no ponds, streams or rivers, and without them, there would be no fishes.

Water is the substance of life and is especially important in the tropical country of Thailand. Many of our major festivals center around water, particularly the colorful Loy Gkratong Festival on the full moon night of the twelfth lunar month, which coincides with the end of the monsoon season. During Loy Gkratong, the water spirits are joyfully thanked for the abundance they have brought to the land and for the life they have given to the people.

I continue to enjoy the legend of raining fishes. It is certainly more credible than the Western expression "raining cats and dogs." What would we do with drenched dogs and cats, falling from the sky and chasing each other around on our front lawns? What a mess that would be! Besides, fishes are nourishing to eat, but cats and dogs falling from the heavens would require us to feed them. Furthermore, I would much rather dream of pretty little fishes falling from the sky than contemplate how Santa Claus squeezes himself down billions of chimneys in one night. I would much rather squat in front of a puddle and marvel at the life within it; I would much rather catch fishes with my brothers and help Mother prepare dinner, sharing the wonderful gifts of heaven and Earth with my family. Those little fishes continue to live within me, as they have nourished my body and soul and have helped me grow. For me, the story of raining fishes brings a richer experience of life and a deeper understanding of the interrelationship of the human family with nature and the land.

I grew up in Bangkok during the early 1950s when the city still had a quaint, small-town feeling, in marked contrast to today's frustratingly overcrowded and polluted metropolis of too many millions. Back then Gkrung Tehp ("City of Angels" or the "Celestial City"), as Thai people call it, was lush and green and still known as the "Venice of the East." People used boats for transportation—through the maze of canals (called *klong*), waterways and the immense Jao Praya River and its tributaries—as much as they drove cars on narrow two-lane roads lined with huge shade trees, *klong* and ponds.

When I was three my family moved out to the suburbs, where the firm my father managed could afford to build company homes, and I lived and grew up there until I went to America for college. During the first years after we moved, few people ventured out to visit us, complaining of the distance and the possibility of encountering snakes and other frightening wildlife in the unfamiliar country. Our property had large ponds on both sides, and beyond one of the ponds were thick woods of rattan, home to huge reptiles and other wild animals that fed off the fishes in our ponds and, occasionally, a duck or two from my mother's flock.

We had a huge expanse of land in front of the house, mostly landscaped as lawn bordered by flower gardens and at least a dozen mango trees among other tropical fruit trees and enormous shade trees. It was a most nurturing environment for me, and I recall it with great fondness. I scooped up fishes on the lawn and fished them out from puddles, and once in a while Mother would have the pond drained so that we could wade in, knee-deep in mud, to catch the larger fishes with nets and woven baskets. I also remember running a muslin-cloth net strung on a rattan frame (which doubled as a butterfly catcher) along the side of the pond to scoop up netfuls of tiny, almost transparent, fresh-water shrimps. Mother would mix them into a batter to fry up as delicious shrimp cakes, so crispy and tasty my mouth waters just thinking about them.

School was only about a mile away, surrounded by rice fields and, beyond them, cornfields. I remember those lazy afternoons when my attention would wander outside of the classroom windows and I would daydream or watch with great interest the farmer with his water buffalo tilling the land. It is hard to believe that today the countryside where I grew up is one of the most prized residential districts of Bangkok, built up with high-rise condos, millionaires' mansions, crowded apartment buildings, modern supermarkets and shopping malls. All the *klong* have been filled in and shade trees cut down to be replaced by more and more lanes of concrete road and pavement, which always seem to be jammed with cars no matter how much they are widened. My parents' home still stands where it used to, old and worn, an oasis amid all the craziness of modern life. Coconut palms, mango and guava trees and banana plants still sway out front along the grassy lawn, but the ponds have disappeared. The fishes do not jump and fill the puddles as they used to, for there are no places for them to live in between the monsoons. When it does flood during the heavy rains, garbage and city refuse fill the puddles instead. I feel sorry that my niece and nephews have not had the benefit of the precious playground that nature used to provide me.

So each year when I return to my homeland, I take off for the country, where wide expanses of greenery still roll endlessly beyond the horizon. There the fishes are still jumping and the people are still living off the bountiful land. But more and more of the precious, fertile farmland and naturally wooded hills are lost each year to encroaching development: condos and look-alike homes built in Western styles, industrial complexes and factories, international hotels and golf courses. In many places, industrial wastes have poisoned the land to the extent that rice no longer grows and the water is too toxic to support life. I only hope that Thailand does not lose sight of the symbols of abundance and prosperity upon which it was founded—a prosperity that gives life rather than takes it away, that gives freedom rather than enslavement, that benefits all and not just a wealthy minority and that reflects a responsible consideration for the interdependence of all life. I hope in the quest to develop the country, my people do not destroy the true roots of our prosperity as the forefathers of our nation so wisely recognized and preserved in writing seven centuries ago. May the leaders of the present and of the future have the foresight to know that when the land and water no longer support life, our children no longer have a home.

Like Bali, where Dewi Sri, the Rice Goddess, reigns supreme among rice-farming villages, the traditional rice-growing communities of Thailand have a high regard for Mae Pra Posop, or the Rice Mother (Mae means "mother," and Pra is "lord" or "goddess"). Elaborate ceremonies are performed in her name during various stages of rice cultivation so that she may bless the fields with bountiful harvests from year to year.

Mae Pra Posop is one of five Thai goddesses who personify the five material elements. The others are Mae Pra Plerng (Fire Mother Goddess); Mae Pra Toronee (Earth Mother Goddess), who is instrumental in helping the Buddha attain enlightenment as depicted in many temple murals; Mae Pra Pai (Wind Mother Goddess) and Mae Pra Kongka (Water Mother Goddess). "Kongka" is derived from the "Ganges" River and is honored each year by the very colorful Loy Gkratong Festival. The very fact that rice is defined as a basic element along with fire, earth, air and water shows how important rice has been in the development of Thai culture.

Rice (kao in Thai) is synonymous with food; it is the basic substance needed to sustain life and ensure survival. From rice, one receives not only nutrition but also a spiritual essence. All other foods served in a meal—meat, fish, vegetables, etc.—are considered gkap kao (gkap meaning "together with"), things that are to be eaten with rice. Unlike Western cuisine, a Thai meal features rice as the main course with meat and vegetable dishes as side courses. When mealtimes are announced, the words used—gkin kao—literally translate as a time to "eat rice."

BLESSED BY THE RICE MOTHER

THANKING THE RICE GODDESS

Most Thai people do not say grace before their meals, thanking a deity in heaven for their food. Children are taught to respect the food on the table and to eat in reverence, in a spirit of thankfulness to elders and parents who provide the gift of nourishment and make it possible for them to be there. Following the meal, they are taught to wai their empty plate (place the two palms of the hands together in a prayer position while bowing the head) to thank the Rice Mother for the nurturance the rice has just given them. Seldom will a Thai, especially in a farm village, leave rice uneaten on the plate out of respect to the Rice Goddess and to the source of the food itself.

Many of my cooking students who have traveled with me in Thailand find it very entertaining to watch my two tour assistants eat their dinner. Hard-working and hardy eaters, they down plate after huge plate of rice each evening with great gusto. Following the deep involvement in the partaking of their favorite food, it is always refreshing to see them silently bow their heads and wai their empty plates in a spirit of reverence and gratitude, thanking the food itself, personified by the Rice Mother in particular. The gratification is immediate, and so is the gratitude.

Among traditional farming families, a symbolic gesture of kindness to all living things is also made preceding a meal. The elder in the family takes some of the rice, gently rolls it in a small ball and places it on the ground outside to feed ants, birds or other small animals.

If there is any rice left after a meal, it is never thrown away but instead is saved and placed on top of the next pot of rice for the next meal. It may also be dried in the sun and preserved for later use in other rice dishes. Throwing rice away would be wasteful and an act of disrespect to the Rice Mother.

The practice of thanking the Rice Mother at the end of a meal is quickly disappearing among the younger generations, particularly among those who live in the cities and have become removed from the cycles of planting and harvesting of rice. As farm children are lured by promises of riches and a "better" life in Bangkok and other booming towns—or are forced by economic hardship to find work in cities to supplement meager farm incomes—and as modern ways of farming continue to challenge age-old agricultural methods, the traditions and ceremonies around Mae Pra Posop are regrettably becoming lost.

"GRANDMA SIX FINGERS" AND HEART VALUES

In my extensive travels throughout Thailand, some of the friendliest, most honest and openly sharing people I have had the good fortune to meet are also the most "destitute" in material terms, living within very modest means, in small villages often passed over by the occasional traveler. I remember particularly well an eighty-plus-year-old grandmother whom I call "Grandma Six Fingers" because her right hand has an additional appendage growing from the side of her small finger.

During one of the first tours I led to Thailand, we stumbled into Grandma Six Fingers's very modest rice shop in a small town above Sukotai to find some lunch. The warm welcome we received from three generations of small-village folk was most touching and much appreciated by the wonderful group of American travelers I had with me. Grandma Six Fingers was very pleased to have the honor of so many white people visiting her all at once. She seemed fascinated by the strange-looking beings from afar and was delighted to have her picture taken with everyone. She told us that she was too old and poor to travel but could perhaps make it in spirit through the photographs to America, that magical land she vaguely recalled hearing others talk about. With that remark, she beamed a most radiant smile toward the cameras pointed in her direction. Curious about foreign lands, she asked question after question of her captivated guests, and we had a lively discussion and a completely unexpected exchange.

Soon after, frail little Grandma busied herself getting this and that for us and made sure her grown children, the cooks, brought the best they had in the house for us to eat. One thing after another came streaming out of their meager kitchen. The younger ones hurried off and soon returned with luscious, tree-ripened fruits from their backyard. Grandma humbly confessed they did not have much to offer us—just simple, country food. "We country folk are poor. We don't have much in the way of material possessions, but we are rich with *näm jai.*" And this she gave us in such big doses that we came away with our spirits joyfully filled.

Näm jai is difficult to translate without losing the fullness of its meaning, for there is no close equivalent in the English language. Literally, it means "water that flows from the heart" or, in short, genuine generosity that comes straight from the heart without any expectation of return. *Näm jai* is a quality highly valued in Thai society, where the deeply rooted Theravada Buddhist tradition encourages the practice of generosity as a spiritual pathway to a more harmonious life. This "heart" quality is especially widespread among the poor rural people of Thailand. In the larger towns and big cities, though friendliness still abounds, the quality of *näm jai* seems less expansive and less profuse.

Because of my deep respect and love for Grandma Six Fingers, I try to stop by her humble abode once each year with one of my tour groups on our way up north to celebrate the festive Loy Gkratong Festival. Grandma tells me she loves those white *farang* (foreigners) and is delighted to have so many of them visit her each year. As for the *farang* who come and are able to see beneath the thin veil of material "poverty," their lives are enriched by the sweet nectar that flows from her heart.

My tour groups also frequently stop to watch farmers plant and harvest rice in the fields. Methods of planting and harvesting have changed little since rice was first cultivated in this part of Asia, and the arduous work is still done today almost entirely by hand, requiring much hard, physical labor of the farmers.

In planting rice, villagers sow rice seeds in a small patch following the first rains. It doesn't take long for the seeds to sprout and turn the patch into a thick carpet of brilliant green. The seedlings are pulled from the ground and tied with bamboo strips in small bundles, which are then distributed in the flooded fields. While the men prepare the fields, the village women, wearing their faded sarongs, long-sleeved shirts and lampshade-shaped bamboo hats for protection from the scorching sun, work together side by side to transplant the seedlings. This grueling work requires them to bend over barefoot and calf-deep in muddy waters and push the young shoots into the mud with their fingers a few at a time in evenly spaced rows.

During the harvest, men and women of the village all help each other work from one field to the next, cutting golden rice stalks heavy with grain with their sickles. The stalks are then bundled and threshed. I recall visiting a small weaving village in the north one December, only to find it deserted because everyone, including the weavers, had taken to the fields to help with the harvest. It's a village activity, a family activity. Very seldom do you see farmers working their fields alone during the major rice planting and harvesting seasons. Though it is hard work, there is much singing and laughter out in the fields. Several of my tour groups have stopped to observe and give a helping hand, only to discover that they provide more amusement than anything else to the good-natured farmers.

Watching such back-breaking activity cannot help but bring out one's compassion for the hard-working farmers and cultivate a greater appreciation for the food we eat. When we thank the food at each meal, we also remember to thank the people whose energies have made it possible for the food to be there.

TRADITIONS AND CEREMONIES AROUND THE RICE MOTHER

Thai people, like many of our neighbors in other parts of Southeast Asia, believe rice to have a "vital spirit" (*kwan*), much like the vital spirit possessed by human beings. Just as the important ceremony of *tam kwan* is performed for major milestones or crises in a person's life—such as a birthday, puberty, the

Rice Stalk (*Kao*)

aftermath of a serious illness or ordination into the monkhood—it is also performed for rice during critical stages in its life cycle, to strengthen and confirm its vital spirit.

When rice plants flower and begin to take seed, farmers look upon the rice as becoming "pregnant." At this important time, a *tam kwan* ceremony is conducted in the fields, invoking the spirit of the Rice Goddess to come and strengthen the vital spirit of the rice plants. An auspicious day is selected for the ceremony; often it will fall on a Friday because the Thai name of the day, *suk*, is a homonym of both the words for "happiness" and "ripe." Various offerings are prepared, including a ripe banana cut in small pieces, a citrus fruit of some kind (to serve as a remedy for morning sickness in pregnancy) and a few small pieces of sugar cane; in some villages the offerings may be an assortment of small cakes. These are placed in a cup made of banana leaf, called *gkratong*. A little wicker basket holding a comb, some cosmetic powder and perfumed ointment is also prepared and brought to the fields.

The farmer hangs the leaf cup with the offerings from the end of a small pole and then takes the powder and ointment, brushes them on the leaves of a rice plant and combs it as if he were dressing the hair of the Rice Mother. Following that, he calls on her, wishing her happiness and fruitfulness on the occasion of her conception, and prays that with his offerings the ancient Rice Mother will thrive and be free from danger.

A marker is then made of small bamboo strips in the figure of two interlaced triangles, called a *chaleaw*, and this is put in place in the fields. The marker serves as an announcement to neighbors and passersby that the rice plants in the fields are in the process of seeding and care should be taken not to allow their water buffaloes, cows and other domestic animals to trample the fields and cause damage to the crop. In ceremonies with ancient roots, the *chaleaw*, which resembles a rudimentary six-pointed star, is a magic symbol often used as a mystical charm to ward off evil spirits. This same magic pentacle is also frequently seen sticking out from the mouth of earthen pots in which medicinal herbs are being brewed or steeped.

Another round of ceremonies takes place at the time of harvest. In some communities, a *tam kwan* ceremony is executed just before the harvest; others perform one at the time of threshing as well. In most communities, after the harvested rice is brought to the threshing floor, farmers return to the fields to ritualistically gather stray heads of fallen rice, all the while calling out to Mae Pra Posop, inviting her to come and reside in the comfort of the barn. This last remaining rice collected from the fields is regarded as the spirit of the Rice Goddess, the life essence of the rice crop. The harvested rice is then threshed.

Following threshing, offerings of food are made to the Rice Goddess, after which all the leftover paddy on the threshing floor is picked up and stored in a bag or basket. This paddy is called Mae Pra Posop's rice and represents the essence of the rice that will be used for propagative purposes. A doll is then made from rice straw mixed with the stray heads of rice paddy gleaned earlier from the fields. This doll is a symbolic representation of the Rice Mother herself and is kept with her bag of rice in the barn. A request is made to her to remain in the barn and guard the rice that has been set aside as seeds for the next planting season.

In addition to the ancient rituals rooted in the land, some farming communities gather for a Buddhist merit-making ceremony at the paddy threshing floor. A simple bamboo pavilion is built, roofed with rice straw and decorated with garlands of golden rice stalks. An altar is set in place, holding a Buddha image and various ceremonial items including a vessel carrying the rice of the Rice Goddess. Monks are invited to come in the evening to pray and to chant verses from the scriptures, blessing the villagers and their rice crop for the next growing season. During the ceremony, the rice of the Rice Goddess and the rice to be kept as seed stock are blessed and proffered magical protection by a sprinkling of holy water before they are taken into the barn to be stored. The ceremony continues the following morning as villagers make merit by presenting offerings of food to the monks.

On the evening prior to all these ceremonial activities, a big feast is put on with lots of merriment. Usually, the more abundant the harvest has been, the more festive the celebration. The whole village gathers to sing and dance, and it is a customary time for the eligible men of the village to court the young ladies. In some areas of the country, special harvest dances and dances in honor of the Rice Goddess are performed with much gaiety.

When the next rice-planting season arrives with the coming of the rains, the Rice Mother doll, together with her stored bag of rice, is brought out from the barn. The doll is ceremonially destroyed; the grain from the heads of paddy in the doll and the special reserved rice are mixed with the other seed rice to be sown. The mixing of the spirit of the Rice Mother with the seed stock gives symbolic assurance that the seeds will be fertile and blessed in the fields. The ritualistic destruction of the doll is said to be reminiscent of the "killing of the corn spirit" in ancient times in other cultures, in which the blood from human or animal sacrifices was mixed with the soil to ensure fertility before the sowing of the grain.

THANKING THE WATER SPIRITS

There is another very important goddess closely allied with Mae Pra Posop and the cycle of rice planting, and she is Mae Pra Kongka, the Mother of the Waters. Without her gracious providence, it would be virtually impossible to grow rice as well as most other crops. Rice cultivation especially is very dependent on an abundant supply of water as the fields have to be flooded and kept wet through most of the growth cycle of the plants. In addition to her essential role in rice production, Mae Pra Kongka makes it possible for villagers to benefit from another important source of food: fish.

By the eleventh and twelfth lunar months each year—following several months of blessed monsoon rains—the rivers and klong are full, and the laborious process of rice planting is usually completed in most areas of the country. The farmers can now settle down to a more relaxed period of time, keeping an eye on their fields, fishing, gathering wild plants for food and waiting for the rice to grow and mature. During this time, villagers celebrate the abundance of the land. On the full moon night of the twelfth lunar month, which falls sometime within the month of November, there is much festivity all around the country as entire villages and towns gather to honor the water spirits and celebrate the Loy Gkratong Festival. Small and large gkratong, artfully made from banana leaves in the shape of lotus blossoms and beautifully decorated with multicolored flowers, incense sticks and lit candles, are floated down rivers and waterways in a glittering procession of lights.

Before a *gkratong* floats away in the water, the candle and sticks of incense are lit and villagers join in silent prayer to thank the Mother of the Waters for the abundance she has brought. Some prayers ask for forgiveness for having polluted the waters; others ask that the wrongdoings committed during the year be washed away so that life can begin anew; still others put forth personal wishes. Some people place a coin in their floats, symbolically wishing that their offering be returned by prosperity in the coming year; and some include a lock of hair from their own head to personalize their offerings. It is said that the prayers and wishes are granted if the candles in the *gkratong* stay lit as they float down the river until they are beyond sight. Following this beautiful and reverent gesture of gratitude and connection with nature, there is much rejoicing as people sing and dance into the night.

A RICE GODDESS FOLK TALE

A distinguished Thai scholar, Phya Anuman Rajadhon, who researched and wrote extensively on folk culture in farming communities, preserved an old folk tale from the central region about Mae Pra Posop in his book on Thai studies.[1] The tale is acutely familiar, bearing a close resemblance to the Greek myth of the Goddess Ceres and her daughter Persephone. In the story, Mae Pra Posop, for some unknown reason, had gone away to live in a faraway land and left the fields barren. In an attempt to restore fertility to the land, the Supreme Deity sent an order to the lesser gods to go find her and invite her to return. The gods searched far and wide and, with the aid of fishes, crossed the Seven Seas and the Seven Mountain Ranges. Finally, they came upon Diamond Mountain, where they found the Rice Mother. At first she was not enthused about going back with the gods, but after much coaxing, she agreed and made her grand return with a large contingent of fishes, bringing fertility and prosperity again to the land of rice fields. The Seven Seas and Seven Mountain Ranges were the legendary seas and mountains that surround the Golden Mount Meru, the cosmic mountain where the deities of the Buddhists dwell.

In rural temples, representations of the Rice Mother are sometimes found alongside statues of other goddesses. She is usually depicted as a beautiful young woman with long, flowing hair and wearing ornate traditional Thai dress. In one hand she carries a luxuriant sheaf of rice, fertile with grain. Statues of her stand on raised platforms, the sides of which are sometimes painted or carved with scenes of ponds abundant with fishes, rice stalks and blossoming lotus plants. She is indeed a symbol of fertility in the land where "in the water, there is fish; in the fields, there is rice."

1. For a detailed discourse on the traditions, customs and way of life of Thai farmers, refer to Phya Anuman Rajadhon's extensive works, published in English in *Popular Buddhism in Siam and Other Essays on Thai Studies* (Thai Inter-Religious Commission for Development and Sathirakoses Nagapradipa Foundation, 1986) and *Essays on Thai Folklore* (1988).

RICE BUCKET WAYS

Often in my growing-up days, Mother would refer to me fondly as a "rice bucket" because I was so easy to feed. As long as there was rice on the table, I was satisfied. If nothing else looked good, soy sauce over rice was enough to keep me content. I loved the taste of the rice! Mother had a way of steaming that brought out the rich taste of the grain and enhanced all the subtleties of its flavors. I learned from her the secret of how to steam "perfect rice" each time (a secret I will share with you later in this chapter).

I remember many mornings when my favorite breakfast was a fried egg over a bowl of fragrant steamed rice. The egg was covered with a sauce made of a sweet black soy sauce mixed with light soy. Mother would break the egg up into smaller pieces and mix it with the rice and sauce—yummy!

Several years ago when my nephew was seven years old, he came to America for the first time to spend his summer vacation with me. His mother had told me that he loved fried eggs for breakfast, so on his first morning in my home I made him one. Instead of digging into it as I had expected he would, he stared at it with a quizzical look for the longest time and then asked what it was that I had fixed for him. "A fried egg, of course, silly; haven't you seen one before?" I thought he was kidding with me. But he seriously replied, "It doesn't look like an egg. It's so pale." It dawned on me that he was right. The yolks of eggs in Thailand are noticeably larger, and their color is a much more vibrant golden orange. He finally took a bite of the egg and a disappointed look came over his face. "This tastes so bland. Do you have any other eggs that look and taste more like a real egg?"

The rice as well as the eggs in Thailand seem to taste much better than the varieties sold today in American supermarkets, perhaps because they are fresher and more naturally grown. Farmers' markets, however, are starting to gain momentum in many cities across California and other states. Besides all kinds of wonderful seasonal fruits and vegetables, truly fresh eggs are available direct from farmers to consumers each week.

Whenever I go to Thailand, I love to walk in the stimulating fresh open markets. They are such exciting and humanizing places to visit. In addition to the exchange of money for food, there seems to be just as much soulful exchange of human energy. The smiles and personal touches; the sweat and labor; the artful bundles and attractive piles of colorful fruits and vegetables; the sellers and buyers of different generations, cheerful young faces and weary old ones, in modern clothes and traditional sarongs; the poor and the more fortunate; the squawkers and the sweet talkers; everything moving and changing, nothing uniform or static—this is the heart and soul of the culture!

Besides rice and eggs, Thai people breakfast on a wide range of noodle soups, stir-fried noodles with vegetables, fried rice and other simple rice dishes. Frequently, breakfast is a mini-version of lunch or dinner, and among laborers, it is just as substantial as any other meal of the day. When I was growing up, leftovers from the evening before plus one or two simple, newly cooked dishes served with rice made a satisfying morning meal before the family headed off for school and office.

Another common breakfast is *kao dtom* (literally, "boiled rice"), a soupy rice mixture. *Kao dtom* can be made plain and served with a variety of salty, pickled and stir-fried dishes; or chicken, pork, fish or shrimp can be cooked in the soup and flavored with garlic, ginger, scallions and cilantro. *Kao dtom* is a breakfast borrowed from the Chinese. If it is cooked down until the rice distintegrates and becomes the texture of creamy rice cereal, it is known as *johk,* much like what the Chinese call rice soup. Both *kao dtom* and *johk* are very nutritious and highly recommended for people suffering from fatigue, digestive problems and illness. They are easy to digest and contain nutrients in ready form to be absorbed and used, thereby enabling quick revitalization of the body. What better way to "break" the "fast" of the night and begin a new day of productive activity than to partake of a vitalizing-bowl of steaming rice soup. (*Kao dtom* and *johk* shops do a brisk business in the late evening and wee hours of the morning in areas frequented by late-night revelers— there's nothing better to sober up a night of drinking!)

In some quarters, and especially in towns with sizable Chinese populations, breakfast rice soups are often served with a lightly salted fried bread called *bpah tong gkoh.* Some people make this chewy bread their main breakfast food, downing it with sweetened Thai-style hot coffee. I particularly like the smaller-size *bpah tong gkoh* that are fried to a crispy golden brown. They are delicious when freshly made. Cold *bpah tong gkoh* that has sat around for a while, however, is soggy, greasy and not worth the calories.

Western breakfasts—coffee and white toast, sausage, ham and eggs and the like—have recently replaced rice-based breakfasts among city dwellers. One of my tour assistants, for instance, thinks its "cool" to have an American breakfast; I do my best to convince my American tour groups of the goodness of Thai breakfasts.

DINING THAI-STYLE

If I am a rice bucket, then many Thais must be rice barrels! My two friends who assist with the cultural tours I lead to Thailand consume at least twice and maybe three times the amount I do at each meal. A mountain of steamed rice on the plate for starters is followed by a second helping (and often a third), after the initial mountain has been completed excavated. People on my tours are always amazed by how much rice they eat and yet remain slender and trim. The truth is that rice as a grain is not in itself fattening—in fact, it is relatively low-cal. The stuff one eats with it usually is what adds substantially to the total calories in the meal.

Unlike the way many Westerners dine, with a large chunk of meat as the main feature on the dinner plate and a small amount of buttered or flavored rice on the side, the Thai diet (and that of most Southeast Asians) consists primarily of plain, unflavored steamed rice, eaten with tidbits of spicy and highly flavored side dishes. A few bite-size pieces of chicken or meat in a curry sauce or stir-fried with chillies and basil, a few spoonfuls of hot-and-sour soup flavored with various herbs, a bite or two of fried or steamed fish and a few helpings of stir-fried vegetables or raw vegies dipped in a hot shrimpy sauce—these are all it takes to help a Thai polish up a large plate of rice and be more than satisfied. Instead of having a little bit of rice to go with the meat, the Thai way is to have a little bit of meat to go with the rice. There is no shortage of chicken, pork or beef in Thailand, but most Thai people prefer to eat more rice than meat. Meat sits heavily in the stomach and can make us sluggish following a meal as the body diverts much energy into digesting it, whereas rice satisfies our hunger without making us feel too heavy, and the spices and herbs of Thai cooking make us feel alive inside out. If you have

Rice Stalk (*Kao*)

found Thai food to be too spicy, try eating smaller amounts of the spicy foods with larger quantities of plain steamed rice.

The higher consumption of grain in the Thai diet may explain why high cholesterol and heart disease are not as prevalent in Thailand as in the Western world. New eating habits (i.e., more meats, less grain) with increasing affluence in Bangkok and other urban centers, however, have brought about a rise in cholesterol levels and the incidence of heart disease in more recent years.

Because Thai people prefer to eat off of plates rather than out of rice bowls as the Chinese and Japanese do, the primary eating utensils are a spoon and a fork. Chopsticks are not particularly practical for picking up tiny rice grains on a plate. Therefore, when you are eating at a Thai restaurant, don't ask for chopsticks. Thais use chopsticks only when they are eating noodles, and only noodles which are served in a bowl, as in noodle shops operated by the ethnic Chinese.

In the past, Thai people ate with their hands without using implements. In rural areas, many farmers and villagers today still use their right-hand fingers to pick up food at mealtimes, and in the north and northeast, where people consume a different kind of rice called sticky rice, eating with the hand is perhaps the most practical way to proceed.

The spoon and fork were first introduced by Western missionaries during the early 1800s. There is a story told of King Rama III of the present Chakri dynasty, whose curiosity about Western tableware prompted him to invite an American missionary and his wife to dinner in the palace so he could observe how they used all their intriguing implements. As international relations expanded, later kings adopted the European style of dining into the court. By the time the absolute monarchy ended in the 1930s, Western tableware had become so popular among the upper strata of society that one of the ruling field marshals decreed the spoon and fork as the nation's official dining implements. The tablespoon has since become accepted as the primary eating implement, and the fork serves the secondary function of helping guide and push morsels of food onto the spoon. So, if one is right-handed, the spoon is held in the right hand and the fork in the left.

Considering the types of food that comprise a Thai meal, it is obvious why the spoon is the primary implement. A mound of rice is piled on the plate. Little bits of food are dished onto the rice, a spoonful at a time, with accompanying sauce. Both spoon and fork mix the bits of food and sauce with some rice, and then a mouthful portion is scooped up by the spoon with the help of the fork and brought to the mouth. This way all the rice grains on the plate, the bits and pieces of accompanying food and the drops of spicy-flavored sauces are easily picked up and eaten. There is no waste, no disrespect shown to the food itself—and no risk of pimples on the face! (Some parents tell their children that if they clean their plates each meal, they will be blessed when they grow up with beautiful or handsome mates who will be dependable and good providers. But if they are untidy and leave a mess of rice grains all over the table, floor and on their plates, they risk attracting mates with faces covered with pimples, or worse yet, they may grow up with a pimple for every rice grain wasted on their own faces.)

The Thai way of dining is a family-style, eat-as-you-go, shared experience. The elder or most respected person at the table usually starts the meal, which normally consists of several non-rice dishes, usually about one dish per person plus one extra, served around rice. The more people there are, the greater the variety of dishes. There is no particular order in which the dishes are served, and this includes the soup.

The non-rice dishes are all set out on the table; they stay on the table through the meal and are not passed around. It is okay to reach over to spoon a little of this and that when desired, or if the table is long and you can't reach, those next to you will help serve you. Dining becomes a joyful ceremony in which everyone at the table seems part of an organic whole rather than separate, unrelated individuals.

When dining, the non-rice food is spooned onto one's plate a small helping at a time, enough for just one or two bites. A large portion of any dish is never taken at once in respect to others sharing the meal. It is regarded as bad manners to do so. When this serving is eaten, a little of something else is then spooned from another serving dish. After each bite, you decide what you feel like eating next, and when you are full, you simply stop. This is a way of nibble-eating; it is a fun way to eat. You become more present with the food, with yourself and your body, and with other people who are dining with you. As you pick and choose, you savor more of each bite than you would by just automatically eating what you had dished onto your plate from earlier in the meal. Also, your rice is kept relatively clean, as the juices from a previous bite of something do not alter the flavors of the present bite. This way, the variety of flavors can be preserved and appreciated. Also, overeating and wasting food are diminished as one does not take too much food on one's plate at the beginning of the meal.

Serving spoons are not often used. Traditional folk believe they separate and create distance among the people sharing the meal. Therefore, be sensitive in asking for a serving spoon (if you must) from your gracious hosts in a Thai village who have welcomed you into the intimacy of their home and accepted you as one of the family. The practice of eating out of the same dishes, of course, is gradually changing in urbanized areas in response to the hygienic concerns of modern-day living.

One of my American friends who spent some time in Thailand a few years ago was very much impressed by the way people served one another through the meal, always looking out for someone else's needs before satisfying oneself. While growing up, I was taught to serve others around me the best of the foods from each serving dish. Mother always gave away the best mangoes from our trees, and in return she received the best of other things from our neighbors and friends. When we look after everyone else around us and offer them the best, we all gain—it is a win-win situation.

"THE BEST RICE IN THE WORLD": JASMINE RICE

One day several years ago, I was in a bank in Berkeley to cash a check. The teller, a young Japanese woman, saw my unusual, long surname on my driver's license and asked where I was from. When I told her Thailand, her eyes immediately lit up and she excitedly asked, "What's your favorite rice?" The totally unexpected question threw me into puzzlement, and I was at a loss of what to say in response. "Uh, well, I like steamed rice," I managed to utter, still unsure of what she was after. "No, no. What *kind* of rice?" "Well, I usually eat a kind of rice from my country." "Yes, yes! Thai rice. Jasmine rice! That's my favorite! It is the best rice in the world! I was introduced to jasmine rice a few years ago by a Thai friend and fell in love with it. It tastes so good! I won't eat any other kind of rice any more. They are all tasteless compared to jasmine rice!" I was quite amused by her conviction and testimonial, which sounded like a miraculous spiritual conversion! But I believe what she said is true. Jasmine rice is so good that I can eat it plain, by itself, without any other flavorings.

Jasmine rice (*kao hom mali*) is a premium-grade rice from Thailand and is alternately labeled as "fragrant rice" or "scented rice." It is not artificially flavored with the essence of sweet jasmine flowers as the name would suggest. What it does have is a delicate, natural fragrance unique to the rice. It is an aromatic grain much like the better-known basmati rice from India, though the price is not anywhere near its expensive Indian counterpart. (As such, I've seen it labeled as "Thai basmati rice.") It is called "jasmine rice" because one of the favorite fragrances in Thailand comes from the *mali* flower, a very sweet variety of jasmine, and frequently those things that carry a sweet natural fragrance are referred to as being as fragrant as *mali*, or jasmine. Jasmine rice is widely available in American Chinatowns and in Thai and Southeast Asian grocery stores, as well as in some chain supermarkets and large food retailers. It is sold in 5-, 10-, 25-, and 50-lb. sacks.

"PERFECT RICE" EVERY TIME

Because of its slightly sticky quality when cooked, jasmine rice tastes best steamed. Steaming fluffs up the rice and retains the fullness of its natural, fragrant flavor. Electric rice cookers can be used for steaming, but I believe that most rice cookers do not truly steam but rather boil or simmer rice. Usually the rice at the bottom of the cooker is boiled and only the portion closer to the surface is steamed, which is why the rice closer to the top tastes much better than the mushy rice at the bottom of the pot.

But steaming rice without a rice cooker is easy, and here is an almost foolproof method to get "perfect" rice each time—with no measuring. All you need is a large pot, a heat-proof bowl that fits inside the pot and a trivet of some kind to lift the bowl off the bottom of the pot (or use an Asian steaming pot and rack set).

First, boil a kettle of water. Rinse the rice in the bowl with cold tap water a couple of times. Drain. Next, place the trivet on the bottom of the large pot and pour boiling water into it a few inches deep. Then, place the bowl with the rinsed rice in the pot, balanced on the trivet. Pour boiling water over the rice to about three-quarters of an inch above the rice line (the rice tastes better when you add hot rather than cold water to it initially). Just estimate the depth with your eye; there is no need to stick your finger into the water to measure if it is "one knuckle deep," as you may have heard from other sources. You don't want to burn yourself in the hot water, and the knuckle technique is flawed simply because some people have longer fingers than others. Don't worry if the water level is a little more or a little less than three-quarters of an inch. Within a range, this technique will work and will produce wonderful steamed rice each time. If the first time you use this method the rice turns out too mushy to your liking, use less water the next time; likewise, if it is too firm and chewy, use more water.

Asian Steamer Set

There is another factor that may effect the degree of firmness of your steamed rice, varying from one sack of rice to another. New-crop rice takes less water to cook whereas old-crop rice will absorb more water. So, if you have been cooking "perfect" rice all along and one day you buy a new bag and it dishes out wet and mushy on your dinner guest's plate, don't blame yourself. It could be that you have happened upon a bag of new-crop rice. Don't blame the rice either and throw it out as bad rice. Just know to use less water the next time you cook from this batch. The reverse situation could also happen, but such experiences are likely to be more occasional than frequent. Fortunately, new-crop rice usually will be labeled as such, so take notice when you purchase each bag of rice.

After you have covered the rice with hot water, cover the pot and steam at medium heat, or at a level where you can still hear the sound of water boiling on the bottom of the pot or see some steam escaping from underneath the lid. The rice will be done in about twenty to twenty-five minutes. You don't have to check it or stir it or watch it. Just let the steam do the job for you. If you forget about the rice and forty minutes later think of it, don't panic—your rice will be fine. Once cooked, the steam only keeps the rice warm. The rice will not overcook unless you have added too much water initially. You are more likely to burn your pot first before you burn your rice, but if you have two to three inches of water on the bottom to start out with, you shouldn't have to worry for about an hour. If you smell metal burning in the kitchen, you may still be able to save your rice. And unless you allow your pot to burn a while before removing it from the heat, you won't have to worry about rice burning into your bowl and a headache of a scrubbing job later.

After the rice is cooked, fluff it up with a spoon while it is still warm to loosen the grains before serving.

The above method will work best if you do not try to steam a small quantity of rice in a large bowl or a large quantity of rice in a small bowl. Remember that rice doubles in volume once cooked; the bowl you use should be a quarter to a half full with rice. Many of my students have developed a kind of kinship with the one particular bowl they use to cook rice for themselves and their families. They have also discovered that they like to steam more rice than is needed for one meal because leftover jasmine rice is so easy to reheat and tastes almost as good the next day or a few days later.

To reheat, put the cold cooked rice in a heat-proof dish and balance it over a trivet in a pot with one to two inches of water at the bottom. Cover and bring the water to a boil, then lower the heat and let steam about five to ten minutes, depending on the quantity you are reheating. If the rice cooked the previous day is too hard and dry to your liking or has dried out in storage, just sprinkle a little water to evenly coat the rice grains before reheating.

All of the rice grains steamed using this technique are steamed intact and none of them is boiled. Because the bowl is lifted from direct contact with the intense source of heat, the hot water added to the rice no longer boils but is gradually absorbed by the grains as they are cooked by the surrounding steam. As such, each grain of rice stays whole and retains its flavor. This method can also be used for steaming other kinds of white rice besides jasmine rice, as well as brown or wild rice, although the latter two will require the addition of more water (one inch or a little more above the rice line) and extra steaming time (about forty minutes or longer).

It is always a good idea to rinse white rice before steaming to remove whatever dust or rice polishing agents that may linger on the grain, especially if the rice is a calrose rice, which is often dusted with talc, a carcinogen. Unless calrose rice is labeled "No Talc," I advise you to stay away from it, or rinse it many times until the rinse water is clear.

Most Thai people do not cook rice using the method I have described, but it has been particular to my family for generations. As Bangkok developed and became more affluent during my years away in college, imported electric rice cookers became fashionable and replaced more traditional ways of cooking. Mother started using one and became accustomed to this modern convenience until she came to visit me a few years ago. She was impressed by how good my steamed rice tasted. When she asked how I cooked it, I told her I have always steamed rice the way she taught me in my youth. The next time I was in Thailand, Mother had put away her rice cooker and had returned to steaming rice the old way.

STICKY RICE—A SPECIAL CHEWY WHITE RICE

The people of northern and northeastern Thailand prefer to consume a variety of rice called *kao niow* or, literally, "sticky rice." Easily cultivated on the hillsides and high plateaus of these two regions, it requires less water to grow than the wet rice of the central lowlands. More commonly known as "sweet" or "glutinous" rice among other Asians, it is usually identified by either of these two names on the labels of rice sacks. (These names will also be used interchangeably to refer to sticky rice throughout this book.)

Sticky rice is a starchy grain. If steamed or boiled the same way as regular rice, the grains will break down and become soft and mushy in consistency. Instead, Thai people like to cook it in such a way that the rice grains remain whole and have a firm, chewy texture. To accomplish this, the rice is soaked for several hours until the grains have absorbed enough water to cook. Then it is drained and steamed dry in a woven bamboo basket without adding any water.

Though the grains remain whole, steamed sticky rice sticks together in a lump. Northerners and northeasterners eat with their hand, pulling off a bite-size chunk at a time and rolling the rice with the fingers and palm of the right hand roughly to form a ball. The rice ball is then dipped in a spicy sauce, or picked up together with morsels of accompanying meat, fish or vegetables. Sticky rice lends itself well to eating by hand. It is not messy because, if done correctly, the grains stick to each other but not to the fingers or the palm. Rolling the last bite of rice at the end of a meal usually sops up the remaining juices and grease from fingers and palm and effectively cleans the hand. In the rural northeast, or the Isahn region—the country's poorest and most traditional region—a recent song likens the togetherness of villagers to the sticky rice they eat, people "sticking" together and helping each other out in contrast with city folk in the central valley who have lost their ties to family and village.

Sticky rice comes in both short-grain and long-grain varieties. Thai people prefer the long-grain rice; the short-grain variety is more commonly used in Chinese and Japanese cooking. Among the long-grain varieties, some have a delicate, aromatic flavor, and these "high-grade" hybrids are distinguished as "jasmine" sweet or glutinous rice, much like their fragrant cousins in the non-glutinous family. The starchiness of sticky rice gives it a distinct opaque whiteness different from the more translucent appearance of regular rice grains, but the reverse is true after the rices are cooked. Soaked and steamed as described, sticky rice becomes translucent, while regular rice turns opaque white when cooked.

Sticky rice is consumed in other parts of Thailand as well, but usually it is sweetened and flavored with coconut milk for sweet snacks or desserts. It is especially popular during the mango and durian season when tons of the coconut-flavored rice are sold to eat along with these precious fruits. In mango season during the hottest months of the year—March through May—streetside vendors, neighborhood fruit stands and *kanom* (sweet snack) shops all over the country do a brisk business selling sticky rice along with their precious golden fruits. Large mounds of glistening grains filling enormous metal bowls may be seen alongside neatly arranged piles of yellow mangoes and odoriferous prickly durians. These are two of the favorite fruits among Thai people, and both go well with rich, creamy sticky rice.

There are many varieties of mangoes in Thailand. Depending on the attributes of the fruits during various stages of growth, some kinds are eaten only when still green, others when partially ripe and still others when fully ripe. Two of the favorites for eating fully ripe with sticky rice are *ohg rawng* and *näm dawg mai*. The first is a small mango that fits easily on the palm of a hand. Though somewhat stringy, its very sweet, juicy and distinct mango flavor make it an excellent companion with coconutty sticky rice.

The second is a delightfully fragrant, juicy mango whose name means "nectar of flowers." With a smooth, thin peel and an almost paper-thin seed, its delicate flesh, absolutely free of stringiness, is ambrosia. It melts in your mouth. Garden-grown *näm dawg mai* mangoes are highly prized and fetch lots of *baht* (Thai currency) at the market. They are worth every bit paid! In my childhood home, Mother grew at least half a dozen of these mango trees around the garden and next to the pond. Smaller and more fragile than other mango trees, they also bear fewer fruits than other varieties. The extra care and attention required during the flowering and fruiting months make their fruits ever more precious. Mother's trees were her pride and joy whenever mango season rolled around. Home-grown and better-tasting than any of the cultivated orchard mangoes, we ate our fill and never had to buy any. Some years, we were blessed with such bountiful harvests that after giving away dozens to neighbors and friends, there would be plenty left for Mother to pack in baskets and take to market to sell and trade with fresh fruit vendors.

Durians are also wonderful with sticky rice, though not all Thais would agree with me. They are controversial fruits, evoking strong emotions of either love or disgust and not much in between, mainly because of their powerful aroma. People who love durians say they are gifts from heaven, while those who dislike them say they come from a rotten-smelling hell. I am bemused by such extreme responses to a truly exotic tropical fruit, which is none other than what it is. I sometimes refer to it as the "Buddha fruit," for it serves to reinforce the teachings of the Buddha that all our worldly experiences are colored by our own personal prejudices and earlier conditionings. Indeed, I have witnessed many people tasting durian for the first time trying to compare it with something they have had in the past (without much success, of course) rather than savoring and accepting it as being just what it is.

Durian

If you have not had durian before and are game enough to try something exotic, I suggest your first experience be a supervised one with someone who knows the fruit and knows when it is at its most likable stage. Don't let the strong odor hold you back. People who like the taste usually regard the odor as fragrant and inoffensive; others cannot get past the odor to even taste the fruit.

Durians are large, oval-round fruits, ranging in size from a small to a mid-size watermelon. Their brownish green peel is thick, hard and spiky. They are pricy, costing from two to five dollars a pound in Southeast Asian markets, the average size weighing about four pounds. Inside, they are divided into podlike sections, each holding delicate, light to deep yellow custardlike fruits that are sweet, creamy and very rich. There are many varieties. Among the ones I personally regard as best-tasting are *mawn tong* ("golden pillow") and *chanee* ("gibbon"). Your first experience ought to be with a fresh whole one that is not overripe rather than with one that has been peeled and frozen. Freezing does undesirable things to a durian's texture and flavor.

Glutinous rice is also milled into flour and used to make a vast array of sweetmeats and desserts. People in the central region, comprising the country's heartland, consider sticky rice to be too heavy to eat in large quantities at a meal; they prefer the nonglutinous type of staple rice (which they commonly call "lordly rice" [*kao jao*] or "beautiful rice" [*kao suai*]). They argue that sticky rice sticks to the stomach and ribs, is hard to digest and, therefore, makes one sleepy and lazy following a meal. Northerners and northeasterners, on the other hand, regard the common rice farmed in the central lowlands to be unsubstantial and insufficient to hold them from meal to meal. The difference in preferences and viewpoints reveals how rice serves not only to unite but also to distinguish the peoples in the different regions.

Since the "greening of Isahn" campaign was launched many years ago in an attempt to restore agricultural productivity to a heavily-deforested and arid land, the cuisine of northeastern Thailand has become increasingly popular in other parts of the country. As cultural awareness of the once little-known region becomes more widespread and as greater numbers of northeasterners are forced to become migrant workers all over the country, bringing with them their food and style of cooking, the intensely fiery and pungent food of the region has been "discovered." Restaurants specializing in Isahn cuisine have popped up everywhere. The food of peasants has become the "in" thing, a fashionable cuisine. Along with the many spicy dishes, sticky rice is now more prevalently served, unsweetened and unflavored, as a main meal rice. It is no longer relegated only to desserts and sweet snacks. The acceptance and incorporation of the region's staple food into the mainstream of Thai cuisine have served to blur the differences among the peoples of the different regions.

When eating Isahn food, steamed sticky rice is a definite must. Barbecued chicken with green papaya salad; various *lahbs* (intensely spicy minced meat salads); fermented sour sausages called *naem*; little round Isahn pork sausages and spicy *näm prik* sauces made with fermented shrimp or fish, accompanied by crisp raw vegetables and pungent and aromatic herbs—all are very good when eaten together with chewy sticky rice. It seems the more you chew, the better everything tastes. Use your hand as the Isahn people do. It makes for a truly delightful finger-licking experience.

To cook sticky rice, Thais use a cone-shaped, woven bamboo basket that looks somewhat like a straw hat. The basket fits over a tall companion pot with a wide collar to hold it in place. Depending on how much rice is to be

Sticky Rice Steamer Set

steamed, any round lid that fits above the rice level in the basket can be used as a cover. A few inches of water in the pot, when heated over a burner, produce the steam which rises and passes through the basket to cook the presoaked rice. Homes and restaurants in the north and northeast serve cooked sticky rice in small round baskets with covers (called *gkra-dtip*), which are placed around the dining table. These baskets come in different sizes; some hold enough rice for one or two people, while larger ones serve four or more.

The special steaming basket and pot are available from Southeast Asian markets and are essential for the even cooking of larger quantities of sticky rice (from a few cups to five pounds of rice at a time.) They are inexpensive, about five dollars apiece, and will last a long, long time, making lots of wonderful batches of delicious sticky rice.

If you are unable to find the special basket, try using a straw or wire-mesh colander placed on a rack over a steamer. Avoid steaming the rice directly on a steamer rack lined with dampened cloth (as suggested by some sources) because the moisture the cloth absorbs is likely to turn the grains touching it into a mushy, gooey mass. If you are making just a small quantity (i.e., less than two cups), you can steam the rice in a dry bowl placed on a steamer rack. Spread the grains out loosely rather than compact them on the dish; this makes it easier for the steam to reach the inner layers and cook all the grains more evenly. Make sure to soak the rice in plenty of water for several hours, or overnight, before steaming. Steam about half an hour or until the rice is thoroughly cooked through.

Don't use the sticky rice cooking method for other sorts of rice. It won't work because nonglutinous rice is a much denser grain and will not absorb water the same way glutinous rice does. Even if soaked all day, when steamed dry, regular rice will not cook and produce the chewy texture of sticky rice.

BLACK STICKY RICE: A NUTTY WHOLE GRAIN

Sometimes identified on the bulk bins of specialty food markets as "Indonesian black rice," black glutinous or sweet rice is a nutty whole grain widely consumed in many of the Indonesian islands. If you have traveled to that part of the world, you may have fond memories of being served delicious black rice pudding for breakfast or dessert. Many Southeast Asian countries also cultivate and consume their fair share of this tasty whole grain. In Thailand, where the rice is known as black sticky rice (*kao* is rice; *niow*, sticky; *däm*, black), I've seen it sold as a sweet snack more often in the marketplaces down south. I first saw beautiful patchwork fields of ripening black rice in the southern region, their dark tops waving in the wind, alternating side by side with patches of golden grain.

In Thailand, black sticky rice is consumed mostly in sweetened form and is not used as the main rice in a meal. In my cooking classes, I introduce the wholesome grain to my students in the form of a simple black rice pudding (see recipe on page 38). Over the years, many of them have grown very fond of this delicious rice and regard it as one of their favorite discoveries in my kitchen. Since taking the classes, some of them have traveled to Thailand but have returned with reports of disappointment and frustration in trying to find black rice pudding on the menus of restaurants there. Thai people seldom have such a rich and substantial dessert following so closely after a meal, prefering instead lighter sweet-soup concoctions or fresh seasonal fruits, or nothing at all. Both white and black sticky rice, as desserts, sit too heavily in the stomach following a meal and are nibbled on more as sweet snacks, in the mid-afternoon or later in the evening after a few hours' break from dinner. If you have a craving for black sticky rice while traveling in Thailand, look for it not in restaurants but in the larger fresh food markets likely to have sizable *kanom* (sweet snack) stalls carrying a wide assortment of sweet treats, including sticky rice. In Bangkok, you might also search for it along the crowded sidewalks near busy commercial centers, bus stations and heavily populated residential neighborhoods, where pushcart vendors and mobile street hawkers set up temporary stalls, offering a wide variety of nibble food to satisfy every craving.

Among the fascinating markets great for walks and a sampling of Thai sweetmeats, the bustling streetside stalls in the Banglampoo area of Bangkok offer an exciting cultural adventure. The nighttime food scene in the Tonglaw area is equally impressive (except on Wednesdays when many vendors take the night off). In Chiangmai, I've found ready-to-eat black sticky rice with regularity in the basement *kanom* section of the extensive Worarot Market near the Bping River and, occasionally, in the colorful early morning market in foggy Mae Hong Sawn near the Burmese border. The vendor in Chiangmai sells many different kinds of sticky rice—white, black, red, yellow, green, brown—and at least half a dozen kinds of toppings. Just point to the rice you wish and choose a topping, and she will wrap your selections on a piece of banana leaf pinned with a bamboo pick. Push-cart *kanom* vendors in the larger towns in the south often will have black rice pudding cut in squares along with other delicious puddings made with cassava root, tapioca, taro and corn.

Black glutinous rice is a natural rice with grains that are unevenly colored and that look like wild rice when dry. Its rich, nutty flavor is distinctly different from the more subtle delicateness of white glutinous rice. Black rice is not the whole-grain version of white sticky rice as some may think, and unlike wild rice, it is fairly easy to cultivate. This is reflected in its reasonable price. Southeast Asian markets in America carry 5-lb. bags for about a dollar per pound. Most frequently, the black rice has been imported from Thailand.

On closer look, you will notice that "black" sticky rice isn't really black at all. After soaking for a few hours, the water will turn into a deep burgundy, showing the rice's true colors. This is the natural color of the rice, not an additive. If you wish to make a reddish sticky rice snack, mix together equal amounts of separately cooked white and black sticky rice and blend in with a coconut sauce. If you make a trip to the old city of Nakon Bpatom southwest of Bangkok to visit the enormous sacred shrine dating back to the fifth century, wander across the street to the lively market and try the town's famous *kao lahm* (sticky rice roasted in bamboo). Besides those stuffed with white sticky rice, there are others with a reddish black-and-white rice mixture, flavored with coconut milk and a sprinkling of black beans—a delectable and wholesome treat.

While black sticky rice is used primarily in sweet snacks and desserts in Asia, some of my cooking students have discovered that this nutty whole grain also makes wonderful salads, much like tabbouleh.

COCONUT-FLAVORED STICKY RICE WITH MANGOES

(Kao Niow Ma-muang)

2 cups long-grain white sticky rice, sweet rice or glutinous rice

2 cups creamy coconut milk (or one 14-oz. can)

½ cup granulated sugar

About 1 tsp. salt

Optional flavoring: 2–3 fresh or frozen pandanus leaves (bai dteuy) or 4–5 drops jasmine (mali) essence

1–2 ripe mangoes, peeled and sliced

Rinse the rice once or twice, cover with water 2–3 inches above the rice line and allow to soak at least 4 hours, or overnight. The grains will absorb much of the water, soften and grow in size.

When ready to cook, drain the rice and steam dry (without any water) in a shallow heat-proof dish, placed on a steamer rack over a pot with 2 or more inches of water on the bottom. (For a make-shift steamer, refer to the section on how to steam jasmine rice on page 27.) Steam about 30 minutes under medium heat, or until the grains are translucent, softened but chewy. If you are making a large quantity, use the special sticky rice steaming basket described in the foregoing section (page 33) so that the rice grains cook more evenly. When making a large batch, it also helps to turn the rice and sprinkle a little water over the top once or twice during the cooking time.

When the rice is about 20 minutes into its steaming, prepare the coconut sauce by heating the coconut milk, sugar and salt together in a saucepan. Warm the milk until the mixture is well blended and smooth. If you wish a *bai dteuy* (pandanus leaf) flavor, add a few fresh or frozen *bai dteuy* leaves and simmer with the sauce for about 10 minutes. Then, remove the leaves, and after they have cooled enough to handle, use your hand to squeeze out all the fragrant juice until the leaves are dry. Add the pressed juice to the sauce. If fresh or frozen leaves are not available, use about ¼ tsp. of the green *bai dteuy* essence. Or, if you wish a more delicate floral scent, use a few drops of *mali* (jasmine) essence instead. Keep the sauce warm.

When the rice is done and while it is still hot out of the steamer, pour half the coconut sauce over the rice. Stir well with a spoon to make sure all the grains are well coated. The rice should be wet but not swimming in sauce. Add more of the sauce if needed, reserving the remainder for dribbling over the top before serving. Let stand for 15–20 minutes to allow the rice grains to absorb the flavorings.

Pandanus Leaf (*Bai Dteuy*)

Matured Coconut (*Ma-prao*)

When ready to serve, dish the rice onto individual serving plates, spoon some of the reserved coconut sauce over each portion and arrange sliced mangoes over the top. Serve warm or at room temperature.

NOTES AND POINTERS

The coconut sauce should have a pronounced saltiness behind the sweetness. The saltiness will help bring forth the rich flavors of coconut milk and the delicate taste of sticky rice. Also, the salty sweetness of the flavored rice enhances rather than distracts from the fruity sweetness of mangoes. For more information about leaf and floral essences, refer to pages 96 and 123.

When mangoes and durians are not in season, coconut-flavored sticky rice is served with a choice of toppings, ranging from a very sweet coconut-egg custard called *sangkaya* (see recipe on page 122) to a salty-sweet, minced dried shrimp mixture. The *kanom* vendor in the market usually has several choices, something to satisfy every mood and palate.

$\mathscr{B}$LACK STICKY RICE PUDDING
(Kao Niow Däm)

2 cups whole-grain black sticky rice, sweet rice or glutinous rice

2 cups (or 1 14-oz. can) coconut milk

½ cup sugar

½ tsp. salt

2 Tbs. toasted sesame seeds and/or toasted unsweetened shredded coconut (optional)

Strawberries and mint leaves (optional)

Measure the rice into a bowl; run your fingers through the rice and check for any pebbles or other noticeable impurities. Rinse the rice a few times until the water clears. Cover with at least 2 inches of water and allow to soak 4 or more hours, or overnight. The grains will absorb water and grow in size.

When ready to cook, drain the rice and place in a heat-proof bowl with room enough for the rice grains to expand about a third more than its uncooked bulk. Add a small amount of boiling water, just enough to barely cover the rice grains. Place the bowl on a steamer rack and steam over medium heat about 30–40 minutes. If you do not have a steamer, use a large pot in which the bowl fits. Place a trivet on the bottom along with 2–3 inches of water. Bring to a boil. Balance the bowl with the rice on the trivet and add hot water to the rice. Cover and steam. Steaming the rice with a small volume of water will leave the top layer of grains intact, retaining a chewy texture that pops in your mouth. If you wish the rice to be softer, add more water.

While the rice is steaming, make the coconut sauce by heating the coconut milk, sugar and salt together in a saucepan. Stir to dissolve the sugar and salt and blend the sauce until smooth. Keep warm.

When the rice is cooked and while still hot out of the steamer, add about half of the sauce or enough to thoroughly coat the rice. Stir and mix well. The rice should be wet but not swimming in sauce. Let stand 15–20 minutes to allow the flavorings to be absorbed. Reserve the remaining sauce for spooning over the rice before serving.

The flavored rice can be molded into a round mound on a serving plate and decorated with toasted sesame seeds and/or coconut shreds, sliced strawberries and mint leaves for color. Or dish into individual serving bowls or custard cups, topped with the reserved sauce, toasted seeds and coconut and a mint leaf.

Matured Coconut (*Ma-prao*)

For a wetter puddinglike texture, the rice may alternatively be cooked by boiling, the same way as you would regular rice. Use 2½–3 cups of water to each cup of rice. Bring to a boil. Reduce heat to simmer and cook partially covered until the grains are cooked and surrounded by a thick sauce, stirring occasionally to prevent sticking and burning. Add sugar to sweeten to your liking. Stir well, cover and place on lowest heat setting for another 5–10 minutes. Make the sauce less sweet but more salty for contrast with the already sweetened rice. When ready to serve, dish the rice into individual serving bowls and dribble some sauce over each serving.

Serve warm or at room temperature.

NOTES AND POINTERS

Because of its rich, nutty flavor, black sticky rice is usually eaten by itself and not served with fruits, like white sticky rice often is with mangoes. For toppings, stronger flavors like toasted sesame seeds or toasted shredded coconut do more to accentuate the natural flavor of the rice. Unsweetened shredded coconut is available in small packages from Asian food markets or sold in bulk in specialty food stores.

STICKY RICE AND CORN PUDDING

(Kao Niow Bpiak Kao Pohd)

1 cup white long-grain sticky rice,
sweet rice or glutinous
rice

3–4 ears fresh sweet corn

4 cups water

1–1½ cups sugar

1 cup coconut cream

1½ tsp. salt

Soak the sticky rice for 3–4 hours. Rinse and drain. With a knife, cut the corn kernels off the cob. Set aside.

Bring 4 cups of water to a boil in a medium-size pot. Add the sticky rice. Bring back up to a boil, then reduce heat and simmer uncovered, stirring occasionally. After about 10–15 minutes, add the corn and cook until the corn is tender. Add the sugar, stirring well to dissolve. Bring to a boil again, then turn off heat.

If using canned coconut milk, spoon the creamiest part off the top of the can, or about one cup, into a saucepan. Heat the coconut cream with the salt until the mixture is blended and smooth.

When ready to serve, spoon the rice and corn mixture into individual serving bowls and top each serving with 1–2 tablespoons of the salted coconut cream. Before eating, stir the coconut cream into the rice and corn mixture. Best served warm.

NOTES AND POINTERS

In many Thai desserts and sweet snacks, the sweet and salty flavors are contrasted in separate layers, as in this pudding. Often the coconut cream topping is salty while the main pudding itself is very sweet. In this recipe, the salty, creamy topping should *not* be eaten by itself (like some people would nibble on cake frosting) but should be swirled into the sweet pudding just before eating.

Once there was a farmer who lived near a prosperous seacoast town. He worked very hard in his fields but earned only a meager living. Wishing a better life for his son, he sent the boy to the temple school nearby to be educated by the monks.

The boy was intelligent and diligent in his studies, learning to read and write well—things both his parents were not able to do. The old abbot of the temple took a keen liking to the boy and in the free afternoons shared with him his newly acquired interest in the great mystery of alchemy. Together, the old monk and young boy spent their time in consuming experimentation, attempting to find a way to convert copper into gold. Their results were close, but there always seemed to be something missing.

The years passed and the boy grew up to be a smart young man. But the interest in alchemy which the old abbot had stirred in him kept him so passionately involved in his research that even after he returned home, he was absorbed day and night with his secret experiments. He refused to help out in the fields and would not take the time to find work in town. His elderly parents, who were still poor, were very disappointed, but there was nothing they could do to pry him away from his mysterious research.

After much thought, the old farmer decided that marriage might help to break the spell that had consumed his son. It so happened that a neighboring farmer's daughter had come of age. Beautiful and bright, she would make a good match for his son. After much persuasion, the son agreed to get married, hoping that by doing so he would cool down his parents' dissatisfaction in him.

The marriage, however, did not change the young man. He continued to be obsessed with alchemy to the alarm of his parents and his new wife's family. Everyone was very displeased with his reluctance to contribute to the well-being of the family and accused him of being lazy, irreverent and ungrateful to his parents.

Not knowing what else to do, the old farmer turned to the respected abbot of the temple for help. "Venerable Abbot!" he said. "My heart is very troubled. I have come to seek your guidance." The farmer related to the abbot his concern for his son's strange behavior and isolation from the family since his return from the temple. "Pray, advise me what to do!"

Disappointed by what he heard, the old monk regretted the teaching he had given to his young disciple. After a moment of deep contemplation, he replied, "Good farmer, you have worked hard all your life and deserve more than what you are receiving. It is the duty of a son to help his parents, especially in their old age, so that they can live out their last days in comfort, joy and security. I have an idea. Let me have a word with your son. Tell him to come and see me tomorrow."

The old farmer thanked the abbot and took his leave. When he returned home, he relayed to his son the old abbot's wish to see him. Thinking that the master might have important advice to give him on his experiments, the young man eagerly prepared to meet with the old monk the next morning.

"My son," the wise monk greeted his student, "I have been given a good omen! The other night while I was meditating late into the night, a hermit in white robes appeared before me in a vision and whispered to me, 'You need one kilogram of silver dust.' I was puzzled by what he said and begged him to explain further what he meant. He was silent and looked deeply into my eyes. Then he turned his head and looked out the window, pointing as he did at something outside. Before I could make out what he was showing me, he vanished." The old abbot paused and then smiled, continuing with his story. "I sat there for a long while, contemplating what the hermit said, and when I finally pulled myself out from my meditation, I walked over to the window in my room to see if there was a clue outside that might explain the hermit's message. I saw only the graceful outlines of a banana plant in the dim, predawn light.

"My son, I didn't know what to make of it, so I returned to where I was sitting and bowed down at the spot where the hermit had appeared and prayed for further guidance. The hermit did not return. After some time in prayer, I got up and walked over to the window again and looked out. There again was the banana plant. This time I could see it better as the day had dawned. Strangely, I felt as if it was looking straight at me. I carefully examined it with my eyes but saw only the porous bark and the handsome green leaves glistening with dew drops, moving gently in the soft morning breeze. I spent a long time looking at this tree from my window before I returned to my morning round of meditations. But my mind was absorbed with the plant, so I went outside and took a closer look. As I examined one of the leaves closely, guess what I saw, my son! Silver dust! The leaves were covered by a fine dusting of silver dust! This must be the missing element to our experimentation!"

The old monk and his disciple discussed the vision and its message for a long time. They went out to the nearby banana grove and examined the leaves very closely. They cut many banana leaves and carefully scraped off the thin film of what appeared to be silvery dust. They took note of which leaves in what stages of maturity carried the thickest deposit of the dust. For days they documented their findings and at last came to the conclusion that the powdery film on banana leaves *must* be the silver dust, the missing element in their alchemical experiments! Excited with their discovery, there remained but one task for them to do, and that was to collect one kilogram of the stuff.

The young man returned home and took an interest in his father's land for the first time. He wasted no time plowing the fields, planting young banana shoots with an earnestness that astonished his parents and wife. He worked the land with great pleasure, and his industriousness soon brought forth from the earth a most beautiful grove of banana plants. He cared for them with the same great passion that he had devoted to his experiments. He watched the plants grow and mature, cutting certain leaves at the proper time and taking them to his private workshop, where he meticulously scraped off the silver dust and secretly stored it in a jar hidden in a safe place. He then gave the leaves to his wife, who bundled them up and sold them at the market.

Because each leaf carried such a scant dusting of the powder, the young man soon realized that if he wished to collect enough of the stuff within a reasonable period of years, he would need to cultivate more groves of bananas. So, with the delighted support of his family, he expanded his production to include all his father's fields as well as his in-law's neighboring land. It wasn't long before he found himself in charge of one of the largest banana plantations around.

While he continued to busy himself with the collection of the silver dust, his bright young wife did not sit idle. Aside from the leaves her husband handed over to her every day, she collected sturdy, well-formed leaves and sold them to snack and dessert vendors at the market to be used in making *gkratongs* (little baskets for holding food and sweetmeats) and decorative wrappers.

Some of the tender leaves she dried and sold to tobacco merchants to use in rolling tobacco. The thicker, mature leaves went to meat and vegetable vendors for wrapping their customers' purchases. Of course, her main source of income from the plantation came from the bananas themselves. She sold them fresh as fruits, and on special weekend market days she set up a stall selling delicious fried bananas, banana chips, banana cakes and other sweet treats made with the fruits. What she couldn't sell fast enough she dried or made into preserves and candies for the larger markets in the nearby town.

Besides cooking with the fruits, the edible purplish-red blossoms of the banana plants made wonderful salads and accompaniments to chilli sauces for family meals. The soft interior of the stems were also good to eat and were cooked in tasty curry sauces as a vegetable. The young wife packed up what the family couldn't eat into baskets to sell at the local market or barter for other produce, fish and meats. As was common practice among banana growers, matured banana plants were cut down after they had fruited to make room for the young shoots to grow so that the next crop would be strong and bear healthy bunches of large bananas. The industrious wife gently sliced the porous trunks of the downed plants into thin lengths and dried them in the sun, later making them into tough strings. These, too, she sold to merchants at the market for everyday use in tying packages and bundling their goods. Just about every part of the banana plants was put to good use.

Together, the young man and his wife worked hard on their plantation. As the years passed, the husband gathered a substantial collection of precious silver dust, while the wife amassed a comfortable fortune from selling the leaves, flowers, fruits and trunks of the banana plants.

Finally, the day came when the silver dust collected amounted to the one kilogram needed to complete the alchemy experiment. Now rich and matured with years of hard work, the banana grower, no longer a young man himself, went to the temple, as he frequently did, to make merit and offerings of food to the monks. He took with him the jar of silver dust to present to the venerated abbot. "Venerable Grandfather!" he cried. "I have gathered the one kilogram of silver dust—the missing element we need in our experiments to produce gold!" The old monk smiled and replied, "My son, you have already produced gold from the silver dust!"

Knowing quite well what the old monk meant, the banana grower bowed reverently and took leave. Returning to his plantation, he continued to work the land with the same passion that had carried him through the years. He soon became one of the wealthiest farmers in the region and was the pride and joy of his family—and of his wise teacher who had initiated him into the mystery of alchemy.[2]

2. Adapted from Dr. Jit-Kasem Sibunruang's retelling (1975) of an old folktale.

THE ART AND JOYS OF THAI COOKING

Like many Asian cuisines, Thai cooking is a "throw-together" style of cooking that allows much room for creativity. Instead of letting a cookbook dictate what goes into a meal, the foods in season and available fresh at the marketplace—as well as whatever ingredients the cook finds in his or her refrigerator—are the important deciding factors of what will appear on the dinner table. Of course, a good sense of what foods and flavors work well together and a comprehensive knowledge of the basics are helpful.

Some of the best dishes I've made, for instance, have been created out of a mishmash of ingredients and leftovers I find at the end of the week in the refrigerator. A few times I have taken such spur-of-the-moment creations to potluck parties and have been surprised by the inquiries generated for the "recipes." All I could do was tell my friends to enjoy the dishes for what they were, for those moments and nothing more, as they could not be duplicated. Much of the goodness of those dishes, in fact, derived from the wonderful energies of many hands that participated in their preparation—a few dabs of this leftover chilli sauce were blended in with a few bits of that leftover pastry filling, ingredients that my students had saved from classes in my kitchen and stuffed in little containers in my refrigerator. Each small quantity of this or that, complete and delicious in itself, was too precious to throw away, and together the little tidbits could play quite a symphony, especially if conducted properly.

I learned to cook by helping my mother in the kitchen from the time I was a little girl. Mother is an excellent cook, and because of her indisputable reputation, many of Father's friends frequently show up for dinner on weekends. Mother enjoys feeding people (a trait I inherited from her) and can whip up an inspiring meal or snack on short notice out of whatever she finds in the refrigerator and cupboard. During those early years, I helped her wash and cut the vegetables, made decorative tomato and chilli flowers and did other little odd jobs to help her in the kitchen. Most of the time, I just stood around and watched her work her magic over the stove, and when she needed something that wasn't close at hand, I fetched it for her.

I never saw her use measuring devices or written recipes out of a book. (In fact, I didn't even know a category of books for cooking existed until I came to America.) It was always a dab of this or a pinch of that, a shake from this bottle of sauce or a sprinkling from that jar of spice, all the while guided by an intuitive sense. Watching her was like watching a master artist at work. Alert to the rhythms and sounds of cooking signaling critical moments of action, she kneaded and felt with her hands as she marinated and mixed, and played with colors and textures as she arranged them into pleasing, mouth-watering renditions. Cooking took on much more than the blending of tastes and aromas: it engaged all the senses. I learned from her what a complete sensual delight it can be, a source of great joy and satisfaction. Those childhood years gave me a most valuable apprenticeship, in addition to countless hours of precious mother-daughter bonding.

Cooking is an art, much like painting. To produce good art, we must rely on our instincts and feelings as much as our knowledge of materials and methods. Recipes in a cookbook can only be rough guidelines in this creative process. The herbs and spices, condiments and flavor ingredients are like the many different kinds and colors of paints. Learning how to combine them is like learning how to mix paints to obtain the color combinations we desire. Some go together better than others, producing very pleasing results; others do not do so well, giving a muddy look and taste. Adding too much or too little of an ingredient can affect the overall picture, but the decision to do so depends on the artist's or the viewer's personal tastes. The cook's "paints" are applied to the "canvases" of meats, seafoods and vegetables; kitchen implements are the "paint brushes" and methods of preparation are different techniques for applying "paint" in order to create the "images" we envision. Over the years, many of my students have been amazed how the same few ingredients used in different combinations or applied in different methods of preparation produce a vast array of dishes, none tasting like any other before them.

As with any art form, the quality of energy the culinary artist puts into a creation is reflected in the finished piece. The tender loving care we put into food preparation, I believe, does make a big difference in the quality of flavors and in the presentation, lending depth and soul to the food. For this reason, I prefer to use traditional methods, such as grinding herbs and spices in a stone mortar rather than in an electric appliance. Hands, too, work much better in mixing certain ingredients, and a discriminating diner can easily pick out the curry made from scratch by hand from one blended in a food processor.

Cooking is an alchemical process. The ingredients are mixed and transformed by fire into edible "alchemical gold." The resulting synergy makes the final dish much more than a sum of its parts. Some exquisite Thai dishes created by master chefs are so magically blended that it is impossible to separate out all the subtle flavors that went into them. Many times students of Thai cooking cannot envision an end result from a seemingly disparate list of ingredients; the final taste test leaves them delightfully surprised.

Art or alchemy, cooking is more importantly a *process* of living, an activity in our daily life capable of providing immense pleasure and enjoyment. The objective of finished dishes is not the sole aim; the process of "getting there," of preparing and cooking, is equally important and vitalizing. Thai people believe everything we do in life ought to be *sanuk*, or fun and pleasurable. This is not a shallow, hedonistic way of looking at things but is a reflection of our penchant for finding the positive expression in whatever we do. This way, we can make the most of every moment and savor the many pleasures of life that come our way, be they great or small. Because one of our joys is good food and the sharing of food, it is only natural that cooking is a *sanuk* activity for many of us.

Over the years, many of my students have developed a new appreciation and respect for cooking which they had not experienced earlier in life. The cooking principles learned in the classes can be applied to other forms of cooking with gratifying results, further increasing confidence and enjoyment in the kitchen. Cooking becomes a welcome opportunity and a cherished avenue for creative expression, rather than a chore.

Some people have come to my classes with absolutely no cooking background, motivated solely by their discovery of Thai cuisine. Dorothy admitted she didn't even know how to fry an egg when she signed up for the classes, but today she can glide gracefully through the making of a complex curry with the freshest ingredients, which, she proudly proclaims, tastes much better than any served in Thai restaurants near her home. She has changed from someone who knew nothing about cooking to a host who joyfully puts together lavish dinner parties for her friends. She and others like her admit their social lives have improved, and the sharing of wonderful meals with close friends and loved ones has brought them much happiness.

Some have found, too, how therapeutic and stress-reducing cooking can be. Mike, for instance, sets aside one day every other weekend to spend just

Stone Mortar and Pestle

by himself, visiting the market in the morning and spending the afternoon in the kitchen with a bottle of wine and some good music, cutting and chopping, grinding and pounding, stewing and steaming, and so on. There is no time pressure, no rush, no goal—the meal is ready when it is done. Cooking becomes meditation, a time alone for contemplation, a time to be present with himself and all the wonderful herbs and spices with aromas awakening his senses as he chops and grinds them. What a reprieve following a hectic week at the office tending to everyone else's needs and demands! Later in the evening, after cleaning up and setting a lovely table decorated with a beautiful bouquet of flowers, pressed tablecloth, tall candles in elegant candlesticks and charming matched place settings, he entertains close friends with an exquisite dinner, the grand finale for the day.

Others prefer cooking with groups of friends. The party is in the kitchen and starts at the cutting board, culminating at the dining table when the many joint creations are devoured with great gusto. These cooking parties are truly *sanuk* occasions. And when there is no party, cooking together with roommates and loved ones brings a special intimacy into the home. Margot, for instance, enjoys cooking Thai food for her family; her husband, Louis, helps her grind herbs and spices in the stone mortar. This teamwork makes each meal special.

Many of the finest dishes in Thai cuisine require a fair amount of preparation in the kitchen. Thai people like to cut vegetables and meats in small pieces because this helps them cook quickly when stir-fried in a wok, retaining their crispness and fresh flavors. Also, smaller pieces mean more surface areas to coat with the flavors of spices, herbs and condiments, making every bite tastier. Additionally, because knives are not traditionally used at the dinner table—they are viewed as symbols of violence and aggression not appropriate at a shared family setting—smaller pieces of foods are essential.

If you are new to the cooking of Thai food, give yourself sufficient time to prepare your first meals. Try not to set a time limit, so that you can flow freely in the process, have a *sanuk* time and not be stressed hurrying to meet a deadline. Leave the deadlines at work. If you are cooking for a dinner party, the prep work for many of the dishes can be done a day or two in advance. Many of the dipping sauces age well and some actually taste better with time; most curries, too, are better when made a day or two ahead, allowing the flavors of the many herbs and spices to meld and pull together.

I have chosen not to include the number of servings for the recipes in this book, because each individual serving depends on how many dishes you are serving in the meal and whether your family and friends are big rice eaters like Thai people. In my experience, a quantity enough to satisfy a dozen Asians frequently leaves half that number of big, meat-eating Americans hungry for more. Therefore, in deciding how much to make, add up the total quantity of meats and seafoods in all the dishes on the menu and allow a quarter pound to a half pound per person. Most of the recipes can be easily doubled and tripled without sacrificing quality.

I hope you enjoy the cooking tips and stories in this book and gain much pleasure from your many exciting adventures into the realm of Thai cooking.

As the popularity of Thai cuisine has soared worldwide, so has the proliferation of Thai cookbooks. Many simplify the recipes for Western kitchens and alter spice flavors to suit milder Western palates. Others present recipes truer to their original form. Then there are those written by chefs in Thailand who have little idea of the availability and degree of potency of the herbs grown and sold in Western markets. Americans who frequent Thai restaurants at home or have visited Thailand and have grown used to the full scale of spicy flavors may have a difficult time trying to duplicate their favorite dishes from recipes in a cookbook.

Often, it is not the recipes in these cookbooks that are inadequate, but the Western habit of taking recipes at face value, using precisely the quantities specified. For those who do experiment, their unfamiliarity with the fundamental principles of Asian cooking limits the range of their creative endeavors. Most cookbooks are largely "recipe books" and assume a basic knowledge of how to work with food; a basic "food sense" is something difficult to communicate with words and is usually acquired from years of experience in working with various kinds of food in a particular style of cooking.

Whether cooking Thai food in an American kitchen or in Thailand, adjustments in recommended specifications are frequently necessary. The batch of herbs today may not be as fresh as a week ago or were grown locally under milder conditions compared to imported ones from hotter, tropical climes. Or, the herbs called for are not available fresh and require you to substitute with dried forms. There are other variables, too; one brand of fish sauce may be saltier or fishier than another, one batch of palm sugar sweeter than the next, and so on. In addition, when making substitutions for ingredients that aren't available, knowing the potential effects of such substitutions on the remaining ingredients is essential in order to avoid major sacrifices in flavor. Ingredients do not work in isolation; rather, they interact with one another to produce results that may be totally unexpected.

CREATING HARMONIES WITH PRIMARY FLAVORS

The complexities (and simplicities) of Thai cooking, owing to the wide range of flavor ingredients employed in the cuisine, require a good understanding of the primary categories of flavors that are registered by the taste receptacles on your tongue and how they interact with one another. The blending of these main flavors will affect how you taste the herbs, vegetables, seafoods, meats and other food items in the dishes you make. For most of the world's cuisines, there are four basic tastes: salty, sweet, sour and bitter. For Thai cuisine, there is a fifth: hot or pungent.

In traditional Oriental medicine, it is believed the human body is made up of five essential elements. Associated with each of them is a category of flavor derived from natural foods. When the five elements are in balance, the body is in good health; when any of them is deficient or excessive, the harmony of the body is disturbed. One way to ensure good health is to include in the diet a balance of natural foods representing the five flavors: salty, sweet, sour, bitter and pungent (or hot). Because Thai cuisine utilizes all five, almost to an equal degree, it may be seen as a health-enhancing cuisine, if one consumes a wide range of Thai foods with rice as the main course and does not selectively indulge in only a few "favorite" dishes, especially the higher-fat curries and fried foods.

By blending the five primary flavors in varying proportions, surprisingly different results can be achieved. Varying their sources, too, will introduce new dimensions, multiplying the number of variables available to you to create a wide range of distinctive tastes. In Thai cuisine, the bitter flavor comes largely from herbs and deep green vegetables; because these ingredients are the primary ingredients in the recipes where they appear, the remaining four flavors are the ones you can adjust to obtain the taste balances you desire. When you have developed a good sense of how these flavors interact, you may be able to "rescue" or perk up dishes put together from cookbook recipes that turn out "blah," fall below your expectations or simply taste as if something is missing.

The most common sources of the four variable flavor categories follow. The different sections, however, are not mutually exclusive, as many prepared sauces, pastes and dried ingredients impart more than one primary flavor. I have arbitrarily assigned some to particular flavor designations to call your attention to a property which may be unexpected. Brief guidelines on how to blend the primary flavors and create harmonies to satisfy a wide range of desires follow the listing of the flavor categories.

THE HOT FLAVOR AND ITS SOURCES

We Thai people love our spicy foods! We also like variety, so not all dishes are made in the full scale of heat. Hotness is just one variable to play around with; the more the variables, the greater the range of possible creations. Some dishes are meant to be mild so that subtle flavors are not overpowered. Other dishes are made in the medium-scale of hotness, and, of course, there are those that make the body sing in more ways than one!

Not all Thai people like fiery hot food. In fact, the ability to eat spicy foods is as much an acquired ability among Thais as it is among many Westerners. Children are not fed spicy foods until they develop a curiosity to try for themselves what they see adults eat and enjoy, usually when they are about seven, eight or nine. Learning to tolerate hot food is part of growing up, not unlike little girls acting grown-up by stepping into their mothers' high-heel shoes or smearing lipstick on their faces. It is an initiation of sorts, an informal rite of passage. When my niece, Baitoey, came to spend her school break with me two years ago, she was eight and just beginning to acquire a taste for spicy foods. One day she tried the massaman curry she saw so many of my students enjoy, and she loved it. Weeks later, when her mother came to fetch her to return home to Thailand, I cooked a dinner that included massaman curry. Her mother was concerned, informing me Baitoey couldn't eat it because it was spicy. "Of course, I can!" she argued and proceeded to show off her newly acquired taste, downing two plates of rice laced with the rich spicy sauce of the curry. It was almost like proving to her mother that she had grown and learned many new things the two months she had been away. She was no longer a little girl.

Green *Prik Chee Fah*
and Orange *Prik Leuang* Peppers

It doesn't take any guessing to know that the main sources of the hot flavor in Thai food come from fresh chilli peppers. About two dozen different varieties are used, from tiny ones no larger than watermelon seeds to big ones the size of fava beans, each with its own unique flavor and degree of heat. Several kinds of chillies are used in their dried forms, too, which differ in taste from fresh chillies—just like sun-dried tomatoes differ from fresh ones. Besides being made into pastes and curry mixes, dried chillies are also roasted and ground up to sit on condiment trays to pep up food at the table as wanted. In addition, there are a number of bottled hot sauces, the most notable called *prik Sriracha* (it originated in the eastern seaboard town of Sriracha). Orange red in color (a less common yellowish blend is also available), this all-purpose table sauce is now made in California under the same name and is the Southeast Asian equivalent of Tabasco sauce, but it is sweeter, garlicky and less vinegary.

Besides chillies, hotness comes from green, black and white peppercorns and various kinds of gingers, onions and garlic. Because of the important roles chillies, peppers and pungent herbs play in Thai cuisine, two other chapters in this book are devoted to them ("Of Chillies, Spices and Mice" and "Fresh Herbal Flavors Distinguish Thai Cuisine").

THE MAGIC ELIXIR OF THAI CUISINE: FISH SAUCE

Top on your first shopping list for Thai ingredients should be none other than the magic elixir that does wonders to most Thai dishes: fish sauce, or in Thai, *näm bplah*. Not only is it an essential ingredient in finished dishes, it appears as a condiment on the dining table at nearly every meal, by itself or mixed with chillies and sometimes lime juice. A prime source of salt in the Thai diet and rich in protein, B vitamins and minerals, this clear brown liquid is to Thai cooking what soy sauce is to Chinese and Japanese cooking. It is a brew made by fermenting anchovies in sea salt and water.

If you are new to Thai cooking, please do not shy away from this very important sauce just because the first time you smell it you may be overcome with disgust. After all, it is not made for wearing as a perfume or using as an air freshener. When used in cooking, its fishiness lessens dramatically as it dissipates and blends in deliciously with aromatic flavor ingredients. If its odor does not diminish, you may consider switching brands because some are markedly stronger while others are mild and more likable to the uninitiated. Most Thais prefer a sauce with a mid-range of fishiness but keep a couple of varieties on hand for various purposes. For instance, an uncooked dipping sauce for the table fares better with a milder sauce, whereas rich curries, spicy soups and seafood dishes are enhanced by a stronger blend.

Whatever strength of fish sauce you purchase, avoid transporting an already opened bottle of it in your car to your friend's house to cook Thai, especially when the bottle is more than half full. No matter how carefully you have closed its lid and made sure it is well balanced and propped up in a sack or box or wrapped tightly in plastic, it is likely that a few drops of the sauce will make their escape. This happens so often that it seems as if the playful spirits of all those anchovies, excited by the motion of the car, are inspired to

Red Fresno and Green Jalapeño Peppers

jump, believing they are being returned to sea! They leave a very potent-smelling trail behind that may take days or even weeks to wear out. Try washing the spilled area with a sponge dampened with soapy water, followed by a liberal sprinkling of baking soda to deodorize. After this "accident" has happened to you once, you will know to bring a new, unopened bottle to your friend's house for your cooking adventure and leave it there.

Most fish sauces come in large 24-oz. (700 ml) bottles; there is little reason to look for anything smaller, unless you are planning to cook at your friend's house or wish to treat yourself with Thai food on your camping trip. The large bottle may seem like an endless supply, but if you cook Thai food with any regularity, you will find it empties quickly. Besides, it is inexpensive at less than a dollar and a half per bottle.

You may discover other creative applications for your bottle of fish sauce besides using it as an ingredient in Thai cooking. One of my students reported an absolutely sensational result when she used fish sauce to make her Caesar salad. Another told a story of how fish sauce saved a meal for his in-laws. His wife had made a big pot of soup, but it tasted as if something was missing. Not having the time to figure it out, she asked Tom if he could "fix" the soup as she hurried out the door to go pick her parents up at the airport. "Don't worry. I'll take care of it," he replied. As soon as she had left, Tom went to the cupboard, pulled out his bottle of fish sauce and shook some into the soup. When dinner was served later that evening, his wife was surprised at how good the soup tasted.

I have often been teased by students for my confident reliance in the magical flavoring qualities of fish sauce. During the classes, we routinely do tastings before the food is served to see if any adjustments are necessary to bring about the optimal harmony in the dishes many hands helped prepare. Whenever something tastes "off" or not quite right, I frequently reach for the fish sauce bottle. Many insist one of the basic principles they have learned from the classes is: "When in doubt, add fish sauce." As they gain experience cooking Thai meals in their own kitchens, they have come to agree that this "magic" sauce can add that special last touch, pulling everything together delightfully.

It should come as no surprise that the saltiness in fish sauce helps bring out flavor from all manner of foods with which it is cooked; after all, since time immemorial salt has been identified as the foremost condiment and flavor enhancer in all cultures. But beyond saltiness, a good blend of fish sauce adds a unique, pleasant taste and fine aroma of its own.

Not all fish sauces are well versed in making "magic," but again, as with other flavors, this is a matter of personal taste and opinion. I can introduce you to a few personal favorites currently available in California; I assume the same brands are imported into other states and other Western countries that support specialty Thai and Southeast Asian markets. My intention is not to promote particular brands over others, as there are many exceptional ones I have yet to see in Bay Area markets. But these are fish sauces I have enjoyed and have used successfully. Remember that fish sauce can vary quite a bit from brand to brand in flavor and level of saltiness and fishiness; therefore, it is best to use your own taste buds to judge how much to use, rather than what a recipe in a cookbook calls for. Once you have found a brand most agreeable to you, it is advisable to stick with it to ensure consistent results.

High up on my list is Tra Chang, meaning "scale brand," identified by a red label depicting a weighing scale with a fish on one end balanced by

"100%" on the other. Another very flavorful brand is labeled as "Golden Boy," picturing a chubby baby holding a bottle of fish sauce rather than a milk bottle. The boy has his right thumb up to give the sauce a number-one rating. These two premium brands are not yet widely distributed in America, so you need to look for them in particular Thai and Southeast Asian markets. More readily available is Tiparos, a brand that has been around in Western markets for a long time. It is fairly good, though I frequently have to use more of it to get the flavor I seek.

Aside from these three, there is a wide range of other brands. Though some show pictures of shrimp, silver pomfret fish or squid on the label, these are only identifying logos; the sauces are made from anchovies. Gourmet specialty markets have started to carry fish sauce along with other convenience Thai food items, specially bottled in Thailand with English names and labels, for the affluent Western cook. Usually in much smaller bottles, these brands carry a hefty price tag, about six times the price of those offered in Asian markets.

Most bottles of fish sauce come capped with plastic. After opening the top lid, cut off the tip of the "nipple" on the inner "cork" a little above its base, so that the slight ridge can help the top cap snap more tightly in place when not in use. Newer bottles on the market come with caps that conveniently snap open the inside tip. The small opening is large enough to shake out the amount you need directly into the food. Because I do not use measuring spoons, my beginning students frequently try to count the number of shakes I make to flavor particular dishes, but I caution them that a shake from a full bottle will release fewer drops than a shake from a bottle closer to empty—a simple law of physics. After they have gotten used to cooking without measuring, they become as "shake-happy" as I am.

Finally, fish sauce does not need to be refrigerated after opening, unless you cook Thai very infrequently. Keep the cap snapped tightly as exposure to air can turn the sauce darker in color and evaporation can intensify its saltiness. If you use your fish sauce very rarely, salt will eventually crystallize on the bottom of the bottle, but it should still be fine to use. The sea salt in fish sauce preserves it indefinitely.

OTHER SOURCES OF SALTINESS

Even among Thai people, there are those (like me) who prefer to use fish sauce to salt just about everything but dessert, and there are those who prefer to use it in combination with salt and a light soy sauce. In fact, a century ago, before roads and the railway system made products from the sea readily available in inland areas, the use of fish sauce was limited to the coastal regions. The landlocked north and northeast depended on other salted ingredients, such as soybean pastes and fermented mudfish. Although these local products still distinguish the food of these regions, the essence of anchovies from the sea has made its way into kitchens throughout the country and transformed the nature of inland cuisines.

If you do not care for the flavor of fish sauce in your Thai dishes after trying out different brands, you may wish to substitute with a light soy sauce that is not so strongly soy flavored like the darker-colored soys. A fairly good and commonly available brand from Thailand has the picture of a dragonfly on the bottle and is labeled "thin soy sauce." Another is the Golden Mountain brand.

If you substitute with salt, you may wish to consider natural, untempered sea salt. Not only is it better tasting than the common supermarket variety, it is rich in natural minerals. If you can't find sea salt at the grocery store, try natural food stores.

There are numerous sauces, pastes and dried ingredients that also add saltiness in addition to their own unique flavors to Thai dishes. Here is a sampling of some that are commonly used.

Gkapi Shrimp Paste

This concentrated product of finely ground fermented shrimps in sea salt has an even more compelling smell than its companion, fish sauce. There are vastly varying qualities, the odor differing accordingly. Many are undeniably foul-smelling, but there are a few brands that actually have a pleasant, albeit very powerful, roasted shrimp aroma. Many Westerners have unknowingly purchased *gkapi* because of its benign name, "shrimp paste," only to discover its true nature. Not having the faintest idea of what it is supposed to be like, some have tried to return the product, complaining to the store that it has rotted and spoiled.

Like fish sauce, *gkapi* is rich in protein and B vitamins. It is an essential ingredient in making chilli pastes and curry pastes. Just about every curry paste has a dab or two of *gkapi* in it. When pounded and blended in with an array of aromatic herbs and spices, its powerful smell dissipates and actually makes the entire concoction very fragrant. When cooked into food, a little bit of this concentrated paste adds a whole lot of delicious shrimp flavor. A favorite use for *gkapi* among Thai people is as the primary ingredient in a very pungent dipping sauce for raw or lightly blanched vegetables and fried fish, called *näm prik gkapi*. Wrapped in a small piece of banana leaf and roasted over hot coals, it is then pounded in a mortar with chillies and garlic, followed by the addition of lime juice, fish sauce and sugar to constitute an intensely hot, shrimpy and limy sauce. Other ingredients may be added to make other *näm prik* (chilli dipping sauces), such as tiny, bitter pea-eggplants; fried dried shrimp; cooked and chopped fresh shrimp; young green peppercorns; sour tamarind and roasted *maengdah*, a roachlike insect with a most unusual fragrance. *Näm prik* sauces are definitely for hard-core Thai food lovers only!

Gkapi is packaged in small plastic containers or glass jars and is labeled as "shrimp paste." The only ingredients listed are shrimp and salt. The color varies from a pinkish or purplish grey to a dark greyish brown. The consistency also varies, from soft and pasty to dry and hard, depending on how long the fermented shrimp was allowed to dry in the sun. Most brands cover the top with a layer of wax to seal in freshness. Remove this waxy layer before using. Once opened, refrigerate the paste to keep it fresh-tasting, for although salty, it can change color over time and become even more concentrated. Refrigerated, it keeps indefinitely. Always cook *gkapi* before consumption. Because different batches vary in saltiness and shrimpiness, make adjustments as necessary in recipes that call for it.

When you visit Thailand, take note of the big mounds of brown-and-grayish matter filling large metal bowls in the fresh marketplaces. As you walk by, you will unmistakably identify it as *gkapi*. A choice of types and grades in differing shades and unit prices are sold by weight to satisfy different users' needs. The bustling markets and roadside stalls in the seacoast towns of

Shrimp (*Gkung*)

Rayong, Hua Hin, Petchburi, Chaiya and Trang sell enormous quantities of their very fresh, high-quality and very fragrant *gkapi* daily to Thai tourists who frequently make stops to buy foodstuffs to take home. I myself bring a couple of large containers of the best *gkapi* back to America each year.

Thai Oyster Sauce (Näm Mân Hoi)

There are a few brands of Thai oyster sauce. The one most readily available in Asian markets in the West has a label depicting a plump woman stir-frying while shaking sauce from a bottle into the wok. Underneath her are the words *Mae Krua*, which means "mother of the kitchen," the Thai way of referring to a female chef. (A male chef is called *paw krua*, "father of the kitchen.") On either side are pictures of oysters. It is quite flavorful and is available in small, medium and large bottles, the largest holding 20 fl. oz. (600 ml). Another very tasty brand that has recently appeared in the U.S. market is the Healthy Boy brand.

These two brands of oyster sauce taste noticeably different from the Chinese brands available in American Chinatowns. The Thai sauces are less salty, have a more pronounced oyster flavor and are not heavily loaded with monosodium glutamate (MSG). Oyster sauce is used extensively to flavor stir-fried vegetables (an easy sample recipe appears on page 66) and as a flavor ingredient in meat, seafood and noodle dishes (see the recipe on page 178 for ideas). Refrigerate after opening to retain fresh taste.

Salted Soy or Yellow Bean Sauce (Dtow Jiow)

Like oyster sauce, *dtow jiow* is a sauce borrowed from the Chinese. It is a concentrated salty mixture of fermented soybeans, which in Asia are known as "yellow beans" because of their natural color. The thick sauce is usually bottled in narrow-neck bottles like those used for wine and does not need to be refrigerated.

There are two varieties of *dtow jiow*, a dark sauce and a lighter one, employed for different purposes, although you may not always have a choice in the market near you. A tasty brand of the lighter sauce is the Healthy Boy brand, showing on its label the picture of a boy holding a bottle of the sauce. For a heavier-tasting dark sauce, the brand commonly available has a dragonfly on the label.

Used as a condiment to flavor dishes with a Chinese origin, *dtow jiow* has also made it into many complex dishes that are distinctly Thai. In such dishes, it is almost impossible to tell that this heavily soy-flavored product has been used. If you find that you like its soy taste, use it to add a robust touch to simple vegetable stir-fries. The lighter-color sauce is more suitable and is especially good with dark-green vegetables (see recipe on page 192 for ideas).

Näm Prik Pow: "Chilli Paste in Bean Oil" (or Roasted Chilli Paste)

I have arbitrarily included a widely used chilli sauce in this section with other "salty" ingredients because it supplies a large part of the salty flavor to the dishes in which it is used. It is also a source of both hot and sweet flavors.

The main ingredient in this sauce is dried red chillies, which gives it its name (*näm* is sauce; *prik*, chilli; *pow*, roasted). The chillies are roasted in soybean oil for a long period of time over low heat to a dark red color along with ground dried shrimp or fish, *gkapi* shrimp paste, garlic, shallots, tamarind, fish sauce and sugar. Some brands contain more chillies and are hotter than others. The most commonly available brand, Pantainorasingh, comes in choices of

Dried Red Chillies

hot, medium and mild (indicated on the bottom left of the label) in two sizes, 8 oz. (227 gm) and 16 oz. (454 gm). Because roasted chillies are the primary flavoring of this sauce, purchase at least a medium-hot jar; the mild version has a lot lacking. There are other brands that are also good, though not as consistently available. Among them, Mae Anong in 17.5-oz. (500 gm) plastic pouches, Mae Ploy in 14-oz. (400 gm) plastic tubs and Mae Pranom in 8-oz. (227 gm) jars. If the Asian markets near you carry a choice of brands, sample a few to find the one you like best. Refrigerate after opening.

Näm prik pow is used to flavor soups, stir-fries with vegetables, meats and seafoods, noodle dishes and sauces for salads. Its sweetness makes it a likable ready-to-use sauce, which you may find tastes delicious as a spread on crackers or toast for a quick snack or on hors d'oeuvres for your party. A good and easy recipe for cooking with string beans appears on page 67.

Dried Shrimp and Salted Fish

Because of the abundant supply of fish and shrimp in the two oceans that lap Thailand's shores, much of the catch is salted, dried in the sun and preserved for future use. This was especially essential in the days before refrigeration and still is among many small fishing villages where modern amenities have not made their advances. These dried seafoods are not only eaten by themselves with rice during off days from fishing, they are also used extensively as flavor ingredients, adding shrimp or fish flavors as well as saltiness.

One of the favorite foods I share with my mother is salted mackerel— dried, then packed in oil to keep moist. It is very salty but has a flavor that is absolutely heavenly (you may not agree). Just a little piece of it fried up, sprinkled with chopped Thai chillies, sliced shallots and fresh lime juice is enough for Mother and me to polish up a big pot of rice. Fried and crumbled, it is also wonderful added to stir-fried Asian broccoli (*ka-nah*). If you like anchovies, you may wish to give salted mackerel a try. Look for it packed in oil in a glass jar or vacuum-sealed in plastic in individual pieces.

There are many kinds of dried and salted fish, and each has its uses for which it is best suited. Some of the smaller varieties are fried or roasted until crispy, then crushed and added to soups, salads or dipping sauces. Dried shrimps are more commonly used in Thai dishes familiar to the Western palate. They come in different grades and sizes; the larger shrimps generally are more expensive, but if you are just starting out in Thai cooking, the small-size dried shrimps should be sufficient for most dishes. Buy ones that have a fresh orangish tinge. Shrimps from tropical Thai waters are generally stronger in flavor than those from colder temperate waters. Store in a cool place in the pantry or refrigerate to keep fresh for a longer time.

For dishes that call for ground dried shrimp, grind the whole shrimps to a fine powder in a clean coffee grinder or blender, or pound in a heavy mortar. Because grinding fluffs up the dehydrated shrimps, you will end up with a greater quantity in the ground form than when you started. Therefore, if a recipe calls for two tablespoons of the ground stuff, start out with about half that amount in whole dried shrimps. You can also buy dried shrimps already ground; look for little jars labeled "shrimp powder." Usually the powder includes crushed dried chillies.

Salted Preserved Vegetables and Salted Radish

Notable among salted preserved vegetables used in Thai cooking are *tâng chai* and *hua chai bpoh*. Both are adapted from Chinese cooking but have become important ingredients in many distinctly Thai dishes; the latter is used in *pad thai* noodles (see page 206 for recipe).

Tâng chai is shredded cabbage preserved with salt and garlic. It originated from a district in China known as Tianjin, which still makes the best-tasting brand. The preserved cabbage is stuffed in squat, round clay crocks and identified as "Tianjin preserved vegetables." A Thai brand comes in a similar jar made of clear plastic. *Tâng chai* is used in a wide range of soups and noodle dishes of Chinese origin. It keeps indefinitely, without refrigeration, as long as it is kept dry in an airtight jar. Because it is very salty and used sparingly, a crock will last you a very long time.

Hua chai bpoh is a salted and preserved daikon-type turnip or radish and may be whole (flattened, elongated pieces about four to five inches long and one and a half inches wide) or shredded in fine strips. There are two varieties; one is highly salty, the other less salty and slightly sweetened and used in many Thai dishes. Look for the words "sweet" or "sweetened" somewhere on the package to make sure you are getting the right one. *Hua chai bpoh* keeps well without refrigeration.

Salted Plum

Although it is sour with a touch of sweetness, pickled plum is an intensely salty ingredient, which is why I have chosen to include it here. Both plum and juice are used to make a sweet-and-sour plum dipping sauce for fried foods and to flavor steamed fish and other dishes with a tangy plum accent.

THE SOUR FLAVOR AND ITS SOURCES

Thai cuisine may utilize more of the sour flavor than any other cuisine in the world. There are numerous kinds of sour salads and sour soups, sour chilli sauces and sour dips, sour appetizers and sour noodles, sour vegetables and sour meat dishes—even sour desserts and sour drinks.

The sour flavor and the main sources from which it is derived, blended in with exotic herbs and spices, distinguish Thai food from much of Chinese food. While vinegar is the primary source of sour in Chinese cuisine, fresh lime juice is all important in Thai food. Another favorite source of sour comes from sour tamarind, prevalently used especially in the southern region. Vinegars—white distilled vinegar ("spirit vinegar") and a clear coconut vinegar—are also widely used. Rice vinegar may be substituted if you find white vinegar too acidic to your liking.

Frequently, the sour flavor is used not to make a dish taste sour but to invigorate and bring about a subtle harmony with other flavors in a dish.

Fresh Lime Juice

Though many Thai cooks, cookbooks and restaurant menus say they use lemon juice in their recipes, they really mean lime juice. The larger yellow lemons are a temperate climate citrus and do not grow in hot tropical Thailand. The mix-up probably came about a long time ago when the Thai word for lime, *manao*, was mistranslated by official sources as "lemon," and the word has stuck in many people's vocabulary since.

For this reason, if you come across a jar of "pickled lemon" on the shelf of a Thai market near your home with the picture on the label clearly depicting green limes, don't think that they have made a mistake in the labeling. They have not. Limes are lemons in Thailand. This is good to know should you be planning a visit there. To order delicious limeade to quench your thirst on a hot afternoon by the beach, ask for lemon juice; "limeade" is likely to get you a quizzical look from the waiter and no ice-cold drink. Better yet, ask for *näm manao* (literally "lime water"), but be prepared to taste salt in your Thai-style limeade, as salt enhances the flavor of lime juice and helps to replenish the large amount of salt you perspire out of your body in the tropical heat.

Thai limes are smaller in size than the limes sold in American supermarkets, but they are full of juice except during the hot dry months of the year (March through May). They are much more intensely sour, too, and half of one can do as much to flavor a sauce as a whole Western lime can. Therefore, it is advisable to rely on your taste buds to judge how much to use rather than follow a recipe amount exactly. A juicy lime that is not very sour can dilute a sauce and affect the quantities needed of other ingredients going into the sauce.

The fresh flavor and sharpness of lime juice dissipate as it is heated and cooked, so I usually add it toward the end of cooking if I wish to retain its original intensity. On the other hand, if I find I've added too much lime juice to my hot-and-sour soup, I let the soup simmer a couple of minutes longer than usual to correct the problem.

In addition to the flavor it imparts, lime juice has a tenderizing quality. Squid and rare meat, for instance, can become very tender and succulent from sitting in a lime sauce. Because of its tenderizing capability, lime juice has been used as a common folk remedy to dislodge a fish bone accidentally stuck in the throat. If this should happen to you, try gargling with lime juice or sucking on a piece of lime, slowly swallowing the juice. It can soften the bone sufficiently in a short while, such that downing a mouthful of rice or water afterward can push the bone away.

If fresh limes are not available during the cold months of the year in your area, lemons make an acceptable substitute, though they lack the intensity of smaller limes. But as you learn how to balance primary flavors, you will be able to increase the intensity of lemon juice by varying a dish's salty and sweet flavors.

Tamarind

Tamarind (*ma-kahm*) is the fruit of large, lacy-leaf trees common in the tropics the world over. It is oblong and curved in shape and looks much like the seed pod of many large flowering trees. When young, the pods are green and fleshy. As they ripen, they turn reddish brown and become brittle on the outside; inside, the rich, dark brown flesh of the fruit is moist and sticky, enveloping a row of beanlike seeds. Because of its widespread habitat and easy cultivation, tamarind has found its way into the cuisines of many countries around the world, from the African and Asian continents to the tropical Americas. In Thailand, tamarind trees are often grown for their shade as much as for their fruit pods. These beautiful trees grace many city parks in Bangkok and other provincial towns. They are also found in the gardens of many Thai homes.

Tamarind (*Ma-kahm*)

There are several varieties of tamarind. Some yield fruits that are very sweet, without the slightest trace of sour. These sweet varieties command a high price at the market and are sold in their ripened pods to be eaten fresh as fruits. The province of Petchaboon in northeastern Thailand is known for its sweet tamarind (*ma-kahm wahn*). Each year, when the fruit comes into season during the dry months, a Sweet Tamarind Fair is held with lots of festivities and lots of delicious tamarind to sample and take home. During this time of year, bags of the plump brown pods are peddled around by street hawkers as well as piled among colorful fruits at fruit stands across the country. The prized good-eating varieties even find their way into prepackaged gift baskets sold in modern Bangkok supermarkets, alongside imported fruits, canned goods and chocolates.

More common varieties produce tart fruits that vary from sweet-and-sour to mouth-puckering sour. The less sour ones—removed from their brittle pods and coated with a mixture of salt, sugar and crushed chillies—are a delight to nibble. They wake up the mouth, get the juices flowing and temporarily quench thirst. Others are cooked in syrup with their seeds strained out and made into candied tamarind. They are great for the digestive tract and have a mild, natural laxative effect. Additionally, tamarind is believed to possess blood purifying properties.

For cooking, sour tamarind is used as a souring agent that adds a pleasant fruity taste. Like lime juice, it also tenderizes. Tamarind pods are sometimes available fresh from Asian markets and other ethnic grocery stores, but they may not always be the sour varieties and, therefore, may not give consistent results in cooking. Occasionally, the pods carried in the stores are immature tamarind; though brown on the outside, they are still green and undeveloped inside. Southeast Asians eat these young pods fresh with a sweet shrimp sauce, or chop and incorporate them into a tamarind chilli sauce called *näm prik ma-kahm*. Young green tamarinds are also pickled and eaten as snacks much like green pickled mango, dipped in a mixture of crushed chillies, salt and sugar.

For more consistent results in cooking, I use "wet tamarind" (*ma-kahm bpiak*). This is the dark brown flesh of ripe sour tamarind removed from the pods, compressed into compact blocks and sold in Thai and Southeast Asian markets. Labeled as "wet tamarind" or simply "tamarind," most brands already have the fibrous strings and most of the seeds removed. In buying wet tamarind, I usually squeeze the package to feel its softness; a softer package generally is fresher, more moist, easier to work with and yields better-tasting tamarind juice.

To use, break off a small chunk of wet tamarind and mix with a few tablespoons of water, using your fingers to knead and mush the soft part of the fruit so that it melts into the water. Gather up the undissolvable pulp and any seeds with your hand, squeeze out the juice and discard. You should end up with a fairly thick brownish fluid called "tamarind water" (translated from the Thai *näm som ma-kahm bpiak*). Use this fluid form in your Thai dishes. If you wish to make a large quantity of tamarind water, soaking the tamarind in warm or hot water first to soften will help speed the process. Use about a quarter cup of water to each one-inch chunk; the amount to use, of course, will depend on whether there are a lot of seeds in the package you buy.

The wet tamarind block, when kept airtight in a cool place, lasts indefinitely and needs no refrigeration. It is like preserved dried fruit. Tamarind is also available already premixed with water, in the form of a ready-to-use concentrate; however, it isn't as fresh-tasting as the tamarind water you make

yourself. Once you open a container of the premixed stuff, you should plan to use it up in a few weeks because it will spoil quickly. Price-wise and quality-wise, you get a lot more for your money with a block of wet tamarind. (Besides using it in cooking, wet tamarind is a valuable silver polisher; the large silver factories in Chiang Mai use plenty of it to shine their beautifully tooled silver bowls and jewelry to an impeccable sheen.)

Besides the tart fruit, the edible leaves and flowers of tamarind trees are also sour and are eaten fresh in salads and with chilli dips. They are used instead of the fruits to add sourness to some types of spicy-sour soups. Tamarind seeds, on the other hand, are roasted and added to other roasted ingredients to make a coffee substitute. They are also roasted, soaked and eaten whole as a folk medicine to drive out intestinal parasites.

Pickled Vegetables and Herbs

Most pickled products contain the sour flavor, though some of them are also quite sweet and salty. Among the pickled vegetables used in Thai cooking that are predominantly sour is pickled mustard. There are a number of varieties, some labeled as "sour mustard greens" and some as "salted mustard." Some are more leafy, others more stemmy, and others are made with the young hearts of mustard. Also sour are pickled plum (though I have chosen to include it in the previous section because of its saltiness) and pickled lime, which is also sweet.

THE SWEET FLAVOR AND ITS SOURCES

Besides adding sweetness to sweet dishes, the sweet flavor is a very important balancing agent. A little bit of it can amazingly change the alchemy of a dish without making it taste sweet. The addition of a little sugar amplifies the fresh flavors of herbs, heightens the potency of spices, creates a lively harmony with other primary flavors and strengthens the overall character of a dish. For many hot-and-sour sauces, it is undoubtedly the "intensifier." On the other hand, in large amounts sweetness can also do the opposite, mellowing and disguising the spicy flavors.

Aside from granulated and processed cane sugar, a tasty source of sweetness in Thai cooking comes from the natural sugars tapped from palm trees. Palm sugar is from sugar palms (palmyra) and coconut sugar from coconut palms. Sweetness also comes from prepared products that contain sugar, such as *nãm prik pow* ("chilli paste in bean oil," see page 55) and sweetened black soy sauce (page 63). Moreover, the natural sweetness in the foods themselves also interacts with other ingredients in a dish to bring about some kind of balance.

Coconut and Palm Sugars

Near the colorful Damnoen Saduak floating market in Rajburi province southwest of Bangkok, there is a small coconut sugar plantation run by an energetic old man. He is visited daily by Thai and foreign tourists who hire paddle boats to tour the quiet country canals. Very early every morning, he climbs the many coconut trees on his plantation to make cuts in the flower buds, under which he straps cylindrical plastic containers to catch the sweet nectar dripping from the cuts. A couple of hours later, he returns and climbs the trees again with great agility to collect the filled containers.

The lightly cloudy fluid is poured into huge woks over an old earthen stove at the edge of the nearby canal. A helper gathers dried coconut husks and leaf ribs for fuel and builds a fire to boil the watery fluid down to a thick, concentrated syrup. Attracted by the fragrance and sweetness of the nectar, honey bees swarm around the woks, dozens giving in to a sweet death in the hot syrup. They are skimmed off before the gooey sugar is whipped to a smooth, creamy texture with a beater attached to a long wooden stick. The light brown coconut sugar is then dropped onto wax paper in small lumps, or spooned onto shallow round molds, and left to set and harden. They are then packaged in plastic bags for sale to Thai tourists and merchants who drop by to visit. This activity takes place every day along the canal; each year I have stopped by the plantation with my groups of American travelers, and the old man has always been there. If he is not atop a tree somewhere, he cheerfully greets us with glasses filled with warm coconut nectar.

In a similar manner, palm sugar is tapped from palmyra or lontar palm trees, commonly known as sugar palm. These tall palm trees have very large leaves that are fan-shaped, extending outward into split leaflets. Driving through the Thai countryside, you will see plenty of these trees growing amid rice fields and in thicker groves down the southern peninsula. With their rounded heads, they always seem to me like the faces of people, and as their trunks sway and leaves move about in the gentle breeze, they seem to be nodding and waving to everyone passing by. They make me smile and silently reply with a "hello" in my heart.

Roadside stalls along the highway passing by the peninsula town of Petchburi sell bottles of tan-colored, fresh sugar palm nectar (which Thais call "fresh palm water" [näm dtahn sod]) along with bags of the mild-tasting, gelatinous young fruits. Fresh palm nectar is a delicious aromatic drink with a distinctly smoky flavor. More flavorful than the lighter-colored coconut nectar, it usually makes a better-tasting, more caramel-flavored sugar than coconut sugar.

In cooking, coconut sugar and palm sugar can be used interchangeably (brown sugar is a poor substitute for either one). Often, you won't have much choice in the small Southeast Asian market near you. The sugars come in glass jars as well as plastic containers, small and large. Usually they are in crystallized form, but if you are lucky, you may find batches that are soft, gooey and easy to spoon out. When I buy palm sugar, I squeeze the plastic containers on the shelf to find one that feels soft. Sometimes, in the same shipment, some containers hold hardened sugar while others may still be moist. That's because palm sugar is not a highly processed sugar, and much of its production is still a cottage industry. Some wokfuls of palm nectar are boiled down more than others before being filled into containers. When cooled, it crystallizes into a block.

The hardened sugar requires scraping with a spoon or a hand-held coconut shredder with sharp teeth. My students tell me placing the whole container into the microwave oven for a brief time helps soften the sugar. I am beginning to see some stores carry hardened palm sugar in round blocks, packaged in cellophane rather than in plastic containers or glass jars. Cutting these blocks down with a knife into chunks is easier than trying to scrape hardened sugar from jars. Palm sugar is also available in tin cans in a more syrupy form. It is quite good, better than crystallized coconut sugar, though some people think it has a tinny taste.

The color of both coconut and palm sugar can vary a bit from batch to batch. Sometimes they are a light cream color; at other times, a rich mocha.

Degree of sweetness, too, can vary; therefore, use your taste buds to guide you in determining how much to use in the recipes. I generally find the darker, stickier palm sugar to be richer and more flavorful. The difference in coloration, sweetness and flavor, again, reflects the fact that these natural sugars are not highly processed like brown sugar, which always seems to be uniform in color and sweetness from box to box. Much depend on the type of palm trees, time of year when the sugar is tapped and, to some degree, the heat and fuel source used to reduce the nectar.

Coconut and palm sugars keep well when stored in a cool dry place and do not need to be refrigerated. They are great sweeteners, balancing agents and flavor enhancers for curries and robust sauces. Many coconut desserts are accentuated by their rich, caramel taste and distinctive aroma.

Black Soy Sauce (See-yew Däm)

This is a rich and thick sauce, made by fermenting soy sauce with sugar or molasses. Black in color, it has a delightful flavor and is used as much to add sweetness as saltiness to rice and noodle dishes, soups and stews and various stir-fries. Although I have included it in this section with sweeteners, it belongs equally in the category with salty ingredients.

Do not mistake this soy sauce with other dark Chinese and Japanese soy sauces that aren't sweetened. To assure that you are getting the right kind, look for a bottle that identifies the product as coming from Thailand. There are a few different brands, but the most commonly carried in Asian markets in the West seems to be one with a dragonfly on the label. Make sure the label says "black soy," as the Dragon Fly brand makes three kinds of soy sauces with almost identical labels, save for the name of the sauce. Although it is sweet, it is not the same as "sweet soy." The latter, used primarily for particular sweet snacks, is even sweeter and is thick like ketchup. Black soy sauce does not need to be refrigerated after opening.

Sweet Pickles

Although they also add a sour flavor, some pickles have a dominant sweetness. Notable among sweet pickles is pickled garlic, available in glass jars from Thai and Southeast Asian markets. The garlic is usually pickled in whole heads. The individual cloves may be removed from their skins for a more pleasing presentation, but the whole head is edible except, perhaps, for the more fibrous stem and core. Pickled garlic has a firm, crisp texture and makes a tasty garnish. It is a delightful sweet ingredient in salads, noodle dishes and stir-fries. I also like to use the sweet brine in which it is packed to flavor dipping sauces and salad dressings.

In Thailand, we have a variety of round, single-clove garlic called *gkratiem toen*, highly prized for its medicinal properties. It is pickled with honey and medicinal herbs and nibbled on by itself as an appetizer or incorporated into salads and stir-fries. Its pungent sweetness is particularly good with the tanginess of sour pork sausage (*naem*), a favored food in the north and northeast and available in some Southeast Asian markets labeled as *nem*.

Other Sweeteners

If you are unable to find coconut or palm sugar and want to stay away from refined white and brown sugars, you may wish to experiment with other natural sweeteners, such as honey and brown rice syrup. Remember that in

Garlic (*Gkratiem*)

many Thai dishes, some kind of sweetener is needed to accentuate herb and spice flavors and bring about an overall balance. To this end, the natural sweetness contained in certain vegetables, meats and seafood also contribute to the harmony.

BALANCING FLAVORS: AN EXERCISE

To demonstrate how balancing the primary flavors can add more to a dish than the sum of its parts, the following is a simple exercise for making a basic hot-and-sour sauce:

1. Chop two cloves of garlic and five Thai chillies or a large hot jalapeño pepper. Crush together with a mortar and pestle to a paste. Transfer to a small sauce dish.
2. Add two tablespoons of fish sauce. Stir well. Taste for reference.
3. Add two tablespoons of freshly squeezed lime juice. Stir and taste. If the sour flavor hits you before the salty, add more fish sauce, and vice versa. Adjust the sauce so that it is equally salty and sour. Note how the sauce tastes overall. (If the sauce is much too hot, tone it down by adding more of both fish sauce and lime juice until it reaches a tolerable level. But remember that you will be serving the sauce with other food and not eating it by itself; therefore, it should be hotter than "to taste.")
4. Add half a teaspoon of sugar. Stir well to dissolve. Taste. Has a change taken place? What has it done to the flavor of the chillies, garlic, fish sauce and lime juice?
5. Add another half a teaspoon of sugar, stir and taste. Again, note the changes, if any. Has the sauce started to taste sweet?
6. Add yet another half a teaspoon of sugar, stir and taste again. Repeat this step until you begin to notice sweetness in the sauce. Note at what point the sauce seems the most intense and lively.
7. Continue to add sugar until the sauce becomes equally sweet, salty and sour. Note all the changes that take place with each addition.

When we do this exercise in my beginning cooking class, varying reactions occur during the different steps. After the first addition of sugar, students are sometimes divided as to whether they like the sauce better or less. With the second and third additions, excitement begins to emerge. Many of them are surprised how the sauce now tastes not just sour but noticeably more limy; some claim they can taste the flavors of the garlic and chillies better, while others report that the sauce has become hotter and more intense. Usually, the intensity of flavors peaks at the point just before the sweet flavor becomes noticeable. From then on, the addition of more sugar sweetens and mellows.

When I balance flavors, I generally start out with the hot (if it is a spicy dish), then the salty. This is followed by the sour (if it is a sour dish). The sweet flavor is added last to balance. Usually, sweet balances both the sour and salty, and vice versa. For instance, if a dish you made turned out too salty, add a little sugar; likewise, if it is too sweet, add a little more saltiness. Use the sour to balance if the dish can benefit from a tangy flavor. Similarly, saltiness and sourness can be used to balance each other. In desserts or sweet snacks, a little salt can bring out flavors from other ingredients, such as coconut milk, in the same way as a little sugar can bring out the flavor of ingredients in salty dishes.

Thai Chillies (*Prik Kee Noo*)

From this above exercise, you can whip up a number of different sauces to accompany different types of dishes. For instance, you may wish a sweeter sauce for your barbecued chicken and a more intensely hot-and-limy concoction for fried fish. Changing the sources of sour to vinegar or tamarind and of hotness to other types of fresh or dried chillies will add new dimensions to your creations. As you continue to experiment with new and different sources as well as new and different combinations of the four flavor groupings and add to these different types of aromatic and pungent herbs, you will soon find an almost infinite range of possibilities opening up to you. Remember that this process of experimentation can be applied to other areas of cooking besides making sauces.

BROCCOLI WITH THAI OYSTER SAUCE

(Broccoli Pad Näm Mân Hoi)

2 medium-size stalks of broccoli

2–3 Tbs. peanut oil for stir-frying

6 cloves garlic, chopped

2–3 Tbs. Thai oyster sauce, to taste

2–3 tsp. fish sauce (näm bplah), to taste

2–3 dashes of ground white pepper

Cut the broccoli into small bite-size pieces. Use the bottom stem also, after peeling off the fibrous outer skin.

Heat a wok over high heat until its surface is hot. Swirl in the oil to coat evenly. When the oil is hot, add the chopped garlic. Sauté 5–10 seconds to flavor the oil, then toss in the broccoli. Stir-fry about a minute. If your stove is very hot, add 1–2 Tbs. of water as needed to help steam the vegetable so that it doesn't burn. Then sprinkle in the oyster sauce and stir-fry another minute. Season to taste with fish sauce. Continue to stir-fry until the broccoli turns vibrant green and is crisply cooked. Sprinkle liberally with white pepper, stir well and transfer to a serving dish. Serve warm along with other dishes and steamed rice.

NOTES AND POINTERS

Most crisp and leafy vegetables taste wonderful cooked in this manner. Try asparagus, snowpeas, cauliflower, cabbage, carrots, zucchini, summer squash, baby bok choy, napa cabbage, spinach, kale, chard and various kinds of mushrooms. You can also combine several vegetables for a delightful mixed vegetable dish. If you wish, spice up the stir-fry with a couple of slivered chillies and some sliced shallots or onion.

Garlic (*Gkratiem*)

STRING BEANS WITH ROASTED CHILLI SAUCE

(Tua Kaek Pad Prik Pow)

1 lb. string beans

2–3 Tbs. peanut oil for stir-frying

6 cloves garlic, chopped

2–3 Tbs. roasted chilli paste (näm prik pow)

1 Tbs. fish sauce (näm bplah), to taste

1/2 to 1 cup whole Thai sweet basil (bai horapa) or holy basil (bai gka-prow) leaves and flowers

Cut and discard the ends of the string beans. Cut the beans at a diagonal slant into segments about 1½ inches long.

Heat a wok over high heat until the surface is hot. Add the oil and swirl to coat evenly. When the oil is hot, stir in the chopped garlic and sauté a few seconds. Toss in the string beans and stir-fry about a minute. Spoon in the roasted chilli paste. Stir to mix well with the beans. Add a quarter cup of water, stir and cover with a lid to allow the beans to steam. Open lid and stir occasionally, adding more water as needed to help cook the beans until they begin to turn tender. Season to taste with fish sauce. Add the basil, stir well into the mixture until wilted and until the beans are tender. Transfer to a serving dish and serve warm along with other dishes with steamed rice.

NOTES AND POINTERS

For a different texture and color and a shorter stir-frying time, blanch the string beans in boiling water 1–2 minutes before tossing them in the wok. Compare with beans cooked without blanching and see which you like better.

For a quick and easy one-dish meal on those evenings when you don't feel much like fussing around the kitchen, add a source of protein to the stir-fry, such as chicken, pork or shrimp (sauté shrimp separately ahead of time and toss back in with the beans during the last few seconds of cooking). Or, for a vegetarian version, use a firm pressed tofu that will stay dry and hold together for the duration of the stir-frying. Sauté tofu with garlic at the start for half a minute before adding the beans.

This recipe is a vegetable adaptation of a common way of quickly cooking fresh seafoods. Particularly good are clams, shrimps, scallops, squid and squid egg sacs (see page 166). Roasted chilli paste is also used to stir-fry with pork; instead of basil, fresh-ground pepper and soy sauce are sprinkled into the meat as it cooks.

Thai Sweet Basil (*Bai Horapa*)

OF CHILLIES, SPICES AND "MICE"

For our love of spicy foods, Thai people have a lot to thank foreign traders. If not for the Portuguese and the Dutch, the Arabs, Indians and Chinese, the chilli peppers from the New World or the spices from the "spice islands" may not have found their way to pep up all of our wonderful dishes.

Since the country's birth more than seven centuries ago, the cuisine has evolved enormously and appears to have gotten spicier. The maritime silk route, the ancient trade channels between India and China and the explorations forged by curious Western adventurers in search of golden treasures brought many wild and exotic ingredients from around the world to Thailand. They were warmly received and eagerly sampled in royal kitchens, and some of the foreign gems were swiftly adopted and skillfully incorporated into the country's cuisine. It is very much in line with Thai character to take an ingredient that is alien to the culture and combine it with native herbs, spices and condiments to create an end product distinctly Thai. Innovative chefs in fine Bangkok restaurants continue to discover and experiment with new and unusual imports—nowadays mostly processed rather than natural foods. You wouldn't know, for instance, that mayonnaise was used in a delicious Thai dish you just ate because it had been taught to sing in a Thai chorus!

OF CHILLIES AND "MICE"

We Thai people love our chillies, and tons of them are generously used every day in restaurants and homes across the kingdom. In rural areas, just about every home grows its own chilli bushes. Historical evidence, however, suggests that the many varieties used in Thailand are not indigenous to Asia but have migrated from the New World, to fulfill their destinies in Thai kitchens. The path of these chillies parallels the history of the Thai people themselves, whose ancestors—a minority people—migrated from Yunnan province in southern China to find a place they could call home.

Of all spicy flavors used in Thai cooking, the most popular comes from the smallest of chillies, *prik kee noo*. Literally translated, the name means (pardon my language) "mouse shit chillies." Or, if you prefer to be more polite, "droppings" can be used instead, though this word does not work as well to define the ubiquitous *kee*, being less able to hold up in metaphorical usage.

The Thai word *kee* is not an impolite, dirty or obscene swear word like "shit." Besides meaning excrement, it is used widely to form compound words that imply some kind of waste or residue. For instance, *kee dta* ("eye shit") refers to the particles of "sleep" in your eyes when you wake up in the morning; *kee hoo* ("ear shit") is ear wax; *kee bu-ree* ("cigarette shit") is cigarette ashes; *kee peung* ("bee shit") is beeswax and *kee reuay* ("saw shit") is sawdust. The word also appears in countless compound words that emphasize the abundance of particular qualities, such as *kee len* ("playful shit"), one who is very playful; *kee mao* ("drunken shit"), someone who likes to drink and get drunk; *kee lerm* ("forget shit"), a very forgetful person; *kee aai* ("shy shit"), a very bashful person; *kee niow* ("sticky shit"), one who is very stingy (stingy people hate to part with anything) and *kee moh* ("bragging shit"), a braggart.

Why mouse shit chillies? Mice are playful little creatures and like to hide. (Thai children are taught from the time they can talk to refer to themselves with the personal pronoun "mouse," or *noo*. We never say "I," but *noo* did this

Thai Chillies (*Prik Kee Noo*)

and *noo* did that.) Sometimes the only clues that tell us they have been around are the tiny food scraps or droppings they leave behind. Thai chillies are little guys much like mice, and they leave behind unseen evidence in the food they touch—but you definitely know they have been there! Like mice, they like to hide, under cilantro leaves and behind pieces of shrimp and other food particles. When you least suspect, they find their way into your mouth and wow! What a sensation! You may even cuss and swear with the "s" word itself.

Prik kee noo is sometimes called "bird pepper." I'm not sure of the origin of this name; someone once told me it is the name of a similar pepper in some African cultures. Maybe birds feed on these peppers and have helped spread them from continent to continent. Birds are immune to the heat in chillies because they do not have taste buds that register the hot sensation like humans and land mammals do. However, chillies do have notable effects on certain birds. They say, for instance, that the hill myna birds, kept as pets by many Thais, especially in the south, are much more gregarious and eloquent in their language skills when fed lots of *prik kee noo* (so are many humans!). These very smart birds from the tropical rain forests can emulate most sounds they hear, much like parrots. Walking down the sidewalks in the southern port town of Krabi, don't be surprised if a shiny black-feathered creature with a bright orange beak, an iridescent yellow stripe on either side of its face and a curtainlike flap of the same bright color extending from the corner of one eye to the other woos you, letting out first *gkaeow jah* ("Hi there, parrot"), followed by "Have you eaten yet?" (in Thai, of course) and a quick, robust, very humanlike laugh.

According to historical accounts, the Portuguese were the "birds" who dropped chilli peppers into the hands of our ancestors in the sixteenth century, after initially transporting them from their place of origin in South America to Europe. Some accounts suggested that chillies, because of their high concentration of vitamin C, were eaten by sailors together with ginger, as a preventative against scurvy, long before it was discovered that oranges could perform the same function.

Researchers believe all the different kinds of chilli peppers around the world are descendants of the original "mother" pepper that grew on Bolivian soil. Having traveled far and wide and having been grown under all kinds of conditions and in different types of soils, the chilli pepper picked up new characteristics and changed. Breeding by various mentors on many continents added innumerable strains. The little *prik kee noo* is a Thai-bred variety, now called "Thai chillies" when sold in Western markets. Small and slender, they are intensely hot. The smaller they are, the hotter they seem to be. In fact, there is a strain of *prik kee noo* called *prik kee noo suan*, which is no larger than the head of a nail but packs a wallop of a bang! So don't look down on little things; there is much spiciness and liveliness concentrated in small, unsuspected packages. Beware of these tiny mice for they can reduce a big and burley meat-and-potatoes man to nothing but a pool of tears. Their hotness, however, is not the only quality that has endeared them to the Thai people: they have a distinctive fragrant taste that spicy food enthusiasts grow to love. Substituting with other kinds of chillies sometimes can be disappointing.

In Thailand, dinner tables are set not with salt and pepper shakers but instead with these tiny chillies cut up and swimming in a dish of fish sauce (*näm bplah*). Try making some for your next Thai meal. Cut the chillies in small thin rounds, place them in a sauce dish and cover with fish sauce. Spoon chillies and sauce over whatever needs pepping up and, after a few times, you may find yourself addicted to these lovable mice. One of my American friends developed such a liking for these little chillies that after spending a few months traveling around Thailand, one of his favorite breakfasts became Thai-style fried eggs over plain steamed rice, which he spiced up with spoonfuls of *näm bplah prik, prik kee noo* in fish sauce. (Thai people like to fry their eggs in very hot oil, making the edges of the whites crispy while the yolks are still partially soft.)

Prik kee noo chillies turn from a deep green to a bright red when they ripen. The green ones have a very strong and immediate bite to them, while some of the red ones may delay releasing their full potency, catching up with you when you least expect. They can be just as hot as the green ones. If you are not using your batch of Thai chillies fast enough, they dry easily for future use by being left out uncovered on a plate in the kitchen. The red ones dry more easily than the green ones, which require more air circulation and light. Placing them on a wire rack out in the sun will speed up their drying. Thai chillies dry well because they are not fleshy like larger varieties such as jalapeños or serranos; they are primarily a bag of seeds held together by a thin skin. Never bother to go through the tedious task of deseeding them. I usually do not remove seeds from any kind of chilli peppers, except when I use the larger dried red chillies for making chilli pastes with a roasted flavor. Then I remove the seeds and discard them since the roasted dried pods are more flavorful, and I add more pods until the desired chilli flavor, roasted aroma and heat level are obtained.

Besides *prik kee noo*, there are many other kinds of chillies used in Thai cooking. Among them are *prik leuang*, an orangish yellow chillie with good flavor and quite hot, though nothing close to a *prik kee noo suan; prik chee fah*, dark green or bright red when ripe, about the same size and hotness as a serrano; and *prik yuak*, a larger, light green pepper similar to the yellow wax pepper. Most are larger than *prik kee noo* and come in varying colors, shapes and spiciness, but none is quite as hot as the little mice. Because these other types of chillies are not yet readily available in Western markets, the jalapeño, serrano, fresno and yellow wax peppers, carried by many American supermarkets, may be substituted, as they have been in many of the recipes in this book.

Because chillies are useful not only for their heat but also for their unique and distinctive flavors, the many different varieties are used in a wide range of dishes and sauces to enhance the tastiness of particular meats, vegetables and seafoods. Thai people do not stick to using only *prik kee noo* for everything just because we are crazy about it. After all, the more flavor variables we have at our disposal, the more possibilities exist for creating masterpieces for the sophisticated palate.

WHICH IS HOT
AND WHICH IS HOTTER

In shopping for chillies, it is helpful to keep in mind that the hotter peppers are generally the smaller and skinnier varieties. (This applies also to dried red chillies.) They say, for instance, that serrano peppers are higher on the heat scale than jalapeños. However, you may find that one batch of jalapeño peppers may be hotter than another carried in a different store or during a differ-

Green *Prik Chee Fah* and
Orange *Prik Leuang* Peppers

ent time of year. Some batches of serrano peppers may be quite mild and milder than jalapeños, but then the next time you buy them, you may be painfully burned.

Another general rule cautions you that among the same variety of chillies, the deep green pods tend to be hotter than the red ones, which have ripened and turned sweeter. Indeed, I have found sunstreaked green chillies to be quite hot, and in Thai cuisine, the hottest of the curries are made with green chillies. But again, this is only a generalization. The heat level of chilli peppers depends a lot on the conditions under which they are grown. Usually, the hotter the climate, the hotter the chillies. Jalapeños bought in the winter months, for instance, may pack very little heat, whereas during the hot months of summer, they may blow you away. If they are imported, their heat level will depend on the country from which they came. Hot peppers pick up much of their heat from the sun. If you grow your own chilli plants, you may notice that the pods exposed to the most hours of direct sunlight tend to be spicier than those that are sheltered, even though they come from the same bush and outwardly look the same.

In recent years, it seems the jalapeño peppers sold in supermarkets have become milder and milder. I am informed by an unconfirmed source that milder jalapeños are being bred to broaden their appeal in a market dominated by less-bold consumers. If this is true, perhaps markets will begin identifying these chillies by a different name so that spicy food lovers know which is which.

There is also a subjective element in determining the relative hotness of different kinds of chilli peppers. In my cooking classes, students frequently disagree about which of several dishes is the hottest. A few may insist that the massaman curry is definitely hotter, while others argue it is undeniably the green curry. There is no right or wrong answer; both are only opinions based on subjective perceptions. Everyone's taste buds are a little different, varying in where the sensitivities lie and how the hot sensations are registered. Some chillies hit the taste buds in the front of the tongue, others in the middle or the back. Some leave their mark on the inner lining of the mouth or on the lips, while others do not. Depending on whether a person is more sensitive in the front or the back of the tongue, or whether he or she has sensitive membranes on the lips or in the mouth, the experience of hotness can be very different for different people. The complexity increases when other spices in the curry combine with the chillies' heat to color a person's perceptions.

Because the heat level of chillies can vary substantially from batch to batch, it is important when using any recipe that calls for chilli peppers to vary the number depending on the particular peppers you have on hand and on your heat tolerance. Test out the chillies first, either by taking a small bite of one or, if you are not that brave, cut the stem off a chilli pod and touch the tip of your tongue lightly on the cut end. The sensation lingering on your tongue will give you a rough idea of how many chillies you ought to use to achieve the heat level you desire.

The hottest part of chilli peppers lies not in the seeds but in the membranes that hold the seeds in place. The seeds pick up their hotness from contact with these membranes. When seeds are removed from fresh chilli peppers, often the membranes are scraped out along with the seeds. Because most Thai people are very heat tolerant, we seldom remove seeds from fresh chillies because by doing so, much of the hotness is lost. But if you are a

Red Fresno and Green Jalapeño Peppers

beginner when it comes to spicy foods, you may wish to deseed the chillies until your tolerance level for hotness has increased sufficiently.

WHAT TO DO WHEN YOU ARE ON FIRE

Many people do not realize that the hotness of chillies, which comes from the natural chemical capsaicin, is not water soluble. Have you ever noticed that when your mouth is on fire, no matter how much ice-cold water or beer you drink, the burning sensations linger? Water or beer only temporarily relieves the burning while you are drinking it, but as soon as you stop, you find the hot flames still leaping.

Instead of water, try milk next time, or something that contains cream or oil— capsaicin is oil soluble. A dessert with coconut milk can end a spicy meal nicely as it douses out the fire in your mouth. Some people have also found a full-bodied red wine to help during a meal, more so than white wine. Chewing and swallowing mouthfuls of plain warm rice is another way to wipe away traces of capsaicin in your mouth—better yet, try rice mixed with sauce from non-spicy stir-fried vegetables as it contains some oil.

If you have sensitive skin, you may wish to take precautions when working with chillies. When slicing the peppers, try not to touch the interior lining because it contains the highest concentration of capsaicin. Hold the peppers by the shiny skin and when deseeding, use the blade of a knife instead of your fingers to scrape out the seeds. Or, you can simply avoid the seeds all together by slicing the peppers lengthwise around the inner core that contains the seeds and hot membranes. But if your mouth can take the heat, don't bother to deseed the chillies at all.

If after taking these precautions you still find your fingers burning and throbbing, wash your hands several times with a soap that contains a high concentration of oil or cream. Fresh sap from the aloe vera plant and oil-based ointments of aloe, comfrey or calendula also help relieve some of the burn. Lime juice can be effective, too, and I have heard that a strong vinegar works equally well. When you prepare a big Thai meal, save the rind of the fresh limes squeezed for a sauce or salad; the remaining drops of juice combined with the essential oils in the zest will help clean your hands later of traces of capsaicin. If you have ultra-sensitive skin, wearing thin rubber gloves when working with chilli peppers is advisable. Just as people with fair complexions tend to get sunburned easily, I believe that they, too, are particularly susceptible to chilli burns.

Whether or not you have sensitive hands, always remember that when cooking Thai, avoid rubbing your eyes with your hands at any time. Your fingers may not burn from touching chillies, but your eyes certainly will. Capsaicin is very easily picked up by your fingers, and even the minutest trace can burn the sensitive linings around the eyes. If this accident does happen, do not panic. Wash with the suggested antidotes and avoid rubbing; the burning will fade away in time.

When roasting chilli peppers, especially the dried variety, make sure there is plenty of ventilation. Dried peppers can burn easily (turn them frequently and watch them carefully), and burnt chilli fumes in the air are painfully irritating to the linings of your throat and lungs. For the same reason, when stir-frying with chillies and chilli pastes over high heat, make sure the fan over your stove is turned on.

Dried Red Chillies

THE LIFE-ENHANCING QUALITIES OF CHILLIES

For the first time that evening, silence descends upon the room as the group of twelve religiously partakes of the scrumptious meal they just helped prepare. On the table before them are four dishes, two laden with hot chillies: one an intensely spicy soup, thick with all kinds of herbs, exotic vegetables and at least twenty *prik kee noo*, enough to make anyone break into a sweat and cough; the other a lovely dish of succulent shrimps and scallops, dressed in a creamy red sauce that at first glance appears tame, but when savored, reveals its true fiery nature that only the soup before it can subdue. Within a matter of minutes, the silence is broken by the sounds of noses sniffling and sighs of satisfaction. Faces glow warmly with rushes of blood and smiles of contentment, while beads of perspiration trickle down reddened cheeks. The energy in the room seems to have risen to a higher octave, exuding a euphoria, a "chilli pepper high." A few in the group appear to be blissed out in a trancelike state, while others announce the aliveness they feel all over their body. Such is the mood that prevails following an advanced Thai cooking class. The students who arrive tired and stressed out leave spirited and laughing, their bodies singing and renewed.

All the fuss chilli lovers go through to satisfy their craving for spicy foods can be baffling to their friends and loved ones who do not share the same gastronomical passions. Recent research on the effects of chillies on the human body can perhaps shed some light. One study has found that capsaicin triggers the release of endorphins in the brain, the body's natural painkillers. This finding explains why so many people feel so alive after they've had a spicy meal, as endorphins induce a natural high, infusing people with good feelings and pleasurable sensations. I often find that when I feel tired, sluggish and disconnected, a good spicy-hot meal will perk me up and bring more clarity.

Thai food is said to have an addicting quality, perhaps owing to some degree the endorphin-generating chilli peppers liberally used in the cuisine. But this "addictive" property of capsaicin, unlike opium, is not one of complete, involuntary physical dependency, for chilli lovers, though they prefer to have most of their meals laced with the hot stuff, can enjoy flavorful non-spicy meals, too, and can do without their chillies for extended periods of time without suffering adverse effects. Furthermore, unlike addictive drugs, chillies are nutritionally loaded with health-enhancing properties.

Besides imparting flavor to food, hot chilli peppers supply the body with large amounts of important vitamins and minerals. Ripe red chillies especially are rich in carotene (more so than carrots) and vitamin A—good for the eyesight and essential to normal cell growth. Fresh peppers are also a rich source of vitamin C (as much as five to six times more than oranges and lemons), helping improve the body's resistance to illnesses. In addition, they are concentrated with potassium and bioflavonoids.

A diet that includes chilli peppers benefits the digestive, respiratory and circulatory systems. Contrary to popular belief, they do not cause damage to the stomach and intestines but instead stimulate the beneficial production of mucous to coat and protect the stomach lining from irritation. As such, they have been used in folk medicine as a remedy against certain kinds of ulcers. They also help increase the rate of digestion by increasing blood circulation to the linings of the stomach and intestines, and they have been prescribed for the treatment of stomach cramps, diarrhea, flatulence and other digestive problems. They also loosen up mucous in the throat and lungs and are an excellent remedy for colds and flus, bronchitis and other respiratory ailments, without the side effects of many pharmaceutical drugs. Because of their natural antiseptic and anesthetic properties, chilli peppers were used in olden days to treat open wounds on soldiers during wartime. Used in foods, they help preserve freshness, and when eaten, they enable the body to rid itself of worms and other unwanted intruders.

Researchers in Thailand have found capsaicin to be an effective preventative against heart disease. It improves the ability of the body to dissolve potentially harmful blood clots and maintains the health of blood vessels, keeping their walls pliable and free from fatty deposits. It promotes the metabolism of fat, the increased metabolism burning up to fifty calories a day. Other studies reveal its anti-cancer properties. Traditionally, chilli peppers are valued blood cleansers, ridding arteries of undesirable cholesterol and impurities. They improve circulation to different parts of the body; as more food and oxygen reach the cells to nourish them, the feeling of alertness and aliveness is promoted. This property also makes them beneficial in ointments for relieving arthritis and treating certain skin conditions. In hot climates, chilli peppers help the body ventilate by opening pores on the surface of the skin. Perspiration is induced and as it evaporates, a cooling effect is gained. Some Thais believe sweating profusely after eating chillies helps rid toxins from the body.

But beyond the medicinal properties of hot chillies, the peppers simply add a depth to food that makes dining much more enjoyable. They stimulate taste buds and nerve endings and sensitize the mouth to feel more of each morsel of food that is being savored—the texture, shape, weight, density, juiciness and a host of flavor dimensions. Instead of killing and desensitizing taste buds as some people believe, the opposite seems to be the case. Many people who have allowed themselves to gradually increase their tolerance level for hot chillies have found that their sense of taste has become greatly heightened. They are able to taste many subtle flavors they couldn't before and can enjoy a wider range of foods, spicy or not.

Because tolerance for spicy foods is an acquired ability for most people, go slowly with yourself and your friends and loved ones, who are just beginning to explore this whole new world of taste sensations, until a comfortable threshold is reached. Over time, you will find this threshold increasing, sometimes without your being aware of it. Along with improved tolerance, you will be reaping more of the health benefits chilli peppers bestow. When you have become used to the burning feeling in your mouth and on your lips, you will find it isn't pain that you feel, but a pleasant, warm sensation all its own. The repertoire of your feeling abilities will have expanded as will your taste sensibilities.

PEPPERCORNS: THE "THAI PEPPER"

The chilli pepper may have been a foreign immigrant, but the peppercorn is thought by many to be indigenous to Thailand; hence it is called *prik thai*, or "Thai pepper." Some food historians disagree, however, insisting it was transplanted a very long time ago from India, where it is indisputably native. The *thai* in the name, they point out, does not refer to Thailand, but to the root meaning of the word itself, which is "free" or "spread out," and refers to the way it grows.

Whether or not it is a true native of Southeast Asia, the tropical peppercorn vine has probably lived on the land that is now Thailand long before the nation was born. The berries peppered up the food of our ancestors for centuries before the Portuguese sailed into the ports of our fabled kingdom of Ayutaya with the fiery chilli pepper. (Black pepper was the treasured spice that secured for Christopher Columbus the financing he needed to discover a shorter route to India. He instead stumbled upon the land of the chilli pepper, which he took back with him to Spain to the dismay of his sponsors. Fortunately, the Portuguese followed in his footsteps, and the chilli pepper made its circuitous journey to the land of the Siamese, later known as Thailand.)

White, black and green peppercorns all come from the same tropical vine, differing only in stages of ripeness and how they are processed after they are harvested. When still young, the clusters of berries hanging from the crawling vine are green and soft, with a mild but highly aromatic flavor. They are used in curries, added to hot stir-fried dishes and mixed into spicy *näm prik* dipping sauces. The next time you are in Thailand, look for short sprigs of these green berries in the spicy dishes you order and chew them along with whatever food they accompany for a refreshing burst of flavor. Because they are perishable, it is difficult to find fresh green peppercorns (*prik tai awn*) in markets in Western countries; more likely, gourmet food stores carry them packed in brine or vinegar or freeze-dried—all of which, unfortunately, alters their delicate flavor. If there is a specialty Thai or Southeast Asian market near you, look in the frozen compartment for small plastic pouches identified as "young pepper." Frozen, they will have turned black but retain their soft texture and most of their fresh taste.

Black pepper (*prik tai däm*), the form best known in the West, comes from pepper berries that have matured to the point where their deep green color has started to turn reddish. Dried in the sun, the outer skin blackens and shrivels, giving black peppercorns their characteristic wrinkled look.

To obtain white pepper, the berries are left on the vine until they fully mature into bright red seeds. The seeds are laid out in a warm place and allowed to ferment naturally for a few days, after which the outer red covering is rubbed off or washed away. What remains are smooth, round white peppercorns. Sometimes they are bleached with lime to a more uniformly white color.

Some people experience black pepper as hotter and more aromatic while others reserve this judgment for white pepper. It really depends on the variety of pepper and the degree of freshness. Just as the chilli pepper has evolved into countless varieties, the peppercorn plant has been bred into many different strains. Some produce a black pepper that seems more pungent than the white; others yield the opposite results. For instance, I have always found the white pepper from Thailand to be spicier and more flavorful than the pepper sold in jars in American supermarkets.

Although most English-version Thai cookbooks routinely call for black pepper in their recipes, it is white pepper that is used the most in Thailand. Derived from unbleached peppercorns, its color is less uniformly white. The next time you purchase a jar of ground *prik thai* from a Thai market, notice that it is a richer shade than an American brand, speckled with a little black. Black

Young Peppercorns (*Priktai Awn*)

pepper, in the form known to the West, is rarely used in mainstream Thai cuisine; only occasionally does it appear in certain regional dishes.

A favorite way Thai people use pepper is to pound it in a mortar with garlic and cilantro roots to make a marinade paste for grilling or deep-frying meats and for spicing up stir-fries and fillings for dumplings, crêpes and pastries. Pepper is an ingredient in many Thai curry pastes and is routinely sprinkled over stir-fried foods, soups and noodle dishes.

Like most spices, ground pepper loses its fragrance quickly, so it is best to buy whole peppercorns and grind them as needed in a pepper mill or a clean coffee grinder used solely for grinding dry spices. Fresh ground pepper has a wonderful perfume that no packaged, preground pepper has. One easy-to-make dish is garlic-peppered shrimps—crispy fried shrimps coated with lots of fresh-ground white pepper and chopped garlic. Try the recipe which follows on page 80, and remember, the crispy tails are the best part. Fish, squid, pork, chicken and just about anything can be garlic-peppered, so play around with the recipe, substituting other foods.

In Thailand, you can order garlic-peppered dishes everywhere you go, whether or not they are listed on the menu. Besides benefiting from the well-known health-enhancing properties of garlic, pepper adds its own medicinal values, approximating those of the chilli pepper in many respects. It is a folk remedy for various kinds of digestive and respiratory problems and has been included in just about every general tonic prescribed by herbal doctors for the maintenance of vital body functioning. Pepper is especially valuable for elderly people in keeping the fire element in balance and maintaining body warmth during the cold winter months.

The pepper trees with beautiful feathery leaves found in California and other warmer states are not related to the tropical vine that produces the spice so widely used around the world. The red and pink berries of these trees are a little sweet, very mild and have a delightful peppery flavor. Though considered edible, some people develop allergic reactions to this pepper, so use it with caution.

THE AROMATIC DRY SPICES

Aside from chilli peppers and peppercorns, myriad aromatic spices found their way to Thailand through foreign traders and immigrants. From the Middle East, Arab merchants introduced coriander and cumin; from India came cardamom and cinnamon; and from the Indonesian "spice islands," nutmeg, mace and cloves. These dry aromatic spices found their way into Thai cooking largely influenced by the cuisine of Indian settlers, who had moved to the region as far back as two thousand years ago with the spread of the ancient Hindu and Buddhist empires. Today, they are primarily used in curry pastes. These spices have also been well integrated into Western cuisines.

Cardamom (Loog Gkra-wahn)

There are a few kinds of cardamom. The variety used in Thai curries with Indian origins is a soft, wrinkled, charcoal black seed loosely held inside a round strawlike shell, ivory in color, which can be easily popped open with the fingers. In massaman curry, cardamoms are roasted in their shells and added to the curry sauce whole as a garnish, imparting a refreshing fragrance; in a Muslim noodle curry, they are shelled, roasted, then ground and pounded into the curry paste.

Cloves (Gkahn Ploo) and Cinnamon (Ohb Cheuy)

The dried flower buds of an evergreen tree and the brown bark of the cassia tree are used mainly in curries and sauces with Indian origins, such as massaman curry and panaeng curry. Cinnamon is also used to add a pleasant flavor to stewed beef and duck dishes and to peanut sauces with a Malay influence.

Coriander Seeds (Mellet Pak Chee)

Thai coriander seeds are smaller (about half the size) than the seeds available in spice jars sold in American supermarkets, but they are much more strongly perfumed. Look for them in small plastic pouches in specialty Thai markets. They are used extensively in various kinds of curry pastes, sauces and marinades for meats. As with other seeds used in curry pastes, the character of the curry can change significantly by roasting or not roasting.

Cumin (Mellet Yirah), also referred to as fennel and caraway

There is confusion about whether fennel is used in Thai cuisine. As far as I know, it is not (neither is caraway). Somehow, cumin has been mistakenly referred to as fennel, most probably because the shape of the seed resembles fennel, though smaller in size. The flavors of the two spices are nothing like each other. If you buy a bag of seeds labeled as "fennel" at a specialty Thai market, you are getting cumin. It is used primarily in curries—sometimes roasted, sometimes not—to effect a wide range of flavor combinations. Because its strong distinctive aroma can overpower the more subtle flavors of some herbs, take care not to overuse it.

Curry Powder (Pong Gka-ree)

Thai people have their version of the Indian yellow curry powder; it is usually a darker brown color. Not usually used for making curries, it is more often an ingredient found in stir-fried dishes, marinades for grilling and peanut sauces.

Nutmeg (Loog Jân) and Mace (Daug Jân)

Mace is the orangish outer covering of nutmeg. The two provide a refreshing flavor when fresh-ground for curries with Indian origins, such as massaman curry, and for peanut sauces with Malay influence.

Star Anise (Bpoy Gkak)

This brown, star-shaped, woody seed pod, with small shiny seeds and a flavor similar to anise seed, is used to stew meats and as a flavoring in dishes with Chinese origins.

GARLIC-PEPPERED SHRIMPS
(Gkung Tod Gkra-tiem Priktai)

*1 lb. small- to medium-size shrimps,
rinsed and drained
(leave shells on)*

*1–2 Tbs. white peppercorns,
coarsely ground*

10 large cloves garlic, chopped

*2 Tbs. tapioca starch,
or corn starch*

1–2 Tbs. fish sauce (näm bplah)

4 cups peanut oil for deep-frying

Lettuce leaves to line serving platter

2 small tomatoes, sliced in rounds

Drain shrimps well after rinsing. Do not remove shells. Grind peppercorns in a spice mill or clean coffee grinder, and chop the garlic evenly.

Heat the oil in a wok. When it is hot and just before you are ready to fry, toss shrimps quickly with the coarsely ground pepper, chopped garlic, tapioca starch or corn starch and fish sauce. Use your hand to mix so that by touch you can make sure that all the shrimps are coated with a thin layer of the flour and that the white pepper and garlic are distributed evenly. The flour will help some of the garlic and pepper to stick to the shrimps during frying.

Test to make sure the oil is hot enough by dropping a small piece of garlic in it. It should sizzle and not sink to the bottom for some time before surfacing. It also should not burn in a matter of seconds—reduce heat if it does. Fry half the shrimps at a time. They should sizzle and turn golden, along with the loose garlic pieces, in a few minutes. Use a fork or a pair of chopsticks to separate those shrimps that are sticking together because of the stickiness of the flour.

Fry until garlic is brown and the shrimps crispy (about 3 minutes). Remove from oil with a slotted spoon or wire spatula (like the kind used in Chinese cooking) and allow to air-drain on a wire-mesh basket or colander balanced over a bowl. Air-cooling will allow the shrimps to stay crispy longer. Use a fine wire-mesh spatula to remove loose garlic pieces from the oil and spread them over the shrimps. Allow oil to reheat, testing again with a piece of garlic to make sure it is hot enough before frying the next batch.

Cool fried shrimps a minute or two and serve while warm on a platter lined with lettuce and encircled by tomato slices. Eat shrimps shell and all, including the crispy tails. Good as an appetizer, or serve with other courses family-style with a hot-and-sour or sweet-and-sour sauce.

Wire Mesh Spatula

Shrimp (*Gkung*)

Allow the oil to cool in the wok, then strain and store in an airtight jar for future use. Refrigerate to keep fresh if you will not be using it again for some time. Because the oil picks up a shrimpy, garlicky and peppery flavor, it can be used with good results for stir-frying vegetables and seafood.

NOTES AND POINTERS

Do try eating the shrimps whole, shells, tails and all. In my ten years of teaching, I've had only two students who could not force themselves to do so, and they definitely missed out. All who have tried crispy whole shrimps love them and make them frequently at home.

Tapioca starch is available in small bags from Southeast Asian markets. In addition to thickening sauces and desserts, it is frequently used to make batters and to coat foods for frying. It is lighter and smoother than corn starch.

Peanut oil is one of the best oils for deep-frying because it can be heated to high temperatures without breaking down. The very hot oil quickly sears the outside surfaces and therefore does not penetrate into the food. After frying the batch of shrimps, you will have almost the same amount of oil left in the wok as when you started out. The crispy shrimps won't taste greasy as they would if you fried them in other types of oil.

If you prefer not to have shrimp shells as a natural source of calcium, this recipe can also be made with shelled shrimp. Fry only about thirty seconds to one minute, so that the shrimps stay juicy and tender. Without the shells, the shrimps will tend to taste a bit oilier. If you wish a crispy coating, roll the shrimps in bread crumbs before frying.

In the hot, humid tropics during the monsoon season, wild plants and herbs spring up everywhere. During my childhood, Mother often would pull handfuls of "weeds" from the vegetable patch and from the edge of the pond that were edible plants and herbs; she used them in our meals. Sometimes she would ask me to look for certain herbs in the backyard, and it was fun to track them down, snapping tender stems off vines and pulling roots out of the ground. These fresh seasonal herbs and vegetables, transported direct from the garden right into the pot and wok, made for a world of difference in the fullness of healthful flavors that enlivened Mother's cooking.

Thai cuisine employs a wide range of pungent roots, aromatic stems and fragrant leafy herbs. Though influences of Indian and Chinese cooking are notable in certain dishes, an unrestrained symphony of fresh herbal flavors distinguishes Thai food from that of Asian neighbors. Some of the herbs are common species known the world over—such as garlic, mint and cilantro—but more of them are exotic and are just now beginning to make their debut on foreign soil.

This chapter details the essential herbs whose flavors are inseparable from Thai cuisine. (There are numeous other seasonal herbs that are important to many Thai dishes, but they are not included here because they have yet to find their way abroad.) As you learn about these herbs, remember that there is no substitute for holding them in your hands—to touch, feel, smell and taste—to come to understand their unique properties well.

FRESH HERBAL FLAVORS DISTINGUISH THAI CUISINE

THE FOUNDATION

Garlic (*gkra-tiem*) and shallots (*hom*, meaning "fragrant") are indispensable in Thai cooking and are likely the most-used herbs. Tons of them in bulging basketfuls are loaded and unloaded every day at wholesale markets across the country. The shallots are a smaller red variety, but like Thai chilli peppers, they are much stronger-tasting than the larger orangish brown shallots commonly found in Western markets.

The garlic we grow is smaller, too, but again, much more potent than the larger-head and larger-clove garlic sold in California. Our garlic's cloves are tiny, and their skin is thin. We often just smash and chop them up whole, using skins and all. There is no need to go through the laborious task of peeling each and every clove, as is necessary with garlic grown in the West. Besides, the skins fry nicely to a crisp in such dishes as garlic-peppered fish or shrimp (see page 80).

From the same family of bulbous herbs, a lot of green onions (scallions) and chives also find their way into Thai food. Onions are used, too, but not nearly as frequently as shallots, which are usually preferred over their larger, paler and sweeter cousins. (Restaurants in America usually substitute yellow onions for shallots simply because they are less expensive.) For making hot-and-sour salads (*yäm*) and chilli pastes of any kind, the stronger-flavored shallots are imperative and should not be substituted.

Along with the garlic and onion family, the leafy and highly aromatic cilantro (also known as coriander or Chinese parsley, or *pak chee* in Thai) is used extensively. Almost all salads and many soups are laced with the refreshing flavor of this bountiful herb. In addition to the leaves and tender stems,

Shallots

the roots are an essential ingredient, enhancing curry pastes and soup stocks. They are also pounded with garlic and white pepper to make a fragrant paste for flavoring a wide range of dishes, from barbecued meats and stir-fries to fillings for savory pastries. Cilantro sold in a market in Thailand includes the entire plant as it is pulled out of the ground, and every part of it is used. Cilantro sold in American supermarkets, however, usually has the muddy roots already cut and discarded, so you may have to visit a farmers' market to find cilantro with the roots still attached (or, ask your local grocer to save the roots for you). Some Thai grocery stores carry frozen "rootlets" imported from Thailand. If you cannot find roots or rootlets, you may substitute with large stem sections, though the effect will not be quite the same.

Some people do not like cilantro, claiming it tastes like soap. This dislike frequently stems from previous experiences with dishes in which the flavor of cilantro is overpowering. When properly balanced with other robust herbal and spice flavors, however, it gives an exquisite dimension that adds depth and character to a Thai dish.

Much has been written about the medicinal qualities of garlics and onions; they have been used medicinally in just about every culture in the world that consumes them. They keep us healthy, and their abundant usage adds to the wholesomeness of Thai cuisine. Garlic, especially, is regarded by some as a cure-all for all kinds of conditions, and research has confirmed that its blood purifying and antioxidant properties make it an effective preventative against heart disease and cancer. In this day and age when we are concerned about blood cholesterol levels, a large daily dose of garlic in our food can help rid unwanted fats from the blood stream and keep the walls of blood vessels supple and healthy. Cilantro, too, is a known medicinal herb in Asia that offers many benefits, including aiding digestion and the removal of toxins from the body.

THE MAGICAL THREE

Of the exotic tropical herbs used in Thai cuisine, the three compatible companions—lemon grass, galanga root and kaffir lime (leaf and peel)—blend together gloriously to produce the magical flavors so captivating to Thai food lovers. The refreshing fragrance of lemon grass, combined with the robust pungency of galanga and the perfumed vigor of kaffir lime leaf, adds exciting dimensions to many Thai soups and salads. Thailand's most widely consumed soup, *dtom yäm* (see recipe on page 98) is an excellent introduction to these herbs and illustrates how their flavors harmonize in wondrous exuberance. Delightfully herbal, spicy and limy and a joyful treat for yearning taste buds, this soup is loaded with beneficial nutrients and healing properties, making for a great-tasting medicinal tonic to restore bodily vitality in time of colds and flus. One could say it is the Thai equivalent of the American "Mother's chicken soup"—packed, of course, with a lot more punch.

Lemon grass and galanga, combined with the extraordinary aroma of kaffir lime peel, form the basis for many Thai curry pastes. Blended in various proportions with other herbs and dry spices, they contribute a luxuriant flavor foundation that makes Thai curries so different from the curries of other cultures.

Cilantro (*Pak Chee*)

Lemon Grass (Dta-krai)

As its name suggests, this herb is naturally scented with a delicate lemon fragrance. The greyish green, multilayered stalk grows straight and tall, opening up into long grasslike blades. But unlike its name, lemon grass does not grow like the grasses in fields, and if you wish to cultivate it, you need not worry that its seeds will be scattered by the wind and take over your entire garden. Instead, lemon grass is bulbous and spreads outward in a clump as it is established, and the clump remains manageable as you pull out the outer stalks and use them in your cooking. It is very easy to grow, even in temperate zones, and requires little care. A fresh stalk from the market roots in a few weeks when placed in a glass of water or dipped in a root hormone and stuck into the ground. Since it is a tropical herb, it should be planted in a hot, sunny location in your garden or in a planter on your sunny deck and kept moist. A single plant will supply you with all the lemon grass you will need.

The wonderful flavor of lemon grass has rapidly earned it a favored reputation around the world. In fact, an international food writer recently dubbed it "the basil of the '90s." This prolific weed has thus been elevated to the status of a "designer" herb. In California, the fresh stalks are available year round in Asian markets. Look for them also at farmers' markets with ethnic stalls. In the Bay Area, many supermarkets and gourmet grocery stores are starting to carry them on a regular basis, but if you cannot find or plant fresh lemon grass where you live, you may substitute with the dried pieces sold at Southeast Asian markets, though their flavors are not as refreshing. Avoid the powdered stuff; it lacks a lot and sometimes can be very salty as salt is used as an abrasive to help reduce the tough fibers. Fresh stalks of lemon grass will keep for two to three weeks when wrapped in plastic and stored in the refrigerator or placed with the root end submerged in water in a glass outside the refrigerator.

Though the long grass blades have a lemon scent, the dense, light green inner stalk, especially the lower inches, hold the strongest flavors, which is why lemon grass is regularly sold with the blades already trimmed off. The stalks you buy from the market are usually twelve to fifteen inches long and average about a half inch to three-quarters of an inch in diameter on the bottom; when they are home-grown in a cooler climate and shadier exposure, they tend to be much shorter and thinner. Lemon grass is very tough and fibrous—almost woody near the root. Use only the dense multilayered part, all the way up to about an inch before the grass blades start, and cut and discard the bottom tip and peel off the loose outer layers.

When used in soups like *dtom yäm*, lemon grass is cut into big chunks, each about an inch and a half long, and smashed with the back of a cleaver to bruise. This helps break the juice sacs in the tough fibers, releasing the essential oils that carry the aromas and flavors and transforming the previously dry chunks into juicy pieces. If you do not have a cleaver, pound the chunks with the end of a large knife handle. The stalk may be cut crosswise, then split in half lengthwise to expose the wetter interior, or easier yet, sliced at a long slanted angle, then bruised. In soups, lemon grass serves as a stock ingredient to flavor the broth; the tough pieces are not meant to be chewed and eaten. Thai people usually do not strain them out before serving; they know what can be eaten and what cannot, and some like to suck on the lemon grass pieces for a delightful hit of flavor. But if you are serving guests who may not be familiar with Thai soups, you may want to strain out these hard pieces so that no one gags on them, especially if you like the flavor of lemon grass and use lots of it, like I do.

Lemon Grass (*Dta-krai*)

As a lover of lemon grass, I find the stalks grown in the less-than-tropical climates of California and Florida to be less full-flavored than the lemon grass from my mother's backyard and the marketplaces of Thailand, and so I use more of it than I would in cooking back home. The strength of flavors of many tropical herbs derive from secretions the plants produce to protect themselves from the intensity of their environments. The more intense the environment, the more intense the herbs' flavors become. Therefore, when cooking Thai food with ingredients grown in more temperate climes, it is best to go by taste rather than specified quantities in a recipe.

Lemon grass also adds an exquisite flavor to Thai salads, especially those with seafoods and meats in them. In order to be able to chew and eat the herb, it is necessary to slice the stalk very thinly. The tough fibers run lengthwise, so slicing crosswise in thin rounds with a sharp knife breaks the fibers into easy-to-chew-and-enjoy pieces. The greener and less woody upper half of the stalk is easier to slice and has a delicate, clean flavor, whereas the bulbous bottom end is more hearty and bitter. Use both for a full range of flavors. After the fiber has been cut in this manner, the thin pieces reduce easily to a paste when pounded in a heavy stone mortar for making various kinds of chilli and curry pastes.

Beyond its popularity as a culinary herb, lemon grass is highly regarded by traditional herbal doctors for its profuse healing qualities. It has been used for centuries to treat colds and flus, stomach cramps and indigestion, flatulence and urinary dysfunctions, fatigue, back pain and menstrual irregularity and yeast infections. Infusions of lemon grass are said to be good for the fire element and an effective treatment for conditions arising from too much wind. Its essential oils are reputed to contain a substance similar to insulin and, therefore, can be used in the treatment of diabetes.

Lemon grass also has become a common ingredient in many Western herbal teas. It is not to be confused with citronella, a close relative with a heavier and noticeably different perfume. Citronella is a valued ingredient in natural cosmetics and is regarded to be an effective mosquito repellent.

Galanga Root (Kah)

Galanga, called *kah* in Thai and known variously as "galangal" and "laos root," is an immensely pungent and fiery rhizome related to the common ginger but with a personality distinctly its own. Its abundant usage in Thai cooking, almost to the exclusion of ginger, has earned it the title of Siamese or Thai ginger. In short, it is to Thai cooking what common ginger is to Chinese cooking.

There are two different varieties, one known as "greater galanga" and the other, "lesser galanga." The first, which is larger in size, lighter in color and subtler in aroma, is the kind most used in Thai cooking. The fresh root is fleshy, knobby and very firm, to the point of being woody when it fully matures. When very fresh, its ivory color, with hardly any separation between skin and flesh, and its young pink shoots are reminiscent of the appearance of young ginger. But unlike its better-known cousin, it is much denser and harder with ringlike markings spaced almost evenly apart, a glossy outer sheen, a unique mustardlike flavor and a much sharper bite. Galanga is a heavy root and carries a hefty price tag, anywhere from four dollars to eight dollars per pound, depending on the season and the market. But you won't need much of it to flavor a dish, and some Southeast Asian markets will cut a small piece for you to suit your needs.

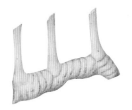

Galanga (*Kah*)

Fresh *kah* is a magical ingredient when it is finely slivered up for hot-and-sour seafood salads and sliced in thin rounds to flavor soups. It helps mask the fishiness of seafoods and the heaviness of red meats, thereby making them taste cleaner, more delicate and more succulent. When you purchase a fresh root, select a smaller and more tender one; the larger roots can be very hard, making slicing and slivering a tedious chore. You will want to sliver the root very finely for salads as it is intensely pungent; in small doses, it adds a hearty spiciness to each bite.

Cultivated in hotter areas of California and Florida, galanga is also imported fresh from countries south of the border and flown in from South Pacific islands. These foreign-grown rhizomes, however, differ somewhat in flavor from the roots grown in the soil of tropical Thailand, which seem to have a wider range of attributes. Imported frozen Thai galanga is readily available in Southeast Asian markets. Although some of its fresh punch is compromised by freezing, it still carries important gradations of flavors lacking in foreign-grown roots, making it my preferred choice for curry pastes with robust characters. Frozen Thai galanga is usually small and has a light reddish tan skin and costs much less than the fresh cream-colored roots. But for salads and refreshing herbal soups like *dtom yäm*, I prefer to use fresh galanga, which is becoming easier to find year-round in the Bay Area. Look for it in Thai and Southeast Asian markets, as well as specialty produce markets.

Much more widely available are the dried pieces of galanga packaged in small plastic bags; these are an acceptable substitute for soups. Many American Thai restaurants use them more often than not in place of the expensive fresh root in their *dtom yäm* soup, but for fresh seafood salads, dried pieces are too woody and do not reconstitute with soaking. If you must substitute for fresh galanga in seafood salads, use frozen Thai roots or common ginger, or do without either.

Dried galanga has a pronounced musky and rooty flavor unlike the sharp bite of the fresh root. It makes a fairly good substitute for the fresh and frozen roots in coconut-based soups, such as *dtom kah* (see page 118), as its strong, earthy flavor blends nicely with the richness of coconut milk. I also like to use the dried pieces in the intensely spicy, northeastern-style minced meat salads called *lahb*. These salads require roasted *kah*, and it is much easier to roast the dried pieces than the fresh root. I do not recommend purchasing powdered galanga for any purposes, as most spices lose flavor rapidly after they have been ground. It is better to buy the dried pieces and grind them when needed.

Galanga has many medicinal properties similar to ginger. It is a digestive stimulant and also helps to settle stomach upsets, ease nausea and curb flatulence. Traditional herbal doctors recommend a tonic made of minced and pounded old galanga root, mixed with tamarind water and salt, for women who have just given birth, as a blood purifier and as an aid in the removal of gas build-up in the intestines. At the same time, its mild, natural laxative effect keeps the bowels regular. Galanga's heat makes it a good agent in reducing cramping and numbness, in healing bruises and swelling, in treating respiratory ailments and skin diseases and in removing toxins from the body.

In addition, *kah* is sometimes classified among the category of herbs we call *wahn*, which are reputed to have magical powers. This belief coincides with an account I once read about its use in medieval Europe among certain medicine people, who wore the dried root as a protection against evil influences and as an enhancer of virility. Known as "galingale" during that period, it was widely used as an aphrodisiac as well as a spice. Somehow, it disappeared from European culinary and medical scenes, and some historians have surmised that it fell out of vogue, along with other spices, as milder foods became the order of the day in the eighteenth century. Today, as Thai cuisine grows in popularity on that continent, perhaps galingale will regain its favored position.

Kaffir Lime Leaf and Peel
(Bai Ma-gkrood, Pew Ma-gkrood)

I once had a student who was elated to discover kaffir lime leaves, the magic ingredient that made Thai food extra special to her. She loved hot-and-sour *dtom yäm* soup and ordered it frequently in Thai restaurants, but whenever she tried making it at home, she couldn't get the flavors to come out quite right. Knowing lemon grass was used in the soup, she added loads of it, but something always seemed to be missing.

It is true that lemon grass is an indispensable flavor in *dtom yäm* soup, but as in many Thai dishes, a favored herb seldom is put on stage to sing a solo. Like the social Thai people, herbs like the company of other herbs, to create together wholesome harmonies in which the individual parts become almost inseparable. Some take the starring roles in certain dishes, supported by their comrades, and switch to supporting roles in other situations. Knowing how to choreograph and orchestrate their performance is the challenge and fun of Thai cooking.

Both the exceptionally fragrant fruits and leaves of the kaffir lime tree play important roles in Thai cooking, imparting unique flavors that have become identified with the cuisine. Any Thai cookbook that alludes to the use of citrus leaves really means kaffir lime leaves, the only citrus leaves used with regularity in a wide array of favorite Thai dishes. The luscious perfume and striking flavor of the leaves cannot be easily substituted with other kinds of citrus leaves. They are worth seeking, as their special attributes are irreplaceable.

Kaffir lime is known in Thailand as *ma-gkrood*. I do not know how the English name came about. I have learned that "kaffir" can be a derogatory word, but my intention in using it in this book is not to offend anyone but to refer to it by that name used most commonly in markets and Thai recipes. Sometimes it is identified as bergamot lime, but this designation is rarely used, especially in America.

The kaffir lime fruit approximates the size of a Western lime. Some are smaller and rounder, and some are larger and more tangelo-shaped, depending on where they are grown. The fruit is dark green in color and has a bumpy surface. Though the juice is seldom used in cooking, the peel of the fruit, with its high concentration of aromatic oils, is indispensable in many curry pastes and is one reason why Thai curries taste refreshingly unique. The zest also imparts a wonderful piquant flavor to such delectable favorites as fried fish cakes, and it blends in powerfully with such spicy, chilli-laden stews as "jungle soup" (*gkaeng bpah*). Because its strong flavor can overpower the more subtle ones in a dish, the rind should be used sparingly, grated or chopped finely and reduced in a mortar with other paste ingredients until indistinguishable.

The leaves of the kaffir lime tree are a dark green color with a glossy sheen. They come in two parts: the top leaflet is lightly pointed at its tip and is attached to another leaflet beneath that is broader on its upper edge. Often, when you buy the leaves in small packages at Thai markets, many of them

Kaffir Lime (*Ma-gkrood*)

may have already become detached from their twin. The size of the leaves can vary quite a bit, from less than an inch to several inches long. The larger leaves are usually darker in color. In recipes that call for them, estimate the number to use according to their size, with the average single leaflet (detached from its double) of about two inches long and an inch wide equaling one leaf. Add more or fewer leaves according to the sizes in the batch you purchased.

Kaffir lime leaves are precious to many Thai dishes, from soups and salads to curries and stir-fried dishes. They are the ingredient that blends marvelously with lemon grass and lime juice in *dtom yäm* to give the soup its wholesome lemony essence. In soupy dishes, add the leaves whole or torn into smaller pieces, using them as one would bay leaves to flavor broth or stew. For dishes in which they are a component to be eaten, such as salads, stir-fries and dry or custardlike curries, cut them in very fine needlelike slivers, so that their strong bouquet can be more evenly distributed. The slivers also provide a pleasing texture and appearance.

To sliver kaffir lime leaves finely, stack three to four leaves of similar size together and slice them very thinly with a sharp knife. It is faster to cut diagonally, which gives the hands better leverage, or roll a few leaves at a time into a tight roll before slicing. If at first this task seems onerous, practice until you develop a sense of how to work with these leaves. It is a good contemplative exercise and a way to become present with a wonderfully aromatic member of our universe. You can also try cutting the leaves with a pair of scissors, but I find this can be a slower process because you usually must cut one leaf at a time in order to get fine slivers. You may be tempted to mince or chop the leaves instead, but these methods add the kaffir lime leaf flavor differently and can overwhelm the more delicate flavors in a dish. Large slivers can be equally overpowering. So, it is best to use fine slivers about an inch long, as Thai chefs have done for generations, to add kaffir lime leaves in the most pleasing balance of flavor, texture and presentation.

Both the fresh fruits and leaves of kaffir lime are sometimes difficult to locate. Because their flavors are uniquely Thai, look for them in Thai grocery stores. Other Southeast Asian markets generally do not carry them, and those that do usually stock the dried form only. Some stores may insist that kaffir limes have been banned from this country; this was true many years ago when U.S. agricultural authorities quarantined the fruits and leaves to protect the vulnerable California citrus crop from possible tropical insects and diseases. Only Thai people and those closely associated with them were able to purchase the leaves (at a high price and "under the counter") from a small handful of shops. But today, they have received full immigrant status and are no longer illegal aliens. Kaffir lime trees are cultivated locally, and groves of them are well established in the hot central valley and southern regions of California and in Florida.

You may want to consider growing your own kaffir lime plant. (In the Bay Area, the Four Winds Nursery in Fremont sells one-gallon-size plants for under twenty dollars.) Unless you live in a frost-free area, it is best to grow your kaffir lime in a container that can be easily moved indoors during the winter months, as cold weather and frost can irreversibly damage it. Give it plenty of sun, warmth and water during the summer months, and once it has become established, prune frequently to encourage bushier growth and a healthier supply of fresh leaves. If the prunings provide you with more leaves than you can use, wrap them in a dry plastic bag and store them in the freezer

Kaffir Lime Leaf (*Bai Ma-gkrood*)

to use later during those months of the year when the plant goes dormant. The leaves freeze well and will keep for a year or longer without losing much of their fresh aroma.

If you do not own or wish to grow a kaffir lime tree, purchase the fresh or fresh-frozen leaves from Thai grocery stores. They are usually packaged in small 1-oz. pouches. Buy several; keep a supply handy in the freezer for those days when you feel like cooking Thai. The leaves are still pricy—about thrity to forty dollars per pound retail. Fortunately, because of their strong fragrance, you will need only a few for each recipe that calls for them. With all my classes and the abundance of Thai meals I cook regularly for my family and friends, I go through less than a pound of the leaves each year.

If you are not able to find the fresh or frozen leaves, you may have to settle for the dried variety. Dried kaffir lime leaves are sufficient in dishes that are soupy, like certain curries and soups. Just rinse the leaves and add them to the dishes; there is no need to reconstitute by soaking, as they will do so themselves while they simmer in the liquid of those dishes. On the other hand, if they are to be used as an ingredient in a paste or need to be slivered finely, reconstitute them by soaking them in warm water until they soften. They will double or triple in size.

As for the peel, fresh or frozen whole kaffir limes can be purchased in the same Thai markets, though they may not always be available. The fruits from trees grown in America are much smaller in size than those grown in Thailand. Their rind, though zestfully fresh, is less pronounced in some of the flavor dimensions especially associated with kaffir lime. For those recipes calling for the peel, I find the dried pieces imported from Thailand to be perfectly fine to use. In fact, the reconstituted dried peel can add more of the exotic kaffir lime flavor than some locally grown limes. A small bag lasts a very long time, doubling and tripling in size when soaked in water. My students sometimes have difficulty locating the dried peel, as packages are not always labeled clearly. One brand is identified as "dried vegetable," accompanied by a drawing that is undeniably the bumpy kaffir lime with its double leaves.

A kaffir lime tree can grow to be a fairly large tree in tropical Thailand (though yours may not). It can be found everywhere. Almost every home in the countryside has one in its yard. Besides supplying great flavor ingredients to enhance food, kaffir lime is also widely used as an indisputably effective cleanser, natural deodorizer and air freshener, even more so than its cousin, the common lime. Small, family-run inns in Thailand often place kaffir limes in the bathrooms. They deodorize and add a sparkling scent, like the sweet bouquet of citrus blossoms, and each scratch of the zest releases another installment of refreshing perfume. Some visitors in my tour groups like the invigorating scent so much that they carry limes around with them; on those afternoons when the heat makes them sluggish, they sniff the limes and are immediately perked up and their spirits are enlivened.

One time my tour group visited the outdoor dining terrace of a meditation center that served delicious homemade vegetarian lunches. On a counter by the entrance were a number of herbal products for sale, including kaffir lime shampoo. Among the twelve in the group, we must have bought out all they had for sale. The juice and essential oils of kaffir lime, added to shampoo, leave the hair squeaky clean and invigorate the scalp and are believed to freshen one's mental outlook and ward off evil spirits. Kaffir lime has also been used for ages as a natural bleach to remove tough stains. When I was growing up, Mother did the wash entirely by hand, and nothing worked better on stubborn stains than a few drops of kaffir lime juice, mixed with a sprinkling of detergent. Not only does it clean effectively, it is inexpensive, natural and sweet-smelling. For rural villagers, a single kaffir lime tree supplies enough limes to keep the whole house and family clean.

In folk medicine, the juice of kaffir lime is said to promote gum health and is recommended for use in brushing teeth and gums. The essential oils in the fruit are incorporated into various ointments, and the rind is an ingredient in medicinal tonics believed to be good for the blood. Like lemon grass and galanga, the rind is also known to have beneficial properties for the digestive system.

MINTS AND BASILS, HOLY AND NOT

Belonging to the same family of fragrant leafy herbs, mints and basils boast an extensive network of relatives growing in various pockets around the world. Some are profuse and have long since made a name for themselves, while others are more obscure, though showing promising futures.

Among several varieties of mints now making their home in Southeast Asia, the one most commonly employed in Thai cuisine is a tropical strain of spearmint, the refreshing herb widely known and long used in Western cuisines. Called *bai saranae*, it is almost always used fresh and uncooked, whether as whole leaves tossed in hot-and-sour seafood salads or chopped and mixed in with spicy minced-meat salads of the northeast, providing a contrast and balance between its coolness and the incendiary heat of chillies. It also makes frequent appearances as sprigs on vegetable platters, along with a forest of other aromatic and pungent herbs (including other kinds of mints) and edible leaves and flowers of trees, to accompany hot dipping sauces and spicy dishes in a meal.

The varieties of basils used in Thai cooking are quite different from the common sweet basil sold in American produce markets and have yet to make a name for themselves. Of the three favorites—*bai horapa* (Thai or anise basil), *bai gka-prow* (holy basil) and *bai maeng-lak* (lemon basil)—only the first has made significant progress in getting established in the U.S., thanks to the growing population of Southeast Asian immigrants and resulting interest in their cuisines. Besides their valued culinary uses, these basils (as well as spearmint) have healing qualities and are used by country folk to alleviate various conditions. Holy basil in particular is said to be beneficial in the treatment of children's illnesses and in promoting tonicity of the body following childbirth. Its aromatic oils are believed to be potent enough to kill insects and prevent the spread of certain types of bacteria.

Thai Sweet Basil, or Anise/Licorice Basil (Bai Horapa)

This tropical variety of sweet basil provides the unusual basil flavor present in so many Thai dishes that it has come to be identified as "Thai basil" in America, even though the Vietnamese and Laotians also use lots of it in their cuisines. Its leaves are deep green, smaller and not as round as Western sweet basil. They grow on purplish stems, topped with pretty, reddish purple flower buds. Both leaves and edible flowers are sweetly perfumed with a mix of a dis-

Thai Sweet Basil (*Bai Horapa*)

tinctly basil scent and that of anise or licorice. Therefore, it is sometimes referred to as "anise basil" or "licorice basil," though it is not the same as the Western strain of these basils stocked by local plant nurseries.

Plentiful in Thailand, *bai horapa* is eaten almost as a vegetable. It is used in large quantities, in whole leaves and sprigs, in many types of dishes, including curries, stir-fried dishes, salads and soups. I am reminded of the wonderful clam dish my mother frequently made during my youth, a favorite of the family. Big handfuls of this basil were tossed in the hot wok with the very sweet, succulent and tasty thin-shelled *hoi lai* ("clams with a patterned shell"), garlic, roasted chilli paste (*näm prik pow*) and fish sauce—delicious! (See the recipe on page 67 for ideas.)

Bai horapa is now readily available year-round wherever there is a sizable Southeast Asian population to support a market of its own. As demand for this great-tasting basil increases, specialty produce markets and gourmet grocery stores are beginning to add it to their herb selections. It is also easy to grow, and seed packets can be be purchased from local nurseries or ordered from national seed catalogues. You can root a fresh stem easily by placing it in a glass of water outside the refrigerator. As with many leafy herbs, this basil can be kept fresh by placing it in a glass with the cut ends in water, covering it with a plastic bag and storing it in the refrigerator. Or, you can wrap the herbs in paper towels before bagging them in plastic for refrigerating. They will stay fresh for about a week.

Holy Basil (Bai Gka-prow)

If I were to name the basil that Thai people love most, it would have to be *bai gka-prow*, or holy basil. Still a relative rarity in the Bay Area, I often have to drive far and wide to a few scattered ethnic shops that carry it on a semi-regular basis, so that I can indulge in a truly heavenly *pad gka-prow* (stir-fry with *bai gka-prow* or holy basil leaves). Almost all Bay Area Thai restaurants list this dish on their menus (their spellings may differ from mine), but they usually substitute *bai horapa* for *bai gka-prow* (the menus should list the dish as *pad horapa*). *Pad gka-prow* can also be ordered in just about every restaurant and food shop you come across in Thailand, but there it is fresh holy basil that makes it taste so special.

This basil is used in simple stir-fries, and together with garlic, fresh chillies and fish sauce, it imparts a wonderful flavor to any meat or seafood you wish to toss up quickly in the wok. The recipe at the end of this chapter for *pad gka-prow* with chicken (see page 100) is also excellent with pork, shrimps and scallops. It is an easy recipe and has become one of the all-time favorites among my students, some of whom have resorted to growing their own *bai gka-prow* to ensure a steady supply of the tasty herb. If you should substitute a different kind of basil for your stir-fry, make sure to change the Thai name, too, by tacking on the name of the basil you use to the word *pad*.

Bai gka-prow is also used in profusion in aptly named *pad kee mao* ("drunken stir-fry") dishes, those very hot, garlic-and-basil-flavored dishes, often for accompanying *Maekong* (Thai rum) drinks or beer. It is not the stir-fry itself that is drunken, but the partaker, who may end up inebriated from excessive attempts to douse the fire brought on by these dishes! (A sample recipe with noodles can be found on page 178.) Use *bai gka-prow* in large amounts especially when it is very fresh as it is a relatively fragile herb and can lose much of its fragrance after a few days in the refrigerator.

Holy Basil (*Bai Gka-prow*)

Thai holy basil has a noticeably different flavor than the variety sold as seedlings under the same name in many Western nurseries that carry specialty culinary herbs. It has less of a sweet floral bouquet and is spicy. There are two varieties: a white (light green) and a red, which has a reddish purple cast around the stems and on the darker green leaves. The lightly hairy leaves of both kinds are jagged along the edges and are smaller and more fragile than Thai sweet basil (*bai horapa*), wilting easily. When freshly picked, the aromatic leaves hold a spicy, peppery bite and a delicious combination of basil and mint flavors. The zestful blend of fragrance and tastes becomes particularly pronounced in cooking; that's why it is preferable to cook *bai gka-prow* rather than eat it raw. The peppery spiciness of holy basil has earned it the name of "hot basil" and it is identified as such in some Thai markets.

I prefer the more concentrated flavors of the red variety, the kind most used in Thailand and that grows profusely everywhere during the wet season. The little herbs pop up along the fences of Mother's garden following drenching rains, and their appearance signals many scrumptious meals featuring dishes laced with their exquisite flavors. In the Bay Area—unless I grow it myself—I seldom have the luxury of a choice, as the red holy basil is apparently more difficult to grow in temperate zones and is, therefore, less readily available.

Other Southeast Asians also love holy basil, and during the hot summer months, you may be able to find big bunches of it at farmers' markets with ethnic stalls. Or, look in Southeast Asian markets located near communities where large numbers of Laotians, Thais, Cambodians and Vietnamese make their home. If you are not able to find fresh holy basil, try the dried leaves imported from Thailand in packages labeled either "holy basil," "kapao" or simply "dried basil." (If the package says "sweet basil," it usually is *bai horapa*.) Though not a complete substitute for the fresh, it gives a touch of the minty *gka-prow* taste when used together with some kind of fresh basil. Soak the dried leaves first to reconstitute; this will bring out more flavor during cooking than if you toss dried leaves into a stir-fry. Use cold tap water to soak the leaves because hot water will leach out some of its already compromised flavor. Remove the hard stems from the softened leaves before using, or your stir-fry will turn out "twiggy."

What makes *bai gka-prow* holy? One source attributes the name to a biblical reference but does not specify which book or verse. Another source traces it to the Hindus in India, who believed this herb to be sacred and planted it around their religious shrines and used it in their cooking, but I have yet to come across Indian food flavored with holy basil. As a lover of holy basil, its divine flavor in *pad gka-prow* dishes make it sacred enough for me!

Lemon Basil (Bai Maeng-lak)

Lemon basil is used much less than sweet basil and holy basil and is available in California only during the warmer months in Southeast Asian markets. The leaves are larger and a lighter green than Thai sweet basil, slightly hairy with serrated edges, and look more like some kind of mint. In Thailand, *bai maeng-lak* adds a special touch to the light, peppery soup we call *gaeng liang*, a nurturing, aromatic brew with vegetables and usually shrimps, said to be good for expectant mothers.

Not only are the leaves (*bai*) used in cooking, but the black poppylike seeds of this herb (*mellet maeng-lak*) are used as well for making sweet snacks and desserts. Soaked in water, the tiny seeds quickly swell into gelatinous rounds, looking much like cooked tapioca pearls, each with a black dot in the center. Mixed with other tasty tidbits in sweet coconut milk soups topped with crushed ice, they make a cooling treat on hot, humid afternoons. My Choice, the neighborhood restaurant on Sukhumvit Soi 38 near my parents' home in Bangkok, serves a delicious, homemade basil seeds ice cream. The subtle flavor of *maeng-lak* seeds and their unusual texture combine splendidly with coconut cream to cool down and clean the mouth and tongue following a spicy meal. *Mellet maeng-lak* may be purchased from Thai and Southeast Asian markets in small bags labeled "basil seeds."

THE SUPPORTING ROLES

Besides the major players in mainstream Thai cuisine, there are numerous other herbs used, either cooked in with food or eaten raw with spicy *näm prik* dipping sauces. Many are used primarily in the cooking of particular regions where they grow. Most have notable nutritional benefits aside from being flavor enhancers, having found their way into the cuisine because of their roots in rural folk medicine.

The following herbs are fairly common in mainstream Thai cooking, and although they are listed under "Supporting Roles," they play significant roles in a number of situations. Turmeric, for instance, is highly valued in the cooking of southern Thailand, while elsewhere it is used on an occasional basis and usually in a supporting capacity to more pungent flavors in a dish.

Common Ginger
The brown-skinned ginger commonly known around the world flavors Thai food to a lesser degree than its cousin, greater galanga. Both the pungent mature root and the milder, ivory-colored young growth with pink shoots are used in a number of Thai dishes, usually ones with Chinese influences. In recipes that call for ginger, always use the fresh root and not the dried powder sold in jars on supermarket shelves. In Thai cuisine ginger is also pickled and eaten as an accompaniment to appetizers and snacks.

Lesser Ginger, "Rhizome" (Gkra-chai)
Gkra-chai is a rhizome composed of several long, slender, fingerlike appendages attached to a small lumpy head. There are three varieties—yellow, red and black—each reflecting the color shade of the root. The first two are more commonly used in cooking, and when you buy the root in frozen packages imported from Thailand, the rhizome will usually be reddish brown.

Although a member of the ginger family, this herb is not so much pungent as it is sweetly aromatic. Its strong and unusual perfume masks the fishiness of seafoods and lightens the heaviness of meats, but it can overpower more delicate flavors if it is used excessively. I like to add it to light, herby seafood curries (such as the green curry on page 140) and to hearty spicy stews to broaden flavor dimensions. In folk medicine, this rhizome is used to treat urinary problems, dysentery, dizziness and inflammations around the mouth. It also makes a tonic for improving bodily strength.

Lesser ginger is usually labeled simply as "rhizome" and sometimes as "kachai." Try to find the frozen roots from Thailand. I prefer to do without rather than use the dried or powdered forms.

Lesser Ginger (*Gkra-chai*)

Turmeric (Ka-min)

Most people in the West are familiar with turmeric in its dried, powdered form as the spice that gives curry powder its characteristic deep yellow color. The dried powder is very mild and, if it has been around for a while, has little flavor, despite the loudness of its color.

Fresh turmeric, on the other hand, has a distinct flavor, very pleasing though delicate. The fleshy rhizome has a cylindrical central root stem from which branches short, fingerlike appendages. These fingers, about two to three inches long, break off easily from the parent. There are several kinds of turmeric. The common variety has a bright orange flesh, just like a carrot—some people swear it smells like carrot and has a sweetness reminding them of carrot. Its aroma is subtle, and it has a root quality to its taste. Though brown-skinned with ringlike markings, tinges of orange show through noticeably on the outside. The deep orange color of this turmeric imparts a rich yellow to curries, soups and stews and rice dishes. It is used extensively to flavor and color the food of southern Thailand, including the delicious turmeric fried fish (see recipe on page 186).

Another variety, known by some as "white" turmeric, is consumed by Southeast Asians and available from some of their markets during late spring and summer. Its flesh is a lighter color than common turmeric; its flavor, however, is not as subtle, and some roots can be quite pungent. Southeast Asian cultures not only cook with this turmeric but eat the young roots raw or blanched, dipped in spicy sauces.

Through the ages, turmeric has been sought as a medicinal herb. Herbalists are familiar with its stimulant and tonic properties and prescribe the juice extracted from the rhizome as an internal antiseptic and antidote to blood poisoning. In traditional folk medicine, the dried root is ground and rubbed on the skin to treat skin diseases; mixed with coconut oil, it speeds the healing of wounds and minimizes scarring. It is also believed to possess magical powers: a piece of the wild rhizome ingested or worn is said to strengthen one's constitution when magic words are chanted to invoke its protective essence. Finally, turmeric has been valued for centuries as a natural cosmetic and dye, coloring the vibrant saffron robes of Buddhist monks. Blended with pomegranate skin, it produces a rich reddish brown color; with acacia leaves, a lovely shade of green; and with lime, a pretty orangish red.

Pandanus Leaf (Dteuy Hom or Bai Dteuy, usually labeled "Bai Toey")

Bai dteuy, a type of pandanus, grows profusely in Thailand. The shiny pleated leaves—long and slender like those of day lilies—are sold along with bunches of orchids for use in floral arrangements, but more importantly, they are the source of a well-loved flavoring that goes into a wide assortment of desserts and sweet treats. The juice extracted from the fresh leaves provides a natural green food coloring as well. Many of the prepackaged green sweetmeats you find in Southeast Asian markets are scented with *bai dteuy* essence, although most of them are tinted with artificial food coloring since the fresh leaves are not always available.

Bai dteuy has an earthy fragrance and taste that enrich coconut milk and syrupy mixtures in the making of sweet foods. A Thai equivalent to vanilla, *bai dteuy* is one of the most popular flavorings for coconut desserts, second only to the sweet essence of *mali* blossoms (jasmine). Country folk use the leaves to

Turmeric (*Ka-min*)

boil with water for drinking purposes, adding a refreshing, almost smoky taste, reminiscent of the juice of roasted coconuts. A few *bai dteuy* leaves frequently find their way into the rice pot as well, to give the rice a lovely fragrance. They are also used to wrap food for cooking, such as *gai haw bai dteuy* ("chicken wrapped in pandanus leaves"), and are neatly folded into small baskets for filling with puddings and cakes.

Besides its culinary value, *bai dteuy* is an herb known for its healing properties. It has a cooling effect and is excellent for the treatment of internal inflammations, urinary infections, colds, coughs, measles, bleeding gums and skin diseases.

Look for fresh pandanus leaves in Southeast Asian markets; they are flown in from Hawaii and are available on a sporadic basis. You need only two to three whole leaves to flavor a couple of cups of coconut milk. Simmer ten to fifteen minutes, or until the milk is richly flavored. Squeeze all the juice out from the leaves before discarding; these last drops are the most fragrant. If you are not able to find the fresh leaves, look for frozen ones carried by Thai markets. Frequently, the imported leaves from Thailand (labeled sometimes as "pandan" or "pandal") are even more fragrant than the fresh Hawaiian ones. Use the dried cut leaves only as a last resort, or substitute with a few drops of the green essence sold in little bottles identified as "bai toey."

I am partial to *bai dteuy*, and not just because it is a wonderful flavoring—it is also my lovable niece's nickname. She has a cousin whose nickname is *Gkati* (coconut milk), so you can see the important role food plays in my family!

Pandanus Leaf (*Bai Dteuy*)

HOT-AND-SOUR PRAWN SOUP
(Dtom Yäm Gkung)

½ lb. prawns, or medium- to large-size shrimps, shells removed and butterflied (save shells for soup stock)

2–3 stalks fresh lemon grass

1 qt. water, or mild soup stock, salted with fish sauce (näm bplah) to the desired saltiness

6 thin slices fresh galanga (kah), or 2 dried pieces

3 fresh or dried kaffir lime leaves (bai ma-gkrood)

8–10 whole Thai chillies (prik kee noo), stem removed and bruised with the back of a cleaver; or substitute with 2–3 sliced jalapeño or serrano peppers

½ a small onion, halved again and sliced crosswise ¼-inch thick

1–2 Tbs. roasted chilli paste (näm prik pow)

3–4 Tbs. tamarind water: a chunk of wet tamarind, about the size of 1 Tbs., with the soft parts dissolved in ¼ cup water, pulp removed

1 cup fresh brown mushrooms, sliced in ¼-inch pieces, or 1 can whole straw mushrooms, drained

1 small tomato, cut in bite-size wedges (optional)

2 green onions, cut in thin rounds

Juice of 1–2 limes, to desired sourness

½ cup cilantro leaves or short cilantro sprigs

Cut the bottom tip off the lemon grass stalks and discard the loose outer layer(s). Then cut each stalk into 1-inch sections at a slanted diagonal all the way up to the greener end, near the start of the grass blades, exposing the inner core. Smash each piece with the side of a cleaver or the end of a large knife handle to bruise, releasing the aromatic oils. Place the cut lemon grass along with the prawn or shrimp shells and the water or stock in a soup pot. Bring to a boil, then reduce heat to low and simmer with a lid on for 15–20 minutes to draw out the flavors. Strain out the shrimp shells and some of the lemon grass.

Add the sliced galanga, kaffir lime leaves, bruised Thai chillies (or substitute) and sliced onion. Simmer a couple of minutes, then add the roasted chilli paste (näm prik pow), tamarind water and fresh brown or straw mushrooms. Heat stock to a boil and simmer for a couple of minutes. Stir in the tomato wedges (if using), green onions and prawns or shrimps. After 20–30 seconds, turn off heat, add lime juice to the desired sourness and the cilantro. Do not let the prawns or shrimps overcook. Serve immediately.

NOTES AND POINTERS

Dtom yäm is a light soup with practically no oil, and it contains the four main flavors—hot, sour, sweet and salty—accentuated with fresh aromatic herbs. It is the most popular soup in Thailand and can be found in the tiniest mom-and-pop village rice shop to the fanciest restaurant in Bangkok. No menu is without it, even in Thai restaurants overseas, and if there is no menu, as is the case in Thailand's rural areas, just speaking the magic words "dtom yäm" is enough to procure a steaming bowl of the fragrant and stimulating soup.

Dtom yäm can be made with just about any type of seafood or meat, or vegetables for vegetarians. You can have a dtom yäm gai (gai is chicken), dtom yäm bplah (fish), dtom yäm talay (mixed seafood), dtom yäm hed (mushrooms), and so on. There are numerous ways of blending flavors, as you will notice from eating dtom yäm in various restaurants here or

Shrimp (*Gkung*)

in Thailand. Flavors vary from place to place, from chef to chef and from pot to pot. But basically, *dtom yäm* is hot and sour—hot from some kind of chilli pepper and sour primarily from lime juice—and has lemon grass as the leading herb flavor.

Most *dtom yäm* in Thailand is made, of course, with Thai people's favorite chillies, *prik kee noo* (see page 69), known now in the Western world as "Thai chillies." In this recipe, the chillies are kept whole, so you and your guests can spot them easily and not bite into one unless you choose to. Simmering the chillies in the broth will flavor the soup with its special spicy flavor. If you can find red ones, they make the soup prettier and are even easier to spot, but if you want to insure a zero chance of a fiery accident, you may wish to simmer the chillies in the soup stock a few minutes and then strain them out entirely. Remember, the longer you cook chillies, the more their heat will cook out into the surrounding broth.

Alternatively, for a stronger roasted flavor, you may wish to use dried red chilli peppers. Roast them on a dry pan directly over a burner until the pods are dark red, turning frequently so they do not burn. Cut each roasted pepper into two or three segments and add to the soup. Keep in mind, however, that the *näm prik pow* in the recipe already provides some roasted flavor. (See page 55 for more information about *näm prik pow*.)

To give the prawns or shrimps a more succulent flavor and a delicate crisp texture, add 1–2 tsp. sea salt and about ½ cup of water to them after the shelling and butterflying. Mix well and let soak 15–20 minutes. The water will turn a dark gray color. Then rinse several times to remove all the salt before cooking.

Kaffir Lime Leaf (*Bai Ma-gkrood*)

$\mathscr{S}$PICY BASIL CHICKEN

(Gkai Pad Gka-prow)

2–3 Tbs. peanut oil for stir-frying

4–6 cloves garlic, finely chopped

2–3 shallots, thinly sliced
(or substitute with
½ cup sliced onion)

1 lb. boneless chicken thighs,
coarsely chopped, or cut
into small bite-size pieces

2–3 fresh jalapeño or fresno
peppers, cut into large
slivers; or 5–10 Thai
chillies (prik kee noo),
chopped and pounded
with a mortar and pestle

2 small kaffir lime leaves
(bai ma-gkrood),
very finely slivered
(optional)

2 tsp. black soy sauce (the semi-
sweet kind; see page 63)

1 cup fresh Thai holy basil
(bai gka-prow),
or substitute with:
¼ cup dried holy basil,
soaked to soften
plus ½ to 1 cup fresh
Thai sweet basil
(bai horapa)

1–2 Tbs. fish sauce (näm bplah),
to taste

Dash of ground white pepper

Prepare the ingredients as indicated. Leave the fresh basil leaves whole; the flowers may also be used. The dried holy basil will soften when soaked in tap water for 10–15 minutes. Pull off and discard the hard stems. Drain.

Heat a wok until the surface is smoking hot. Swirl in the oil to coat the wok surface. Wait a few seconds for the oil to heat, then stir in the garlic, followed a few seconds later with shallots. Stir another few seconds before adding the chicken. Stir-fry a minute or two, or until most of the chicken has started to change color on the outside and is no longer pink. Toss in the peppers or chillies, slivered kaffir lime leaves and reconstituted dried holy basil (if using). Sprinkle black soy sauce over the mixture and stir-fry another 15–20 seconds. Then add fresh basil leaves and fish sauce to taste. Stir and mix well. Stir-fry another half a minute, or until the basil is wilted and the chicken is cooked through. Sprinkle with white pepper. Stir and transfer to a serving dish, or spoon directly over individual plates of plain steamed rice.

NOTES AND POINTERS

This is a good and easy stir-fried dish and one of the favorites among Thai people. It is served over rice as a one-dish meal for breakfast or for lunch, often topped with a crispy fried egg. Of course, it also appears frequently as one of the courses in a shared family-style meal.

If you are not able to find fresh holy basil, this recipe can be substituted with any fresh basil. I have also tried it with a mixture of fresh Thai sweet basil (bai horapa) and fresh mint leaves with good results.

The smaller the chicken is cut, the greater the surface area will be to coat with the flavors of the aromatic herbs and sauces, and the more flavorful the stir-fry will be. Some of my students have reported good results using ground turkey. In Thailand, this dish is often made with chopped pork or bird meat, especially in fast-food, curry-rice shops (rahn kao gkaeng), where an enormous variety of dishes are prepared

Red Fresno and Green Jalapeño Peppers

Holy Basil (*Bai Gka-prow*)

ahead of time and served over steaming white rice to order. When I travel in the rural areas, I often stop at such rice shops in small towns for lunch. Some of the best *pad gka-prow* can be had at these inconspicuous, no-frills, open-air places. They are made particularly spicy to help preserve the meat, as the dishes are prepared early in the morning and served throughout the day until they are sold out.

Try the above recipe also with fresh seafood, such as shrimps, scallops, mussels, clams, crab (all of which require no chopping) and firm-flesh fish, such as fresh halibut and salmon.

The image of a swaying coconut palm evokes in many a vision of a faraway tropical paradise. Perhaps Thailand is one such paradise, as many travelers repeatedly visit there to replenish their souls. All through the Thai countryside—in the various regions, along the two expansive coastlines, on countless offshore islands, in woodlands, amid rice fields, in villages and backyards of residences—tall, handsome coconut palms hold their leonine heads high, gracefully nod and bow to the rhythm of the wind and, from time to time, play their gentle, rustling music.

In addition to their gracious appearance, coconut palms hold even greater value in paradise for their usefulness. Their most apparent benefits derive from their fruit—the lovable coconut itself—as an important source of food. But beyond the food value of the "nuts," there are numerous other ways in which coconut palms contribute to the well-being of their human relatives. The fibrous outer husks of the nuts and the dense stems of palm fronds are convenient sources of fuel. Used to smoke fish and meats in barbecues, the dry husks impart a wonderful roasted aroma. They are also used to make coconut matting and rope and are a superb planting medium for such exotic plants as orchids.

The hard shells of old coconuts can be carved and made into everyday kitchen implements, cooking utensils and containers, such as ladles, spatulas and bowls. Rich dark brown in color and speckled with lovely markings, they are also polished and made into decorative items and jewelry and, in the north, musical instruments and playthings. I remember when I was in grade school, I was fascinated with my older brother's project with coconut shells for his art class. I watched him saw sanded-down pieces of shell with a bowlike instrument into decorative designs, some animal-shaped, others vegetable-shaped. The pieces were then made into pins, broaches and display items.

The tender new growth atop coconut palms, much like bamboo shoots, is good to eat in curries and stir-fried dishes and is a delicacy in the south. The blossoms of coconut trees store a sweet, fragrant nectar, which is tapped and used in making a natural sugar, a well-liked and tasty sweetener for flavoring various Thai dishes and desserts. If allowed to ferment a few days, the sweet sap turns into a rich palm wine enjoyed by many villagers following a hard day's work. The long fronds of the leaves make sturdy woven baskets, hats, mats and roofing materials for the simple thatched houses and storage sheds of rural folk. The stripped ribs of the leaflets can be bundled together to form sturdy brooms. The trunks of the trees themselves are strong enough to be used as posts and as wood for building homes and making furniture. Practically every part of the coconut palm is useful; it is a precious gift of nature to the natives in paradise.

Although grown all over the country, coconut palms are found in great abundance along wide stretches of Thailand's two coastlines, one bordering the Gulf of Thailand on the Pacific Ocean side and the other, the Andaman Sea in the Indian Ocean. They like the sandy soil and flourish in thick groves, which become more and more widespread as one travels down the narrow peninsula to the southern region. Large coconut palm plantations stand alongside groves of rubber trees, sugar palms (from which palm sugar is tapped) and oil palms (elegant, lacy-leaf palms bearing large clusters of small, reddish brown nuts from which palm oil is extracted), pineapples (the best in the world!), bananas, cashews, coffee and cocoa, and orchards of the prized durians, jackfruits, rambutans, mangoes and other exotic tropical fruits, adding to the agricultural richness of the south.

Things Your Mother Never Told You About Coconut

Several islands off the southern gulf coast are lushly covered with coconut groves. One of these is Koh Samui, Thailand's third-largest island and better known today among Western travelers as the place to go for vacationing in a tropical beach paradise. For most of this century, Samui has been more important among agricultural circles as a prolific producer of coconuts, shipping millions to ports in Bangkok each month. But now, although coconuts are still a main source of income for Samui folk, tourism is becoming an increasing source of revenue, and developers have invaded the once remote island, clearing coconut plantations to make way for resort developments. Soon the number of annual visiting tourists may rival the number of coconuts exported from the island!

MONKEY BUSINESS

Although a coconut tree is a great source of refreshment and food as well as other benefits as described, owning one does pose some problems. Because of the height of most trees, access to the fruits is not easy. I remember the many occasions when my mother would eye the voluptuous bunches of coconuts on the trees in our front yard and wonder how to harvest them. She and most of our family love to have cold, refreshing coconut juice and tender young coconut meat for snacks on hot afternoons. Often she would have to depend on our courageous gardener to climb the trees to cut the coconuts for us.

Fallen coconuts are not always good for eating; they may be too old or may have become rancid and spoiled. Good coconuts are picked fresh from the trees. Aside from the obvious danger of being hit by one, shaking the tree or using long poles to poke and prod coconuts to fall is not a wise idea: the long fall may crack them, thereby losing the juice and shortening the length of time they can be kept. Coconuts bruise, too, like other fruits that fall off trees. Falling coconuts may also cause damage to roofs and cars. For this reason, smart people do not plant coconut trees next to their houses or park cars in their shade. And though it may sound idyllic, napping under the shade of a coconut palm along the beach does have its risks!

With their long, willowy trunks, coconut trees are not easy to climb, although coconut grove workers make it look like a breeze as they scurry up the trunks using both feet and both hands as if they were monkeys, without the help of ropes or safety belts. Dtahng, one of my tour assistants who is from southern Thailand, is one such great climber. He had plentiful opportunities when he was a boy to climb and pick coconuts for his family. Whenever our tour settles in on the charming island homes in the enchanting Andaman Sea, he heads for the grove to gather coconuts for us to have for refreshments. He is quite a sight to watch and a great source of thrilling entertainment.

Because of the inherent dangers of picking coconuts and the resultant shortage of labor as people gravitate to better jobs in the cities, many plantation owners nowadays employ monkeys to do the job. On long drives to the south, one frequently sees proud monkeys sitting in the backs of pick-up trucks filled with the coconuts they have picked. Although there are four main species of monkeys in Thailand, the pig-tailed macaque (*ling gkang*), now referred to among Thais as "the coconut-picking monkey," is most trainable and efficient for this line of work. A well-trained macaque is worth quite a bit of money, costing a minimum of six hundred dollars (U.S.). But they do earn their keep, picking as many as seven hundred to eight hundred coconuts a day.

The best pickers are said to be male monkeys born in the wild, caught when still very young and brought into training schools before they reach the age of two. (Females are regarded as slower and lacking the strength and stamina of the males and are usually released back into the wild.) Compared with their brothers bred in captivity, these wild creatures possess a greater innate vitality, sharper instincts and a restless nature that makes them tireless workers. With a glance, expert trainers can sum up their personalities from the size of their hands, the thickness of their fur, the shape of their mouths and teeth, the details of their fingerprints and the color and thickness of their eyebrows and judge how well they will do as coconut pickers. For instance, monkeys with white brows are believed to be near-sighted, stubborn and lazy. Prized ones have large, sturdy hands, a healthy coat of fur, sharp straight teeth, a wide mouth and fingerprints that resemble a human's. The training takes three to six months.

It is not known where the employment of monkeys in plantation work started—Thailand, Malaysia or Indonesia—but in Thailand, monkeys are known to have helped humans pick coconuts for some eighty years. Today, in the southern province of Surat Tani, where coconuts are a major agricultural export, some nine hundred macaques are on the job daily. The numbers are growing, as training monkeys has become a profitable business.

I know a monkey trainer in Surat's Kanchanadit district and have stopped to observe his training regimen. Endowed with funds granted by Crown Princess Sirindhorn to the provincial agriculture department, Sompon established his "Monkey Training College" in July 1985. He is perhaps the most prolific and best-known trainer in the area, and he seems to have a special touch with monkeys. Regarding them as individuals, each with its own temperament and personality, he tailors the training to meet the particular needs, habits and idiosyncrasies of each monkey.

Sompon teaches his monkeys in a playful way, thirty to sixty minutes each day. Instead of using a system of reward and punishment, he shows the monkeys the fun of playing with coconuts. He coaches them on how to bite, twirl and push ripe coconuts around to loosen them from the trees and to throw them down as if they were balls. Trained to play, these monkeys do not expect a tangible reward for behavior reinforcement, as the act of picking coconuts becomes a reward in itself.

Sompon has told me that he is against the keeping of monkeys—or any wild animals for that matter—solely as pets for the pure enjoyment of the owners. However, because of the dangers coconut plantation workers face, these monkeys have become a solution to a serious problem. Sompon teaches the owners to love and respect their monkeys, to learn about their individual temperaments and to care and provide for their particular needs. He encourages them to retire their monkeys from strenuous work at the age of fifteen (their average life expectancy is twenty to twenty-five years).

Fortunately for home growers, there are many varieties of coconut trees. Though most are slender and tall, there are also coconut palms that are short and squat. Some dwarfed varieties are hybrids developed by agriculturists to make the picking of their fruits easier. Others have been bred so that the juice and meat of the young fruits are especially sweet and fragrant. For apparent reasons, the fragrant-juice dwarves (*ma-prao näm hom*) are highly prized for the home garden. These, however, are harder to find, do not produce as many fruits as the taller varieties and usually require more care.

....

COCONUT—A NATURAL FOOD-AND-REFRESHMENT PACKAGE

In the West, most people know coconuts primarily in the sweetened, shredded form they've had in such desserts as coconut cake or coconut macaroons, or as sweetened milk for making piña coladas. Neither is a fair representation of what fresh coconuts really are like and the many different ways they can be used in cooking. Whenever I've had new cooking students who insist that they do not like coconuts, they are always surprised by how delicious Thai curries, coconut soups and desserts taste. Almost invariably, their prior gastronomical experiences with coconuts have been limited to the highly processed and sweetened products.

In tropical Asia, coconuts are eaten in different stages of ripeness. When they are young and green, the clear juice inside some varieties is sweet and refreshing, sometimes naturally fragrant with a subtle hint of flowers. Not only is it a good thirst quencher, the juice is also good for reducing heat in the body. On hot days in the tropics when you feel sluggish and overheated, drink lots of young coconut juice. It will revive you and replenish your energies. In folk medicine, the fresh juice of young coconuts is also recommended for reducing fevers and relieving headaches, stomach upsets, diarrhea and dysentery, for strengthening the heart and for restoring energy to weakened bodies recovering from illness. It is believed that expectant mothers who regularly drink young coconut juice will help the fetus grow stronger and with greater vitality.

In its development, the meat inside coconuts starts out being gelatinous and translucent, growing thicker and whiter as the fruit matures. When it is still a soft, thin layer, it can be easily spooned out and eaten along with the juice. A good variety will have tender meat that is smooth and tasty, lightly sweet and creamy. It slides down your throat with a most pleasing cooling effect.

Palms that bear coconuts with sweet, fragrant juice (*ma-prao näm hom*) are highly prized. Their fruits seldom are allowed to develop to maturity and are picked young and green, fetching a good price at refreshment stands, restaurants and marketplaces around the country. Beneath the outer layer of green, the soft husks are a light cream color. They are pared back in such a way that the top is pointed and the bottom (eye or stem end) cut flat to sit level on a surface. When ready to serve, a heavy knife or cleaver is used to whack around the pointed tip to make a small, round opening. With the aid of a straw and a spoon, the juice and soft flesh can be sipped and scraped out for eating. When you are in Thailand, try these young coconuts and ask for both spoon and straw. The flesh may range from very light, translucent and gelatinous to thick, white and firm, depending on the age of the coconut. Too many unknowing tourists leave the coconut meat untouched, wasting a wonderful, nutritious treat.

Some fragrant coconut palms bear fruits that are golden yellow in color rather than green. There is one such precious tree standing regally by itself in front of an old wooden house along an isolated stretch of the Chumpon coastline. The house belongs to the family of Gkaron, the very friendly young man who manages a rustic resort where my tour groups stay a few kilometers

Young Coconut (*Ma-prao Awn*)

around the bend. He frequently invites us to his family property to pick fresh coconuts from this tree for refreshments. Though he speaks no English, his smiles are the sweetest and most heartwarming, and he is always eager to go through all kinds of trouble to cut down the golden fruits for us to taste.

Once, both his elderly mother and father were home to greet us. We were overwhelmed by the generous doses of southern hospitality that poured forth from these humble souls, whose faces never were short on smiles. They happily rigged a long bamboo pole with a knife tied to one end, which Gkaron skillfully wielded to cut down a few of the coconuts, dodging as they fell. Luckily, his young, fearless nephew, who loves to climb trees, soon came home from school, and in a few short seconds he was up the tree among the bunches of coconuts. One at a time, he twirled them off the stems and threw them down for Gkaron to catch. The father fetched a machete, shaving the husks and chopping off the tips of the shells so we could sip the deliciously sweet juice inside. Thin wedges of the husk's tough outer skin were carved to make spoons for scraping out the tender meat.

Before we were through feasting on the coconuts, Gkaron's mother brought out sliced papayas, freshly picked from the tree behind the house, and bowls of stewed aloe vera, cultivated in a nearby plot. Gkaron's father, an herbal doctor, talked to us about the medicinal uses of local plants and fruits. The juice of fragrant coconuts, he explained, is medicinal, particularly a variety known as "fire coconut," whose shell is a deep reddish brown color. He brought one out from the icebox and chopped it open for us to taste. I was astonished by its strong flavor; it was without a doubt the most fragrant coconut I have ever tasted. He told us of his long journey to Prachuab Kiri Kan province to search for these coconuts. Fire coconuts are rare, but their juice is most valuable and when steeped with herbs can treat many kinds of illnesses.

We left the peaceful house along the lovely stretch of private beach that afternoon with our van loaded with golden fruits. They had cut down all the coconuts for us, even though this lone coconut tree is the only one that bears sweet, fragrant fruits in all the groves for miles around. I was so touched by these people whose hearts flowed with kindness and generosity, even to strangers from a foreign land who did not speak their language, know their names or offer a thing in exchange.

Young coconuts are occasionally sold in specialty produce markets in California and large Asian markets in American Chinatowns. They are recognizable by their spongy, cream-colored husks, sculpted to a pointed top and flat bottom. Their appearance is very different from the more widely available hard, round and brown coconuts, which are matured with their husks already removed. Young coconuts spoil easily when not refrigerated, so do not buy them if they have dried out and turned brownish on the outside or look moldy. You may also sample sweet young coconut juice and meat already removed from the shell, packaged in plastic pouches or cups. Imported from Thailand, these are sold in the frozen foods section of many large Asian food markets. They come in cans, too, but the canned variety is sweetened with sugar and is not as fresh-tasting.

Young coconuts also yield delicious juice and meat when they are roasted in their husks, which are then peeled back to reveal their whitish round shell (ma-prao pow). Roasting turns the juice even sweeter and adds a subtle, but delightful, smoked aroma. The cooked tender meat loosens from the shell and can be pulled out easily with the fingers. It has a richer and creamier taste than the meat of fresh coconuts. Roasted young coconuts rank high on my list of favorite refreshments, and the best I've had are from a roadside vendor on the road from Lopburi to Saraburi. If you are in Thailand, you must look for them and give them a try.

Not all young coconuts have juice that is sweet and fragrant. In some varieties the juice can be rather bland, sour and uninteresting. The mature fruits of these varieties are more delectable; as they ripen, the meat inside becomes thicker and richer, firmer and more pulpy. Its oil content increases, and it becomes a closer approximation of a nut. Most coconuts are grown for their mature fruits, which yield shredded coconut meat for making desserts and snacks; coconut milk for curries, soups and desserts; and coconut oil for cooking and for making soaps, candles, protective skin lotions and cosmetics. Copra, the dried meat of matured coconuts, is one of Thailand's major exports, providing an important source of food and raw material to other parts of Asia and the world.

"CREAM OF THE CROP"— COCONUT MILK

Some people unfamiliar with coconuts think coconut milk is the liquid inside the shell, and that to obtain the milk, all they have to do is poke holes in the eyes and drain out the milk. However, the liquid inside the shell is not the milk but a light, almost clear juice. Fresh coconut milk is not obtained so easily. It has to be pressed and extracted from the finely grated meat of well-matured coconuts—a long, involved process if you start out from scratch with a whole coconut (instructions to follow).

In Thailand, much of the work is already done for the home cook by vendors in the markets, who sell very finely grated coconut by the kilogram fresh each day. If you take a walk in one of Thailand's marketplaces, you may notice a wooden, boxlike machine with a chute on one side, which makes a sound similar to a power saw when it grates coconut. Dense coconut chunks are pushed into the machine from the top and fall down the chute into a bowl, after having been reduced to fine flakes. Today, the newer boxes are made out of metal rather than wood.

When I was a little girl and my mother's kitchen helper, I loved watching and helping her make coconut milk. It was such fun! She added hot water to the grated coconut she brought home from the nearby market. The coconut was allowed to steep in the hot water for a short while and then strained. When it was cool enough to handle, she gathered up the pulp with her hands a fistful at a time and squeezed until all the juice was pressed out. The fluid from the first pressing was very rich and creamy, and we called it "head of the coconut milk" (*hua gkati*). More hot water was added to the pulp to steep, and then it was strained and squeezed again. This second pressing yielded lighter milk and was kept in a separate bowl. A third pressing gave us a very light milk, like skim milk, which we called the "tail of the coconut milk" (*hahng gkati*). Mother kept the three separated for use in different dishes or for adding during different stages of cooking.

The pulp was never thrown away. It was my job to go scatter it by the handfuls into our pond to feed the fishes. They loved coconut and sometimes

Matured Coconut (*Ma-prao*)

would jump for it as I swung my arm over the water. (Mother also fed the fishes grass mown from our lawn, and they grew nice and fat from all the feedings. Every few years when she would have the pond drained, we happily trampled into the mud to catch them.)

Freshly made coconut milk is one of those fine things in life that is hard to beat. Some of the best curries and coconut soups I've had in restaurants back home have been made with coconut milk specially pressed moments before it is needed. One fabulous place to experience such delights is a small, cozy restaurant in the southern seaport town of Krabi. Named Reuan Mai or "Wooden House," the restaurant is, as its name suggests, in an old wooden home, decorated with antiques and souvenirs from all around Thailand—nothing fancy, but very homey. Their curries are absolutely heavenly because of the genuinely fresh flavor of the rich, freshly pressed coconut milk—the nectar of the gods!

Another place that always reminds me of the ambroisial taste of fresh coconut milk is the small, very friendly, family-run resort Gkaron manages along a secluded stretch of the gulf coast in Chumpon province. My tour groups make overnight stops there. The setting is very quiet and serene, caressed by a cooling wind that plays gentle music with the palm fronds of the grove. The rustic islander bungalows are tastefully built and blend in charmingly with the environment. We are almost always the only visitors there.

The best part of being there, however, is experiencing the genuine friendliness of the unpretentious country folk who take care of the place. Smiles beaming, they melt my heart as they serve homecooked meals that are always a big treat. One dish I order whenever I visit is their coconut seafood soup (*dtom kah talay*; see the recipe on page 118). The seafood is fresh-caught by fishermen just a few meters down the beach, and the coconut milk is freshly made from coconuts picked shortly before dinner is served. Every time I've asked them to make the soup, I have seen the cook head off for the grove and return a few minutes later with a big smile on her face, carrying a coconut she specially picked. Nothing can beat coconuts fresh from grove to stove! Eating that coconut seafood soup in the setting of an open-air, thatched pavilion, surrounded by graceful coconut palms alongside a wide expanse of a secluded beach could describe a perfect meal.

Nothing compares with the flavor of fresh-pressed coconut milk. Though there are several brands of rather good canned coconut milk now available on the market, freshly pressed milk will have a fragrant, naturally sweet and delightfully nutty flavor lacking in the canned products. But finding a fully developed and reasonably fresh coconut in American markets is sometimes not as easy as it may seem. Many of those you see in supermarkets or Asian stores near your home are not quite old enough; they have been grown for the meat itself and harvested at a slightly earlier stage of maturity. Frequently, these coconuts are not very fresh, unless the store receives regular shipments each week.

Unlike nuts such as almonds and walnuts, coconuts are more delicate than most people realize and do not have a long shelf life, especially after the outer husks have been removed. The fibrous husks are nature's protective cushion and are integral parts of coconuts, but because of their bulkiness, they usually have been pulled off and discarded. If stores do carry coconuts with husks still on, they may have trouble selling them. The dried, brown husks of matured coconuts aren't particularly attractive, and how would consumers here figure out how to get inside of one? It seems difficult enough to deal with the hard shell.

Without the outer husks, the shells bang against each other in transport and often crack or develop leaks. The eyes on one end are also exposed and subject to puncture and air seepage or mold growing inward. Air and mold entering the coconut will make the rich meat spoil quickly. That's why when purchasing a coconut at the store, be careful to choose one that is still heavy with juice. Shake it, and if it seems dry, chances are there is a crack or leak in the shell, or it may have sat on the shelf too long, the juice having all but evaporated through the eyes. Check the eyes; they shouldn't look dark or moldy. Though they are often sealed with wax to prevent leakage, this does not guarantee that leakage has not occurred.

When looking for a coconut to buy, search first for a batch with an over-all appearance that suggests freshness. If there are several that are moldy and cracked, try another store. From a fresh-looking batch, choose the best-looking one, and if you wish to be doubly sure, take home an extra as back-up. If the market carries more than one kind of coconut, select from those with rich brown shells if you wish to press fresh milk. Inside, the thick flesh should be a pure white color; if it has started to yellow, it most probably is rancid. Besides the thickness of the flesh, you can usually tell whether a coconut is old enough to yield creamy milk by looking at a cross-section of the shell. A well-matured nut will have developed a very hard, chocolate-brown inner shell; this is the shell that can be carved to make implements and decorative items.

Coconuts with lighter brown shells generally are not as fully matured; the meat is delicious as a snack in itself or can be shredded to make fillings and toppings for snack foods, appetizers and desserts. Milk pressed from these coconuts may be less creamy than good brands of canned coconut milk, but its flavor can be fresher and tastier if you happened to have chosen coconuts from a shipment just off the boat from Asia. And although this milk is not quite creamy enough for curries and certain kinds of desserts, it adds a fragrant nuttiness to coconut soups that makes them heavenly!

TO CRACK A COCONUT

Some people try to get into a coconut by banging on it with a hammer. Others suggest poking holes in the eyes to drain the liquid before hammering. This sounds like a good idea, but if you have tried it before, you may have discovered it isn't so easy. The eyes are small and the surrounding shell quite thick and hard. After much effort to jab them with a sharp object or puncture them with a nail, you may end up with a slow trickle, taking a lot longer to drain all the liquid out than you may have patience for.

A quick and easy, no-nonsense way to crack a coconut is to use a cleaver. Holding it with one hand such that the "midriff" rests in the middle of your palm, with the tip on one end and the eyes on the other, whack the coconut with the back of the cleaver a few times all around the center until it cracks open cleanly into two nearly equal halves. Do this over a bowl in the sink to catch the juice as it drains from the cracks. If the juice tastes fresh and sweet, enjoy it as a refreshment by itself or reserve it for use in extracting cream from the flesh.

After the coconut is cracked in two round halves, the white flesh can be scraped out in long thin shreds using a small implement with a row of sharp teeth, available from Southeast Asian markets. (My little niece and nephew

Toey and Baitoey, find this activity to be great fun. Whenever they come to visit and want to help in the kitchen, I keep them out of trouble by asking them to shred coconut. That usually is worth half an hour of silence and undivided attention. Later, when I incorporate the fruit of their effort into a simple appetizer or dessert, they feel so proud to have contributed; they have learned that cooking is fun and a way to give of themselves to their loved ones.) Alternatively, you can first remove coconut meat from the shell and then grate or shred it in the food processor (see the next section, "To Prepare a Coconut for Pressing Milk," for tips on how to deshell coconut meat).

In Thailand, there are shredders that are attached to wooden stools, so that you can shred coconut while sitting down. If you have one, sit on the stool with the flat round shredder head sticking out in front of you and between your legs. Simply hold the coconut half with the white meat on the sharp-toothed head and move your hands swiftly up and down, scraping it out in fine shreds. With practice, you may find that a whole coconut shreds up in no time at all. You may also develop strong wrists from the exercise!

In olden days, the wooden stools were carved into elaborate animal shapes (such graters are called *gkra-dtai*, meaning "rabbit"). The National Museum in the southern city of Nakon Si Tämmarahj and the extensive Institute of Southern Thailand Studies in Songkla display interesting collections of antique coconut shredders among their folk exhibits. Some are people-shaped, with the shredder sticking out of the mouth or, more comically, out of the rear end. These artfully carved stools make fascinating decorative pieces and have become collector's items. Look for them in Bangkok's enormous Chatuchak Weekend Market—a bustling bazaar where almost everything imaginable is available—or in antique shops.

Aside from hand scrapers and stool shredders, there are a number of mechanical contraptions for grating coconut. Many of these can reduce the pulpy meat of old coconuts into very fine, snowlike flakes, perfect for extracting coconut milk and for making chewy sweetmeats. Along with the wooden, boxlike machine mentioned earlier, another common device used by vendors in marketplaces consists of a large, round, aluminum basin with a torchlike shredder head sticking out through a hole in the center. With the basin tilted on its side, the shredder head is hooked on the back to a machine that powers it to turn like an osterizer. The sides of the basin catch the grated coconut so it doesn't fly all over the place.

Long, thin coconut shreds are sprinkled over various snacks and desserts, used as an ingredient in the fillings of crispy crêpes and dumplings, and rolled into sweetmeats. For my niece and nephew, I sometimes toss toasted sesame seeds, some sugar and a little bit of salt with the coconut shreds they have helped scrape out of the shells and serve the mixture to them for a snack or light dessert. Cooked sweet corn kernels added to such a mixture also make a very nutritious snack.

Along the streets of Thai cities and in snack shops, a tasty coconut cake called *kanom bah bin* (see recipe on page 120) is a popular treat. Made primarily of finely grated fresh coconut with rice flour, sugar and flavorings, it is shaped into little flat round pancakes and grilled. Some street vendors fill the sweet coconut mixture in tiny metal rings atop a hot griddle to make uniform little round bites—reminiscent of chewy coconut macaroons.

PREPARING A COCONUT
FOR PRESSING MILK

If you wish to make coconut milk from scratch and would rather use a food processor or blender than a hand-held implement to shred the thick flesh, whack the shell when you first crack it just enough to make a small fissure sufficient for draining the liquid, but keep the coconut whole. (The taste and smell of the juice will tell whether the coconut is good or whether it has gone rancid.) Place the coconut in a hot oven (400–450 degrees) for fifteen to twenty minutes. The heat from the oven loosens the flesh inside from the shell. Do not leave the coconut in the oven too long because you do not want to cook the flesh; cooked coconut meat will not yield fresh-tasting coconut milk. Cracking the shell and draining the liquid before placing in the hot oven prevent the heated coconut from exploding, an experience you want to avoid in your kitchen.

After the coconut has been in the hot oven long enough, remove it and allow it to cool until you are able to handle it without burning your hands. Then whack the coconut all around the center line with the back of a cleaver, as described earlier, to crack into two halves. Using a knife or screwdriver, pry the meat out from the shell. If it is hard to do, whack the shell into smaller sections.

If you wish, peel off the brown skin attached to the shell side of the white meat. Break the meat into smaller chunks and chop as finely as possible in your blender or food processor. Transfer the chopped meat to a bowl and add two cups of hot water. Allow it to steep about ten minutes, then strain through a fine-mesh strainer into another bowl. Gather the pulp with your hands and squeeze all the fluid out from it; this fluid will be the creamiest part of the milk. You may wish to wrap the pulp with a dampened muslin cloth to ease the task of pressing.

Add another two cups of hot water to the pulp, steep, strain and press again. This will be lighter milk. Judging from the consistency from this second pressing, you may decide whether or not to do a third. In Thai cooking, coconut cream from the first pressing is used to make rich coconut desserts (try the coconut custard recipe on page 122). It is also reserved for frying pastes in the making of curries, with the lighter milk added later during cooking to constitute the sauce. The lighter milk is also saved for soup stocks and to stew or precook various meats.

COCONUT MILK—
CANNED AND FROZEN

If you do not wish to go through the trouble of making fresh coconut milk, there are many brands of canned coconut milk available in Southeast Asian markets from which to choose. Some are better tasting than others, and a few are downright awful. They come from a few different countries, but there are probably more on the market today imported from Thailand than elsewhere.

Over the years, my cooking students have sampled and compared different brands of coconut milk. The two which most of them consistently like better than others are Mae Ploy ("Mother Ploy") and Chao Koh ("Island

Matured Coconut (*Ma-prao*)

Folk"). These two brands also happen to be the best sellers among Southeast Asian immigrants. Mae Ploy, with a rich and nutty flavor, has been voted most frequently as the creamiest brand, while Chao Koh, also tasty and with a delightful natural sweetness, is favored by those who prefer a lighter milk.

Mae Ploy for years has been available in the larger 19-oz. (560 ml) cans, and more recently I've also seen it in the standard 14-oz. (400 ml) size, the size of most other brands. Chao Koh, in 13.5-oz. cans, has been around for a long time and is more widely distributed. As one of the first good brands of coconut milk to appear in the American market, it has enjoyed widespread popularity and has made its way into some American supermarkets. Occasionally, I've seen Chao Koh in a small 6-oz. size, which is great for those occasions when just a light touch of coconut milk is desired. Costing under a dollar a can (less if you can buy by the case), these two brands are a great buy.

Brands packaged for gourmet Western markets are starting to pop up here and there. These are usually very pricy and not necessarily as good as the two recommended above. Be wary of words such as "natural," "virgin" and "extra-virgin" on the labels. These are only marketing catchwords to entice unknowing consumers; the products themselves may not have been processed any differently than others not making such claims. Often, you end up paying more for less flavor. Shop around, taste and compare before you decide on your preferred brand.

Many Thai recipes call for the coconut cream and lighter milk to be added during different stages of cooking; some require cream only. When using canned coconut milk in these recipes, do not shake the can before opening. The cream can be separated easily from the lighter milk since it floats at the top of the can. In many brands the cream coagulates in cooler weather, making it easy to spoon out from the top. The most watery part of the milk sits at the bottom of the can. On hot summer days, the cream may dissolve, making the mixture in the can more uniform, but refrigerating helps to separate the cream. Other brands of coconut milk are homogenized, with no separation between the cream and the lighter milk. This milk often has an artificial taste from the additives included to keep the milk homogenized.

Unlike fresh coconut milk, canned milk can curdle when it is cooked over very high heat, when it is mixed with water and boiled or when it is simmered covered for a prolonged period. If this should happen, try adding cream from another can to help bind the water and cream back together.

Frozen coconut milk, available in plastic pouches in some Southeast Asian markets, seems to have an even greater tendency to curdle. Take care not to boil or simmer it for very long; heat it just enough to warm it, and if you must cook with it longer than that, do so at a very low temperature in an uncovered pan. You may also minimize curdling in both canned and frozen milks by reserving the creamiest part of the milk for adding toward the end of cooking.

I recall the first time I tried frozen coconut milk. I thought I had stumbled onto a great find at the market; surely, frozen milk would be closest in flavor to fresh-pressed, especially made and imported from Asia. It turned out to be an embarrassing experience. I made the mistake of trying it out on the first session of a beginner's course, with a group of new students. The dessert we cooked, bananas in coconut milk (see recipe on page 123), looked rather strange and totally unappetizing. The milk had curdled in almost no time at all—"bananas with coconut curds" would have been a more appropriate name!

Coconut milk spoils quickly. Fresh milk should be used within a few days after pressing. Opened cans and defrosted bags start turning sour in about a week or less. Always refrigerate after opening.

COCONUT MILK:
HIGH IN CHOLESTEROL? NO!

Tropical oils, including coconut oil and coconut milk, have been stuck with an unfair bad reputation as "villains" to good health, with a high saturated fat content contributing to unhealthy blood cholesterol levels. I never believed this to be true. People in tropical Asia have always consumed a lot of coconut products —from using the oil in cooking to coconut milk in making soups, curries and all kinds of desserts—but their incidence of high blood cholesterol and heart disease remains very low. On the other hand, meat, cow's milk, butter and other animal fats are high in cholesterol and figure largely in the Western diet.

Scientists have since found that coconut oil, while high in saturated fat, is easier to digest and metabolize than other fats and tends to be burned as fuel rather than dumped into the blood stream. Just as there is good cholesterol and bad cholesterol, there is good saturated fat and bad saturated fat. It so happens that tropical oils like coconut oil are good saturated fats. These scientific findings support what traditional herbal doctors in Asia have known for a very long time, that coconut is a good energy food and can help increase the vitality of people suffering from fatigue or recovering from prolonged illness.

If you are a health-conscious consumer, you need not worry about the fat content in coconut milk as long as your diet is not high in other forms of saturated fats, especially from animal products. If your diet contains a lot of other saturated fats, you probably should worry about them instead, as the oil in coconut milk is quickly burned up as fuel. In fact, some of the oils that replaced tropical oils in processed foods have proven to be worse for the body than those they replaced.

Thai cooking uses lots of garlic, chillies and various kinds of gingers and herbs with health-enhancing and balancing qualities. Many of these ingredients are known to be blood cleansers and to help reduce cholesterol in the blood. A curry made with rich coconut milk also provides a dose of natural medicine that helps the body stay in balance. In addition, just two cups of coconut milk in a curry is enough to feed several people; this amount is certainly not enough to endanger their cholesterol levels on its own.

COCONUT:
A FRUIT, A NUT OR A SEED?

Though its name suggests that it is a nut, I've always regarded coconut as a fruit. When the coconut is young, it has properties like fruit, and as it matures, it becomes more nutty. But in fact it is not a nut; it is a seed.

Unless it is picked, a matured coconut eventually drops from the tree. The fully developed hard shell does not crack easily. Dry and brown, the coconut may sit underneath the tree for months and appear as if it were dead, until one day a green shoot pushes its way out of the shell. The whole time the old coconut has been sitting under the tree, changes have been slowly taking place inside. At one end of the coconut (where the eyes are), an embryo starts growing, feeding off the juice and nutrition of the thick white flesh. This embryo develops into a creamy mass that gradually fills much of the empty space inside. It is good to eat—sweet, somewhat spongy and less fibrous than the matured meat.

The embryo eventually sprouts out of the shell and becomes a young coconut seedling. At this point, the plant can survive for several more weeks or months on the food and water inside as roots gradually develop and extend out of the shell to anchor the plant in the ground. Nutritious coconut meat can sustain life for a long time; one of my students, who is a horticulturist, has successfully used coconut milk to nurse seedlings of other plants in his greenhouse. Coconut palms lead a long productive life. They begin bearing fruits at the age of five to seven years and continue to do so until they are seventy to eighty years old.

As complete seed packages, coconuts have been known to travel to faraway lands to find new homesteads. Stories abound of coconuts floating their way across seas and oceans to be washed ashore on distant islands, rooting themselves in handsome groves to greet visiting humans in search of paradise. The dehusked coconuts you buy at the supermarket, however, are no longer productive seed packages. Once the husk is removed, the seed dies.

Coconut Seedling (*Ma-prao Ngawk*)

COCONUT SEAFOOD SOUP WITH GALANGA

(Dtom Kah Talay)

*A 2- to 3-inch section fresh or
frozen Thai galanga,
or 6–8 dried pieces*

2 stalks lemon grass

3 cups rich coconut milk

3 cups water

8 medium-size prawns

½ tsp. salt

4–5 whole squid

8–10 mussels in the shell

½ tsp. baking soda

*½ a dungeness crab,
preferably uncooked*

8 large sea scallops

*1 small onion, quartered and
sliced crosswise
¼ inch thick*

*3–4 red jalapeño or fresno
peppers of desired
hotness cut in large
slivers*

*4 fresh kaffir lime leaves,
thinly slivered*

*2 cups fresh mushrooms,
sliced about
¼ inch thick*

*4–6 Tbs. fish sauce
(näm bplah),
to taste*

*Juice of 1–2 limes, to desired
sourness*

1–2 Tbs. palm sugar, to taste

*¼ tsp. freshly ground
white pepper*

*A handful of cilantro leaves
or short sprigs*

With a sharp knife, slice the galanga root thinly; it is not necessary to peel unless the outside has turned old and brown. Cut and discard the bottom tip of the lemon grass and remove the loose outer leaf or leaves. Slice at a long slanted angle, about an inch apart, all the way up the stalk close to where the grass blade starts. Smash and bruise with the flat side of a cleaver to release the aromatic oils and flavor. Place both galanga and lemon grass in a soup pot.

Spoon as much of the thick cream off the top of the coconut milk as you can and reserve for later use. Add the remaining watery part along with 3 cups of water to the herbs in the pot. Bring to a boil, then simmer covered over low heat for 10–15 minutes.

In the meantime, prepare the seafood and remaining ingredients. Shell and butterfly the prawns. Sprinkle with ½ tsp. of salt and 2 Tbs. of water. Mix well and set aside for about 10 minutes. Then rinse a few times to remove all the salt. Clean the squid, cutting the tubelike body into 3–4 circles about an inch apart. Leave the tentacles whole. Store in cold water until ready to use.

Scrub the mussels to remove any sand and mud from the shells. Cover with cold water with ½ tsp. of baking soda added, to induce the live mussels to spit out unwanted sand. Pull off the crab legs and claw. Use only the top half of the legs; disjoint the claw into two pieces. Crack each leg and claw piece with the back of a cleaver or heavy knife. Cut the body into 2–3 pieces. Leave the scallops whole. Prepare the remaining ingredients as indicated on the ingredients list.

When the herbs have simmered sufficiently to draw out their flavors, add the sliced onion, slivered peppers and kaffir lime leaves. Simmer 2–3 more minutes. Then add the mushrooms and reserved coconut cream. Stir well to blend into the broth and season to taste with fish sauce. Bring to a slow boil over medium heat. Drain the mussels and squid. When the soup has just reached the boiling point, add the mussels and crab pieces. Stir. After 15 seconds, stir in the remaining

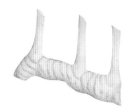

Galanga (*Kah*)

seafood. Add half the lime juice. Stir, then taste; if you wish the soup to be more limy, add more lime juice. Adjust the sour and salty flavors with enough palm sugar to return the sweet, rich taste of the coconut milk.

The seafood should be ready in about a minute or so. Turn off heat and sprinkle with freshly ground white pepper. Stir well, then transfer to a soup tureen, or ladle into individual serving bowls, and garnish the top with cilantro.

NOTES AND POINTERS

This recipe is written with canned coconut milk in mind. Either the Mae Ploy or Chao Koh brand, with a rich-tasting, nutty flavor, is preferred, or use an equivalent brand that you like. If you are using freshly made coconut milk, start with the lighter milk from the second or third pressing to simmer the herbs, reserving the richer cream for the later addition.

This recipe is rich, using one part coconut milk to one part water. For a lighter soup, blend one part milk to two parts water. Because it is a rich soup, Thai people eat it more like a curry—just a few spoonfuls with some rice—and seldom will eat an entire bowl by themselves; Westerners, who are used to rich cream soups, will.

Reversed from *dtom yäm* soup (see page 98) in which lemon grass is the main herb flavor and galanga is used in a supporting capacity, this soup is accentuated with the hearty taste of galanga, hence the name *dtom kah* ("boiled galanga"). Use lots of galanga so that the herb's flavor comes through the rich taste of the coconut milk.

Thai people usually do not strain herbs out of their soups, but if you find the fibrous lemon grass and strong galanga to be distracting, you may wish to remove them before adding the rest of the ingredients. This may be a wise idea if you are having guests for dinner who have never had Thai food and may not know what to do should they bite into a piece of hard lemon grass or pungent galanga.

$\mathscr{G}$RILLED COCONUT CAKE

(Kanom Bah Bin)

1 cup glutinous rice flour

½ cup rice flour

1 cup granulated sugar

¼ tsp. salt

1 large egg

2 cups finely shredded fresh coconut

1 cup limestone water, scented with ¼ tsp. bai dteuy (pandanus leaf) essence, or 1 tsp. vanilla

2–3 Tbs. peanut oil

Mix the two kinds of rice flour, sugar and salt together and knead with the egg and shredded coconut. Slowly add the limestone water, which has been scented with *bai dteuy* essence or vanilla, and continue to knead until the mixture is wet and the cream from the coconut meat is pressed out and blended in with all the other ingredients.

Grease the heated surface of a griddle with the peanut oil. Drop the coconut mixture in spoonfuls onto the hot griddle, molding them into small, flat rounds. Grill over low to medium heat until golden brown. Flip over and grill the other side until also browned. Best when served warm.

The coconut mixture can also be baked in a well-greased pan in the oven, at about 350° for 20–30 minutes, depending on the thickness of the cake. Brush a beaten egg yolk over the top after the cake is cooked through and bake another 5 minutes at 400°. Cut into small squares.

NOTES AND POINTERS

I prefer the cakes grilled in flat pancakes. They brown and pick up a light crispiness which is lacking when baked. The baked cake will tend to be more gooey in texture.

The two kinds of rice flour can be purchased in small bags in Chinese or Southeast Asian markets. For information on limestone water, see page 201.

For information about *bai dteuy* or pandanus leaf essence, see page 96. Instead of *bai dteuy* flavoring, the coconut mixture can also be "smoked" with a special incense candle (*tien ohb*) made of organic matter including herbs and flower petals. Such a candle is commonly used in the making of sweetmeats and desserts to add a spicy fragrance and smokiness. Brown in color, it has a curved shape and can be lit on both ends. This exotic item may not be easy to find in Western countries; ask for it in specialty Thai markets in cities with sizable Thai populations. If you travel to Thailand, look in stores that carry incense and merit-making supplies.

Matured Coconut (*Ma-prao*)

There are several different kinds from which to choose. Sniff and discover which fragrance you like. One candle will last a long time; it will burn very slowly and produce a lot of scented smoke.

To smoke with an incense candle, put the uncooked coconut mixture loosely in a bowl and place the bowl inside a large pot. Light the candle on both ends and position alongside the bowl. Close the lid tightly, adding extra weight over the top if necessary—such as an inverted stone mortar—to prevent smoke from escaping. Allow to smoke 30 minutes to one hour. For a stronger smoky flavor, relight the candle after 30 minutes to produce more smoke.

COCONUT EGG CUSTARD

(Sangkaya)

1 cup thick coconut cream

1 cup palm or coconut sugar

5 eggs

¼ tsp. bai dteuy (pandanus leaf) essence (optional)

a small yellow squash, such as kabocha squash

Heat the coconut cream and palm sugar in a saucepan just enough to dissolve the sugar and blend with the cream into a smooth mixture. Allow to cool to room temperature.

Beat the eggs well and mix in with the cooled, sweetened coconut cream. If you wish, add a few drops of flavor essence. Stir well. Strain the mixture through a dampened muslin cloth or through a fine wire mesh colander. Spoon out any bubbles that may have formed over the top.

Pour the mixture into a heat-proof dish or a hollowed-out yellow squash with a small round opening cut on top. Steam over medium-high heat until the custard is set, about 20 minutes in a dish and up to an hour inside a squash, depending on its size and thickness. Let cool.

If steamed by itself, spoon the custard into serving bowls and serve at room temperature. The sweet custard is more frequently served as a topping over coconut-flavored white sticky rice (see page 36). If steamed in a yellow squash, slice the squash and custard into wedges like you would a cake. The custard is wonderful eaten along with the golden squash.

NOTES AND POINTERS

See page 96 for information about *bai dteuy* essence. As with the foregoing recipe for grilled coconut cakes, a scented smokiness can also be added to enhance the flavor of the custard. Smoke the coconut cream with an incense candle the same way as described for the shredded coconut mixture.

Pandanus Leaf (*Bai Dteuy*)

BANANAS IN COCONUT MILK

(Gkluey Buad Chi)

*4 burro cooking bananas, or firm
red bananas*

2–3 cups creamy coconut milk

¼–½ cup granulated sugar

⅛–¼ tsp. sea salt

A few drops of mali (*Thai jasmine*)
essence (optional)

Peel the bananas just before you are ready to cook. Cut them in half lengthwise, then each half into 4 pieces crosswise.

In a saucepan, heat the coconut milk. Add sugar to the desired sweetness and a little bit of salt. The salt enhances the rich creamy taste of coconut milk, especially if you are using canned milk. Sprinkle in a few drops of *mali* essence if you wish a delicate floral scent in the background. When the mixture is hot and smooth, add the bananas and simmer about five minutes, or until the bananas are cooked but still in whole pieces. Serve warm for best flavor.

NOTES AND POINTERS

Thai people like many of their desserts to be laced with the delicate fragrance of fresh flowers, the favorite being *mali*, a very sweet-smelling jasmine. *Mali* flowers are used profusely in Thailand in beautiful, fragrant leis sold by street vendors for people to take home to hang on shrines and spirit houses. In Thailand, fresh *mali* flowers are soaked in water, and the scented water is used to press coconut milk. For overseas Thais, a *mali* concentrate is available to duplicate the sweet fragrance of home. Look for little bottles labeled *"mali"* in specialty Thai markets. It is highly perfumed, so use it sparingly; a few drops will usually suffice and one bottle should last for years—that is, if you don't take to it like some of my students have, who add the luxurious aroma to their bath water.

There are many kinds of bananas, some more suitable for cooking than others. The common eating banana sold in American supermarkets (known in Thailand as *gkluey hom*, or "fragrant banana") does not hold up very well in cooking. It quickly falls apart after a few minutes and becomes soggy, though the flavor is sweetly fragrant.

For this particular dessert, the variety called *gkluey näm wah* is best. Small, short and delicious with a thin peel and a firm texture even when very ripe, its firmness holds up well in cooking. It is great when grilled, fried, boiled and turned into all sorts of snacks and desserts; it is also wonderful eaten as fresh fruit. *Gkluey näm wah* contains the most vitamins of all the different kinds cultivated in Thailand, and because of this it is often mashed up and fed to infants as they are weaned from mother's milk in rural villages. Unfortunately, I have not yet seen this banana imported into American markets.

Another variety frequently used for this dessert is *gkluey kai* ("egg banana"). Some Asian markets carry it during the spring and summer months. It is short and small, like a miniature banana, with a thin and shiny, deep yellow peel. Inside, the flesh is lightly tinged with orange when very ripe. Sweet and tasty, it is one of Thailand's favorite eating bananas and holds up relatively well in cooking.

I wrote this recipe using "burro" bananas because they are good cooking bananas and more readily available in ethnic markets and specialty produce stores. Large and fat, they look much like plantains but are shorter. For this dessert, I buy ones that are fully ripe—with the peel starting to turn dark on the outside—but that are still firm to the touch. These bananas have a thick peel, so even if they are dark and slightly soft on the outside, the fruits are protected on the inside. If they are cooked before they are fully ripe, their texture will be more like potatoes, and they won't taste much like bananas. However, when ripe and ready for eating, they cook up nicely and add a thick creaminess to the coconut milk. Their sweet and tart flavors blend well with the sweet coconut sauce, and their firmness holds up very well in cooking. This type of banana is also good when roasted over coals. To do so, place the banana over medium to low coals, turning occasionally until the peel browns and begins to sweat. Take a sharp knife and slit the peel along the full length of the banana, exposing part of the flesh. Continue to roast till the outside is black and charred and the inside a deep yellow color.

Red bananas, which are becoming more widely distributed, also cook up nicely in this dessert. However, if the common yellow bananas are the only variety available to you, use firm ones and be careful not to overcook them—usually a couple of minutes is ample time. They will have a soggier texture than the other cooking bananas and the coconut sauce will be less thick, but the flavor will be delightfully fragrant.

Matured Coconut (*Ma-prao*)

The Thai name for this dessert is rather humorous if translated literally into English. *Gkluey* stands for bananas; *buad*, to ordain; and *chi*, nuns (as in monks and nuns). My students fondly refer to this simple dessert as "ordained bananas" or "sacred bananas." Just as nuns in Thailand take on white robes, in this recipe the bananas are cooked and dressed in a white coconut sauce. Bananas are not the only foods that get "ordained": pumpkin and taro, among other things, are similarly cooked in coconut milk. Such sweet, soupy concoctions are referred to as *gkaeng buad* (*gkaeng* is soup or curry). The color of coconut milk changes when other things are cooked in it; when pumpkin is used, for instance, the coconut sauce becomes lightly tinged with orange, reminiscent of monks' robes. Whatever the true origin of the name of this sweet food may be, it suggests that food is sacred and the sacred is part of everyday life.

Over the years, a number of beginners in my cooking classes have initially insisted that they do not like curries and do not want to learn to make them. Invariably, most of them have had minimal previous exposure, if any, to Thai curries and know little about curry beyond the yellow powder sold in small jars on the spice racks of supermarkets. Upon sampling the curries made in class, however, they have been happily surprised by a whole new world of taste sensations bearing no resemblance to the stuff they had always known as curry. The robust flavors of chillies and numerous herbs, blended with fragrant spices in a rich coconut sauce, add up to an experience that almost always leaves a favorable impression.

The yellow powder most Americans have come to identify as curry is actually just one kind of curry. There are hundreds of different kinds, spanning the wide Asian continent from India to the outer Indonesian islands. Thailand has several dozens of her own, with flavor combinations unmatched in the cuisines of her neighbors. The word curry, therefore, could be aptly defined as a way of cooking, a technique of stewing meats, seafoods and vegetables in a tantalizing combination of spices and herbs that have been ground and prepared into paste or powder form. It is a method of cooking that originated in India and that has spread throughout the world through trade and migration over the centuries.

People from India began migrating to Southeast Asia more than two thousand years ago. They brought with them not only their religion, ceremonies and healing practices—many of which have become intricately interwoven into the fabric of Thai life—but also their food and way of cooking. Much of Thai cuisine has roots traceable to Indian cuisine, though over time the adopted ingredients and styles of cooking have changed and evolved as they have been combined with influences from other cultures as well as molded by Thai creativity. Over time Thai people have added their own herbs and favored condiments—blending them together in unique ways—to the Indian curries introduced centuries ago. Dry spices and aromatic seeds accentuate the flavors of India's cuisine, but in Thailand, we rely on a large number of fresh herbs and roots to make our curry pastes. Lemon grass, galanga, kaffir lime peel, cilantro roots, garlic, shallots and chillies, for instance, are found in most Thai curry pastes. *Gkapi*, a concentrated fermented shrimp paste, is also an essential ingredient and reflects our country's dependence on the sea.

The dominance of "wet" ingredients makes the combinations for our curries moist pastes rather than dry powders. Occasionally you may come across ready-made, dried Thai curry mixes; to be expected, these are inferior to those in paste form, as the fresh taste of herbs is lost in the process of dehydration.

Curries constitute the richest part of Thai cuisine, as most of them are made with coconut milk. Because of this, usually not more than one curry is served at each meal, and when a rich curry is included on the menu, it is unlikely that other coconut-milk-based dishes will be served in the same meal. Though they are rich, curries are also very spicy and should be eaten with lots of rice and never by themselves.

CURRY— A WAY OF COOKING, NOT A YELLOW POWDER

THE MANY FACES OF THAI CURRIES

With all the fresh herbs and dry spices available in Thailand, an abundantly diverse range of curries has come about. They vary in character from one end of the kingdom to the other. Some are unique to particular regions, such as the fiery *gkaeng prik* ("chilli curry") of the south and the gingery *gkaeng hâng-leh* of the north; others are in the mainstream of Thai cuisine and can be found in restaurants from border to border.

There are so many kinds of curries that to adequately cover the subject would require an entire volume. This brief chapter seeks only to introduce a few ideas on the basic process of curry making to augment what you may have learned or gathered from other sources.

A handful of basic curries—green curry, red curry, yellow curry, massaman curry and panaeng curry—are the usual selections available in the West. These distinctive curries reflect not only different combinations of herbs and spices but also varying methods of preparation. They have developed as means to enhance the cooking of particular meats, seafoods and vegetables to bring out their special flavors. Hence, you find green curry most frequently accompanied with pork as it seems to work best with pork; however, its fresh herb flavors also make it very good with seafood. Red curry suits poultry well and is especially wonderful with roast duck. The heavier spice flavors of massaman and panaeng curries, traceable to Muslim origins in the south, go well with red meats, such as beef and lamb. (The Muslim people, who comprise five percent of the total poulation of Thailand, form the majority of the population in the southernmost provinces. They are known to be the beef eaters in the country.) Yellow curry (the Thai version of Indian yellow curry) can include either beef or chicken along with potatoes in its sauce.

Among the mainstream curries, green curry (*gkaeng kiow wahn*) is the most popular among Thai people and perhaps the most "Thai" in the sense that it is so different from the curries of other countries. Full of refreshing herb flavors, it is one of our hottest curries, made with lots of fresh green chillies at the peak of their hotness. Sometimes, the green leaves of chilli plants are bruised and added to deepen the green color of the sauce. Green curry is generally one of the lighter curries; its sauce is soupy rather than thick. (The Thai word for curry, *gkaeng*, is also used to refer to soup.)

Red curry (*gkaeng ped*) is also very common in Thailand. It gets its color from dried red chillies and is made and served in a way similar to green curry, with a soupy coconut sauce. Red curry paste is used to make other forms of curries as well, such as steamed curried seafood mousse (*haw moek*) and stir-fried fish or meat in dry red curry sauce (*pad ped*). The recipe for a popular *pad ped* with crispy fried catfish appears on page 146.

In contrast to the green and red, massaman and panaeng curries are richer and sweeter. Panaeng curry is usually served on a plate rather than in a bowl, and the meat pieces are coated in thick, creamy sauce. These two curries are most like Indian curries as they include many of the dry spices prevalently used in Indian cuisine. They are rich and sweet, and Westerners are more familiar with their taste than the lighter green and red curries.

A number of very spicy curries are not coconut-milk based. Two popular ones are "sour curry" (*gkaeng som*), which employs sour tamarind, and "jungle curry" (*gkaeng bpah*), translated by some sources as "country-style red curry."

Although they are like soup, they are thick with vegetables, herbs and fish or meat of some kind, and immensely pungent. The hard-core can slurp them down like chowders, but most people prefer to spoon them over rice and eat them like they would curry.

In Bangkok, menus of fine restaurants usually have entire sections devoted to curries, some running the length of a few pages. Curry rice shops in towns all over Thailand also offer an extensive selection of fast-food curries, including regional favorites and provincial specialties. The next time you are in Thailand, try not to limit yourself to the familiar selections you can get in restaurants back home, but instead sample some of the rare jewels of Thai cuisine that have yet to be known beyond the country's boundaries.

CURRIES SIMPLIFIED

Curries taste best when made with freshly prepared pastes. However, if you don't have time to make a paste from scratch, you can still put together delicious curries at home if you know which brands of ready-made pastes to select and what to do to heighten their spice and herb flavors during cooking.

Not all brands of a particular kind of curry paste work the same. For instance, although green curry is a specific combination of herbs and spices, different brands may use varying proportions of the same ingredients, add their own secret ingredients or process the ingredients in special ways that affect the final products. In making comparisons, one paste may seem to taste better than others, but when made into curry, the flavors are disappointing.

To choose a paste that will satisfy your needs, taste three to four different brands of a particular kind to compare their similarities and differences. Try to separate out the spice and herb flavors from the hot, salty, sour and sweet flavors. These four primary flavors can be added, reduced or changed later on during cooking, whereas the totality of the spice and herb flavors is what you need the curry paste to provide. Some brands of massaman paste, for instance, have a pleasing sweet and nutty taste because palm sugar and ground peanuts have already been added, but these are two ingredients you can easily add yourself. Try to ascertain how strong the spice flavors are and whether they are coming through beyond the mask of the sweet and nutty taste. Generally, if a paste tastes great by itself and makes a good cracker spread, it will tend to make a mild, less interesting curry when cooked in coconut sauce with a host of other ingredients. To make a stimulating curry, the paste should taste intense and too strong to eat by itself with a spoon.

Ready-made pastes come packaged in several different ways: plastic pouches (e.g., Mae Anong brand), small and big plastic tubs (e.g., Mae Ploy brand), small cans (e.g., Mae Sri brand) and small jars (e.g., Mae Pranom brand). Incidentally, you will notice that many of the brands are identified with a picture of a woman on the label. Some of these women are real and have been known for their curry pastes long before they were packaged and exported. Their names begin with *Mae*, which means "mother."

The two brands my students like best are Mae Ploy and Mae Anong. Both make fairly good curry pastes. When I don't make my own paste from scratch, I prefer to use Mae Anong for green curry, as the herb flavors come through fuller and fresher. For massaman curry, Mae Ploy is more robust, though it lacks the roasted aromas characteristic of this kind of curry, aromas that are present in the other brand. Therefore, I sometimes combine the two to take advantage of the strengths of each. Mae Ploy's pastes are generally more fiery and salty and don't require the addition of any fish sauce or extra chillies. Another fairly good brand, Pa-Siam, has a chicken rather than a "mom" as its logo and comes in plastic tubs.

In my experience, pastes in cans don't seem to make curries that are particularly exciting; canning causes a chemical change in the herbs that prohibits their flavors from coming through fully when cooked in coconut sauce. But because the cans are small units, many beginners in Thai cooking use them. Canned pastes have also been around longer than other packaged curries and enjoy a wider distribution. To the unaccustomed and unsophisticated palate, curries made from these pastes may still be regarded as very tasty and enjoyable.

Curry pastes keep well; the spices themselves are natural preservatives, and most also contain salt to maintain freshness. After they are opened, they should be kept airtight and refrigerated. They will stay good for a few months, or freeze them to keep indefinitely. Always use a clean implement to spoon out the amount needed; if mold grows on a curry paste, it usually has been introduced from outside food particles. Mold does not like chillies or garlic, as they are natural antiseptics.

ASSEMBLING A CURRY

Once you have a paste, assembling the curry is a simple process, but there are a few things you can do to optimize the final result. For a coconut-milk-based curry, start out by heating a saucepan over medium to high heat. Pour in about a cup of coconut cream. If you are using canned coconut milk, do not shake the can before opening, and spoon the creamiest part at the top of the can into the saucepan. Heat and reduce until it is smooth and bubbly. You may be able to detect the oil beginning to separate from the cream; this sometimes shows as a texture developing in the cream. At this point, add the curry paste. Fry the paste in the heated cream, mashing and mushing the paste into the cream until it becomes a smooth mixture. Fry over medium heat until the paste is fragrant and darkens, about three to five minutes. This helps release the spice and herb flavors.

Stir in the lighter coconut milk, enough to make the volume of sauce needed. Mix well till smooth and even. Taste and add fish sauce to the saltiness desired. Add palm sugar as a balancing agent to heighten the spice and herb flavors further and to sweeten to the desired balance. The amount to use will depend on the type of curry you are making. Add the meat or seafood and vegetables, according to cooking times required, so that they are tender at the same time. For curries that call for fresh basil, add this in the last couple of minutes of cooking so that its fresh taste does not cook away. For curries that benefit from a touch of tanginess, add the souring agent as well toward the end of cooking. Taste before serving to determine whether any final adjustments are necessary to balance the hot, salty, sour and sweet flavors to optimally harmonize with the herb and spice flavors.

Curries taste even better a day later, giving a whole new meaning to leftovers. Allowing the multitude of ingredients to mingle and marry for a period of time integrates the myriad flavors, such that they become a whole

Matured Coconut (*Ma-prao*)

much greater than the sum of its parts. Curries are perfect for entertaining, as they can be made ahead of time. Make a big pot, enough to enjoy for days to follow.

PASTE MAKING: A GRATIFYING EXPERIENCE

There are few gastronomic delights more satisfying than curries made from freshly ground pastes. The flavors of a good, homemade paste surpass even the very best pastes imported from the kitchens of Bangkok. Moreover, paste making is a fun activity and a deeply stimulating experience. The aromas of all the spices and herbs are released as they are pounded in the stone mortar, and the olfactory nerves are rewarded with unexpected pleasures.

One of my students regained her sense of smell—which she had lost following an accident—as her nose was stimulated by the aromas from the herbs used in paste making. Others have found the process of pounding and grinding to be therapeutic in itself, regarding it as a safe way to release pent-up tension and suppressed aggression. One of these students, who had traveled extensively in Thailand, swore that the Thai people she met were as gentle as they were because they spent so much time pounding and chopping and cooking in the kitchen. She stayed with families in rural areas and awoke each morning to the sound of the rhythmic pounding of the mortar and pestle coming from the kitchen. It seemed to her that their aggressions and frustrations were directed and transformed into something useful and creative.

Pounding up a storm in the kitchen certainly can relieve frustration, anger and depression as well as produce a great meal and the resulting feeling of accomplishment. The sharing of the meal restores a sense of harmony and connectedness with others. Energy is transformed from negative to positive, and everyone gains.

These therapeutic benefits are not forthcoming, however, if you are rushing against time in the kitchen. Paste making can be a very engaging process, and time constraints will only produce stress rather than relieve it. The benefits are also lost if you try to take a short-cut by using a food processor, rather than the age-old mortar and pestle.

A food processor mainly chops and shreds, and unless liquid is added, you end up with a coarsely chopped mixture, not a paste. Grinding and pounding with a heavy mortar and pestle, on the other hand, crush the fibers of herbs, releasing the essential oils that hold the flavors and aromas. That is why herbs that appear fibrous and dry become very moist when pounded. A pounded paste is immensely aromatic and has a breadth and depth of flavor lacking in a processed mixture.

One of my students—who would have preferred to make everything in the food processor—decided to make two pots of curries using the same recipe. One was made with the paste created entirely by pounding in a stone mortar, and the other was made with paste produced in the food processor. Upon tasting, his wife immediately identified the curry made the traditional way; the flavors were just so much more alive.

When you are short on time, you may need to use short-cuts. Just be aware of the trade-offs and decide if you are willing to sacrifice taste for an

Stone Mortar and Pestle

extra half hour of your time. Also, remember that not all short-cuts work and may, instead, lead to frustration. As you are learning the intricacies of Thai cooking, it is important to follow guidelines as closely as possible and learn what each step contributes to the final result. When you have gained a better understanding of the whys and hows of the traditional methods, then you can begin to take short-cuts, noting as you do what is being sacrificed along the way. You may find certain steps are not as crucial as others and discover a short-cut that works well for you in your kitchen without compromising flavor—it may even add a special twist that you prefer. But unless you already know the way to get some place, you may get lost taking a short-cut.

Tips on Equipment and Technique

As already suggested, the one indispensable piece of equipment needed to make exceptional curry pastes is a good, strong, large and heavy mortar and pestle, one that allows you to pound with vigor and twirl in grinding frenzy. It should give you much pleasure with little limitation. In Thailand, there are a few different kinds of mortar and pestle suited for particular purposes. The most efficient for making curry pastes is cut and polished out of granite. It can reduce hard seeds and fibrous herbs down in no time. The pestle and the inside surface of the mortar are polished smooth and are not rough, coarse or porous. Very dense and heavy, they do not chip and last for years even when subjected to vigorous daily pounding. Look for this dark grey stone mortar and pestle set in a Thai or Southeast Asian market near you. It is available in small, medium and large sizes and ranges from about sixteen to twenty-four dollars.

If you are not able to locate a stone mortar and pestle, the more readily available large clay mortar with hardwood pestle works almost as well. It is tall and deep, dark brown in color, has a fairly smooth surface and is much less expensive, averaging around seven dollars a set. Because wood against clay is not as hard as stone against stone, this mortar and pestle works better pounding a small quantity of fibrous herbs at a time, so that the herbs are not cushioned by themselves in a soft bed. Use a straight pounding motion as well as a grinding motion up and down the rougher sides of the mortar. It also helps to have the hardier ingredients chopped or cut in smaller pieces before pounding.

Some of my students prefer the clay-and-wood combination to the stone because it makes a pleasing and much gentler sound and vibration than the louder and harsher stone-against-stone banging tones. The rhythmic sound of pounding with the clay-and-wood mortar and pestle has brought these students meditative calm. To them, it is worth the extra time.

In Thailand, ingredients that go into a curry paste are pounded together all at once in the mortar. Often, the softer and wetter ingredients like garlic and shallots are placed in whole as they mash up relatively easily. Coarse salt crystals provide some abrasion to reduce the harder and more fibrous herbs and spices as well as pull their flavors together. The pounding goes on until everything in the mortar is mashed into a paste and is no longer distinguishable. This can take a long time for someone inexperienced in mortar and pestle techniques.

If you are a beginner with mortar and pestle, work on one ingredient at a time, starting with the dry spices. They are easily pulverized with a rolling motion of the pestle around the bottom and sides of the mortar while its surface is still dry. Remove them from the mortar before proceeding with the most fibrous of the herbs. Pound one ingredient at a time, a small amount at a

Clay Mortar and Hardwood Pestle

time, moving from the hardiest to the softest and wettest. Herbs reduce more quickly when pounded with a sturdy up and down motion; only after their fibers have been adequately crushed does a rolling wrist motion contribute to their reduction. When all the ingredients have been reduced to powder or paste, combine them and pound together until they are well blended and no longer distinguishable. This process takes less time overall and, for the less experienced, produces a paste that is more uniform.

Tips on Prepping Herbs and Spices

Herbs reduce easier in the mortar when they are cut into small pieces or chopped ahead of time. This is especially true with lemon grass, which has tough fibers running the length of the stalk. Slice it into thin rounds before pounding, or your paste may end up with a stringy texture. Reconstituted dried ingredients, such as kaffir lime peel, also benefit from cutting with a sharp knife beforehand. Although softened by soaking, the once-dried zest can still be tough and sometimes pounds to a flat piece without breaking down. If you can, avoid pounding dry spices with fibrous herbs because they frequently cushion one another and end up taking longer to reduce. For those who seek short-cuts, the wetter herbs like garlic and shallots chop easily with the aid of a chopper or miniprocessor, and the dry spices pulverize quickly in a coffee grinder designated specifically for grinding spices—but *always* pound them afterward to release their flavors fully.

For curries with roasted fragrances, such as massaman and panaeng curries, roast the dry spices in a dry pan over a medium flame and cool before pulverizing. I usually roast the different seeds separately, as the smaller ones like cumin take less time than the larger ones, like coriander seeds. While roasting, seeds release their perfume into the air before they brown, so let them go a while longer after you begin to smell their roasted aromas, or until they are uniformly dark, but not burned. This way the seeds are roasted through to the core and not just toasted on the surface. Stir or shake the pan frequently for even browning. Darkly roasted seeds will permeate a curry with stronger roasted flavors than lightly toasted seeds; burned seeds will make the curry bitter.

Dried red chillies are dry-roasted the same way as seeds, by placing them on a dry pan over the stove, but be careful to watch them closely. They may do nothing the first minute, then all of a sudden burn quickly. Turn often so they darken evenly. You *do not* want to burn chillies as they release fumes into the air that irritate the mucous linings of the throat all the way down to the lungs. Make sure you have good ventilation. Burning fumes are less likely if the chillies are roasted before deseeding, as chilli dust from the inside membranes of punctured chillies burns easily on the hot pan. If there are several ingredients that require roasting, I always save the chillies for last, to avoid the possibility of burning traces of them on the pan while I roast the seeds.

For recipes that call for dried chillies, I usually remove and discard the seeds. The flavor of most dried chillies lies mainly in the red skin and dried pods; the seeds are hot but hold less flavor. Deseeding allows you to use more pods for added flavor (as well as for a redder color) without the paste becoming too hot. There are two ways to prepare dried chillies for paste making. They can be ground dried to a fine powder, then pounded with other wet ingredients to form a paste; or they can be soaked first to soften, then chopped and pounded into paste. The latter method seems to produce a curry

Dried Red Chillies

paste with a fresher-tasting chilli flavor. I usually use the soaking method for pastes using chillies that are not roasted, and the dried-ground method when roasted chillies are called for, to preserve the roasted flavor. To soak, cut off the stem end, turn the chilli head down and squeeze out the seeds before putting the chilli in a bowl of water. This allows the water to penetrate to the inside, thereby softening the chillies faster. Avoid using hot water for soaking as it leaches out the more delicate flavors in the chilli pods.

For recipes that call for roasted garlic and shallots, the roasting can be more conveniently accomplished in a toaster oven rather than over charcoal, as traditionally done. Cut the root ends of the garlic cloves and shallots, leaving the skins on (this prevents them from bursting and creating a sticky mess in your oven). Place them on a tray in a hot oven (450 degrees). Check after five to ten minutes and remove the garlic cloves once they have softened and started to ooze out. Shallots usually take longer, depending on their size. Roasted garlic and shallots pop out of their skins when squeezed with the fingers; they mash up easily in the mortar.

Almost all Thai curry pastes are flavored with *gkapi* shrimp paste (see page 54 for description). For recipes that call for roasting *gkapi*, wrap the amount needed in a small section of banana leaf, hold the packet with tongs and stick it directly into the gas flame of a burner. Turn frequently until the leaf is well charred and the odor of *gkapi* begins to escape. Remove from the wrapping and pound into the curry paste. In Thailand, *gkapi* is roasted in charcoal embers; this is easy to do in kitchens equipped with charcoal stoves. If you do not have a banana leaf, substitute with aluminum foil, though this will dry the paste out considerably.

* * * * *

In your paste-making adventure, you may want to consider making a larger quantity than needed because once you get started, it usually doesn't take much more time to make an extra amount. Roasting two tablespoons of coriander seeds, for instance, doesn't take any more time than one tablespoon, and homemade paste keeps for several weeks in the refrigerator without losing much of its fresh flavors. Remember, too, that the paste freezes fairly well for an indefinite period of time.

After you have tried out recipes for several different kinds of curry pastes, you will notice that many of the same ingredients are used, yet the resulting pastes are far from similar. Varying the proportions of ingredients, prepping them differently (e.g., roasting or not roasting beforehand), deleting an ingredient and adding a new one or introducing a new twist somewhere in the process—all of these variations can produce entirely different curries, unlike anything a comparison of the lists of ingredients may suggest. A good curry has a distinct character of its own, its flavors so well harmonized that only a sophisticated palate is able to separate out the players. Such integration is a hallmark of Thai cuisine.

To give you an idea of the diversity of Thai curries, recipes for two very different kinds follow: the lighter, refreshing green curry and the richer, sweeter massaman curry. Two versions of each are presented; one is simplified and uses prepackaged curry paste, and the other includes instructions for making the paste from scratch with fresh ingredients.

The recipe for green curry with fish/shrimp dumplings on page 140 is adapted from the absolutely divine curry served by a family-run, riverside restaurant in Ayutaya called Pae Gkrung Gkao ("Raft in the Old Capital City").

Shallots

Very spicy and full of robust herbal flavors, it is a specialty of the house and is made fresh daily with the finest ingredients, from the fish dumplings to the very sweet and tasty, long, green eggplants. They also serve delicious crisp-fried fish with chilli sauce, spicy roast beef salad, hot-and-sour seafood soup, salads and stir-fries with fresh hearts of palm and many daily specials.

Though fortune has blessed it with expanded quarters over the years, Pae Gkrung Gkao remains a cozy and charming, open-air garden restaurant with superb home-cooked food. It is a great place to relax and watch the rice barges float up and down the river on their way to and from Bangkok. Whenever I pass through this town on my way up north, I make a point to stop by for a delightful meal and to visit the sweet, giggly girls who provide excellent service. Evening is the best time to go; it is quiet, peaceful and cool. Morning, too, is pleasant, when the air is clean and refreshing, and although the place ordinarily is not open for breakfast, they will serve you if you give them advance notice. During midday hours, however, the place loses its serenity as throngs of noisy tourists on day-trips from Bangkok are herded in for lunch. They are served fairly bland Chinese food at a premium price, while the Thai tour guides and bus drivers, who seat themselves in a different corner of the raft, receive some of the best Thai food of the house. If you find yourself traveling in a large tour group, ask to eat with the bus driver at lunchtime.

This chapter closes with a recipe for scrumptious crispy fried catfish coated with freshly made red curry. This is one of my very favorite dishes and has become a favorite among many of my advanced cooking students who enjoy making pastes from scratch. The dish is also popular among Thais and is available in most fine restaurants.

There is one place in particular in Bangkok where I thoroughly enjoy this dry, crispy red-curried catfish. Though the restaurant is seldom frequented by foreign diners, it bears a name distinctly English, "My Choice," spelled in Thai phonetics to match the English pronunciation. Because most Thai people have a hard time with the "s" sound at the end of a word, it is more often called "My Choy." My Choice has a fabulous menu with a great variety of dishes not found in other restaurants, all very reasonably priced. The visitor who cannot read Thai, however, is at a disadvantage as the English-version menu is limited and the translations from Thai into English unfortunately make some exquisite dishes sound awful. If you go there by yourself, look around to see what the locals are eating and be prepared to do some pointing. Better yet, befriend a Thai who frequents the place and have him or her order you his favorite dishes from the menu.

I never miss the chance to take my tour groups to My Choice. Besides their crispy red-curried catfish, many dishes are out of this world, including their salted-crab-and-coconut dipping sauce for vegetables, roasted eggplant salad, fried crispy bitter melon with chilli sauce, spicy lime beef, winged bean salad, *labbs* (very pungent minced meat salads) of all kinds, stewed duck with viny greens called *pak dtum leung*, coconut-seafood soup and many more. They also have some of the best coconut ice cream (nondairy), taro ice cream and the unusual basil seeds ice cream.

Another place where I've had unforgettable crispy red-curried catfish is at a no-frills truck stop next to a gas station near the small town of Ang Tong, a short distance north of the historical ruins of old Ayutaya. My tour assistant who drives one of the vans introduced me to the funky place many years ago. We had just left Ayutaya with our tour group and were planning to drive up to

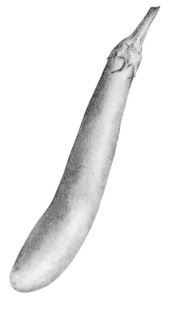

Long Green Eggplant (*Ma-Keua Yao*)

the city of Nakon Sawan to look for a place to lunch, when all of a sudden, Ong made a quick left turn and parked right in front of this nondescript, rural rice shop. I had told the tour members only a few minutes earlier that we weren't going to eat for at least another hour, and some of them had already begun to snack on the bananas and other *kanoms* I had supplied for them in the van, to hold them over until we made it to Nakon Sawan.

But Ong pleaded that we *must* have lunch there. He had forgotten about this precious little place until he saw the gas station. It wasn't quite noon yet, and I was not hungry or inclined to change plans. But Ong refused to take "no" for an answer and had already proceeded into the shop to order food. I was forced to announce the change of plans to the tour members, and we all followed Ong into the rice shop.

We had barely ordered our food when it appeared in front of us in great profusion. Everything looked and smelled so good that no one could resist digging in. Before long, we had cleaned up three large pots of rice and every bit of sauce on the serving dishes. We enjoyed with gusto the fried curried catfish as well as the roasted eggplant salad; the eggplants were grilled to perfection on small charcoal braziers on the floor of the open kitchen. Someone finally broke the silence and remarked that this was the best meal of the tour thus far.

So when you visit Thailand, don't disregard those cheap, broken-down shacks next to gas stations on Thailand's major highways. Just look for noontime crowds—local folk, truckers and long-distance Thai travelers—enjoying a feast of delicious homemade curries and other regional favorites.

Whatever recipes and creative inspiration you choose to bring to your kitchen, enjoy your paste-making adventure. While you busily pound away with your mortar and pestle, smell all the wonderful aromas of the delightful herbs, get in rhythm with your hand movements and have a timeless afternoon of sensual pleasure. The process of getting there is just as rewarding as the destination.

EASY GREEN CURRY WITH PORK

(Gkaeng Kiow Wahn Moo)

*2 cups or 1 14-oz. can
coconut milk*

2–3 Tbs. green curry paste

*1 lb. pork, cut against the grain
of the muscle
into bite-size strips
about 2 x 1 x ¼ in.*

*½ cup small pea eggplants
(ma-keua puang), or
substitute with shelled
fresh peas*

*½ lb. small, round Thai eggplants
(ma-keua bprawh), cut
in halves or quarters, or
substitute with 2 long
Asian eggplants, cut in
bite-size chunks*

*2 kaffir lime leaves
(bai ma-gkrood)*

Fish sauce (näm bplah) to taste

2 tsp. palm sugar, or to taste

*½ to 1 cup fresh Thai sweet basil
leaves and flowers
(bai horapa)*

Slivered chillies, to desired hotness

Do not shake the can of coconut milk before opening, so that the cream remains on top. Spoon about ⅔ cup of this thick cream into a medium-size saucepan and heat over medium to high heat. Reduce until smooth and bubbly and until oil begins to separate from the cream. Add the curry paste and fry in the cream for a few minutes to release the aromas. Then pour in the remaining milk.

Bring to a boil and add the pork and the pea eggplants. Return to a boil, reduce heat and simmer 5–10 minutes uncovered before adding the Thai (or Asian) eggplants. Simmer a few minutes more, then stir in the peas (if using instead of pea eggplants) and kaffir lime leaves. Season to taste with fish sauce (may not be needed if the curry paste is already salted). Add palm sugar to balance and enhance the spice and herb flavors to your liking. Continue to simmer until eggplants and peas are tender. Stir in the basil and chillies (as desired for added hotness) and cook another minute. Serve hot over plain steamed rice.

NOTES AND POINTERS

The preferred canned coconut milk for this recipe is Chao Koh, and Mae Anong is a good choice for a prepackaged paste. It comes in plastic pouches with the picture of a young woman (Mae Anong herself) on the upper right hand corner and is also identified as "Lemon Grass Brand." Rather than the translated name of "green curry," this brand labels the curry with the Thai name, "Kang Kiew Wan" (a different spelling from mine).

There are many kinds of small eggplants in Thailand. Round ones the size of tomatillas, which we call *ma-keua bprawh*, are very good in this curry. Deeper green on top and graduating to a lighter bottom, these are seedy eggplants and taste nothing like the large purple aubergines. Cooked until softened, they soak in the curry flavors and add a thickness to the sauce. Other smaller members of the eggplant family are *ma-keua puang*, which resemble large green peas, though their taste is entirely different. They are bitter, but when simmered in the curry sauce they impart an extraordinary roundedness to the sauce. Much of their bitter

Thai Eggplant (*Ma-keua Bprawh*)

Pea Eggplant (*Ma-keua Puang*)

bite dissipates when they have completely softened with sufficient cooking. Both these eggplants are available in Thai and Southeast Asian markets, especially during the warmer months of the year, though the latter is usually harder to find. Specialty produce markets and gourmet supermarkets have also started to carry them.

If you do not eat red meat, try this recipe with shrimps and fish fillets, cut into bite-size chunks. Cook the eggplants and peas until they are almost tender before adding the seafood. Fish chunks take only about 1–2 minutes to cook; shrimps a minute or less. For a special treat, make the green curry with salmon chunks and lots of basil.

Using this recipe, a red curry can be easily made by substituting a red curry paste and cut-up boneless chicken. For a fabulous roasted duck curry, buy a roasted duck the next time you visit the Chinatown near your home and use it instead of the pork and with a red curry paste. Toward the end of cooking, skim off the fat that has cooked out of the duck and add two small, firm and still slightly green tomatoes, cut in bite-size wedges.

GREEN CURRY WITH FISH/SHRIMP DUMPLINGS

(Gkaeng Kiow Wahn Loogchin Bplah/Gkung)

⅔ lb. ground fish paste, or small white fish fillets

⅔ lb. fresh shrimp, shelled and chopped finely

¼ tsp. ground white pepper

3–4 Tbs. fish sauce (näm bplah), to taste

1–2 Tbs. tapioca flour

4 cups coconut milk (about 2 cans)

Homemade curry paste (see facing page)

1–2 Tbs. palm or coconut sugar, to taste

2 long Asian eggplants, sliced at a slanted angle ¼-inch thick; or 12 round Thai eggplants (ma-keua bproh), halved or quartered

½ cup pea eggplants (ma-keua puang), if available; or use fresh shelled peas

2–3 kaffir lime leaves; tear each into 2–3 pieces

1–2 green jalapeño peppers, each cut into 6–8 long slivers

1–2 fingers gkra-chai root (lesser ginger), thinly sliced in diagonal pieces

1 cup Thai sweet basil leaves and flowers (bai horapa)

Lesser Ginger (Gkra-chai)

Prepare the paste ingredients. If using dried kaffir lime peel, soak first to soften. For galanga, use the fuller-flavored, reddish tan root imported from Thailand, available in frozen form. Grind the dry spices finely in a dry stone mortar or spice grinder. Set aside. Pound the herbs a little at a time, starting with the hardier ones, until each is reduced to a paste. Combine the pounded herbs and ground dry spices and pound together with the *gkapi* shrimp paste to form a fine, well-blended paste. Set aside.

If ground fish paste is not available in Asian fish markets in your area, use small, white-flesh fish fillets and chop as finely as possible with a cleaver or in a food processor or blender. Then pound the fish with a heavy stone mortar and pestle until it is completely reduced to paste and no longer distinguishable as fish. Do likewise with the shrimp. Keeping them separate, sprinkle some ground white pepper, a little fish sauce and about one tablespoon tapioca flour to each. (You do not need to add these ingredients to ground fish paste bought from the fish market.) Knead into the ground fish until sticky, then the shrimp. Set aside.

In a large pot, heat about a cup of the thick coconut cream from the top of a can of coconut milk (or the rich milk from the first pressing of coconut pulp) over medium to high heat. Reduce until oil begins to separate or the cream looks thick and bubbly. Add the curry paste and fry in the cream for a few minutes until aromatic. Pour in the remaining coconut milk and bring to a boil. Season to taste with fish sauce and balance with palm sugar. If using pea-eggplants, add them next and simmer about 10 minutes over low heat, uncovered, before adding the other eggplants and kaffir lime leaves. If substituting with peas, add them together with the sliced eggplants. Bring sauce back up to a boil and simmer a few minutes or until the eggplants begin to soften.

Using two teaspoons, drop the fish and shrimp paste mixtures in small, bite-size chunks into the curry sauce. Return to a boil and add the slivered jalapeño peppers and *gkra-chai* pieces. Continue to cook until eggplants are tender and the dumplings cooked through (they float when cooked). Stir in the basil until it wilts. Remove from heat and serve hot with lots of plain steamed rice.

NOTES AND POINTERS

See notes about Thai eggplants on page 138.

There is a variety of long eggplants in Thailand that is green in color rather than purple like the ones you find in Chinese and Japanese markets. They are sweet and very flavorful and are excellent in green curry. From time to time, I have seen them sold at farmers' markets. If you can find them, try them in this recipe.

Green Curry Paste:

4 dark green jalapeño or serrano peppers, chopped

15–20 green Thai chillies (prik kee noo), chopped

10 white peppercorns, finely ground

1 Tbs. coriander seeds, lightly toasted until aromatic, then ground

½ tsp. cumin seeds, ground

1 tsp. course sea salt

2 Tbs. chopped lemon grass (use the bottom end of stalk, sliced thinly in rounds before chopping)

1 tsp. chopped Thai galanga

1 tsp. grated zest of fresh kaffir lime; or substitute with finely chopped reconstituted dried kaffir lime peel

2 tsp. finely chopped cilantro roots, or substitute with 1 Tbs. chopped stems

3 shallots, chopped

6 cloves garlic, chopped

2 tsp. gkapi shrimp paste

Long Green Eggplant (*Ma-Keua Yao*)

EASY MASSAMAN CURRY WITH CHICKEN

(Gkaeng Massaman Gkai)

1–2 cups coconut milk

2–3 Tbs. massaman curry paste, or to taste

2–3 Tbs. unsalted roasted peanuts, ground finely

Fish sauce (näm bplah), to taste

About 1 Tbs. palm or coconut sugar, or to taste

1 lb. boneless chicken thigh meat, cut into bite-size chunks

1 medium-size potato, cut in 1-inch cubes

2 Tbs. whole raw peanuts (optional)

8–10 baby pearl onions, or about half a dozen small boiling onions, skin removed

Slivered fresh hot peppers as desired

1–2 tsp. tamarind water (about a ½-inch chunk of wet tamarind dissolved in 1–2 Tbs. water, pulp removed)

Spoon about ⅔ cup of thick coconut cream from the top of the can of milk into a medium-size saucepan. Heat over medium to high heat. Reduce until bubbly and oil begins to separate (3–5 minutes). Add the curry paste, mashing it to mix with the cream. Fry the paste in the cream a few minutes until it is aromatic. Add the ground peanuts and some of the remaining milk, enough to make a smooth, thick sauce. Season with fish sauce and palm sugar.

Add the cut chicken and cook it over medium heat in the creamy sauce, until the pieces change color and are no longer pink and raw on the outside. At this point the chicken will start to let out the juices inside. The mixture may appear wetter, but if it is still dry and there is little sauce, add more coconut milk to constitute a sauce to the lightness or thickness you desire. Toss in the potato pieces and raw peanuts and stir into the curry mixture. Cover the saucepan with a lid and lower heat.

Simmer for about 10 minutes. Stir the curry and check its consistency. The chicken should be in a rich sauce. If the sauce is too thick, add more coconut milk. Stir in the baby pearl onions. If using boiling onions, cut in halves or in quarters, depending on their size, before adding. Cover and allow to simmer another 5–10 minutes, or until the potatoes and onions are tender.

Taste the curry sauce. Sprinkle in more fish sauce and palm sugar as needed to adjust the flavors to your liking. (Some brands of paste already have a lot of salt and sugar added.) The curry should be on the sweet side. If you wish the curry to be hotter, add the slivered hot peppers. Stir in a small amount of tamarind water and simmer a minute more to blend in its flavor. Serve hot with plain steamed rice.

NOTES AND POINTERS

As a Muslim curry, massaman curry is usually made with beef and goat meat, stewed in a rich and sweet peanut-based coconut sauce. I have adapted this recipe for chicken, but it is also delicious made with

Tamarind (*Ma-kahm*)

lamb (see the next recipe). Vegetarians can try this curry with a firm, pressed tofu and string beans, or with mixed vegetables, such as eggplant, cauliflower, potatoes, mushrooms and golden squash (kabocha, banana or butternut squash). You can also make the sauce by itself to spoon over grilled fish or shrimp. In fact, by following the first few steps you can make a quick peanut sauce for your satay, but use an extra amount of ground roasted peanuts for added nuttiness.

Always use freshly ground, unsalted, roasted peanuts rather than peanut butter to make peanut sauces that are fresher and more natural tasting. Use a clean coffee grinder to grind the nuts, shaking it as you do so to keep the nuts as loose as possible, so they grind evenly.

If you wish to make this curry with beef, use a chuck roast or stew meat. Precook the beef 1–1½ hours in a small volume of water, or use the light, watery part of the coconut milk at the bottom of the can. For 1–2 pounds of meat, use about ¼ cup of liquid. You won't need much, as beef has lots of its own juices which will cook out in a matter of minutes. Heat the meat with the liquid in a pot; cover and simmer over low heat until the meat is well cooked but still slightly chewy. Stir occasionally. Check after an hour. If the beef is stewing in a lot of juices, cook uncovered over a higher heat the balance of the time to dry up most of the juices. Follow the recipe, substituting the precooked meat and its juices for the chicken.

For a fuller flavored curry, I like to combine two different brands of massaman paste, Mae Ploy and Mae Anong, to take advantage of the strengths of each. But if you want to stick to only one brand, Mae Ploy makes a more pungent curry, while Mae Anong is mellow with a roasted fragrance. Pa-Siam (with a chicken as its logo) is also good and more like Mae Ploy. The preferred canned coconut milk for this recipe is the richer Mae Ploy brand.

Massaman curry is not a sour curry; use only a small amount of tamarind water for a subtle fruity tang, which helps pull together some of the spice flavors and gives the curry a distinctive character. Just as the sweet flavor is often used as a balancing agent, in this case the sour, too, adds its own balance.

$\mathscr{M}$ASSAMAN CURRY WITH GOAT OR LAMB

(Gkaeng Massaman Pae/Gkae)

1½ lbs. goat or stew-grade lamb meat, cut into 1- to 1½-inch cubes

3–4 cups coconut milk (about 1½–2 cans)

Homemade curry paste (see facing page)

2 Tbs. ground unsalted roasted peanuts

2 medium-size potatoes, cut in 1- to 1½-inch cubes

6 whole Thai cardamoms, cracked and roasted in their shells

1-inch section cinnamon bark, roasted until aromatic

½ cup whole raw peanuts

10 small boiling onions, halved; or 15–20 whole miniature pearl onions

2–3 Tbs. fish sauce, or to taste

2–3 Tbs. palm sugar, or to taste

1 Tbs. thick tamarind water

Place the goat or lamb pieces in a saucepan and add ¼ to ½ cup of light coconut milk (i.e., the watery part on the bottom of the can). Bring to a boil, reduce heat to low and simmer covered for 1–1½ hours, or until the meat is just starting to become tender but is still chewy. Goat meat will take longer than lamb. Stir occasionally during simmering. If the liquid dries up, add a little more, but more likely, juices will cook out from the meat and add broth to the mixture. If the meat is simmering in a lot of broth, boil uncovered at a higher heat during the last 15 minutes of cooking to reduce the liquid and thicken the juices.

While the meat is cooking, make the curry paste. Prepare the ingredients as indicated. If using dried kaffir lime peel, soak first to soften. For galanga, use the fuller-flavored, reddish tan root imported from Thailand, available in frozen form. Grind the dried ingredients as finely as possible in a stone mortar or spice grinder. Pound the herbs and roots separately, a little at a time, until they are pasty. Use the coarse sea salt to provide some abrasion to reduce the tougher and more fibrous ingredients. Then, combine all the curry ingredients and pound together into a well-blended paste.

Heat a cup of the thickest cream from the top of a can of coconut milk (or use rich milk from the first pressing of coconut pulp) in a large saucepan over medium to high heat. Reduce, and when the oil begins to separate from the cream, fry the curry paste in it until the mixture is aromatic and darkens (about 5 minutes). Add the ground peanuts and enough coconut milk to make a smooth, rich sauce. Then add the precooked goat or lamb meat with its juices. Stir well to mix with the curry sauce. Return to a boil, cover and simmer 5–7 minutes over low heat.

Add the potatoes, roasted whole cardamoms still in their shell, roasted cinnamon bark and the whole raw peanuts. Stir well. Simmer covered for another 10 minutes, stirring occasionally. Then toss in the boiling or pearl onions and add more coconut milk if the sauce

Stone Mortar and Pestle

Kaffir Lime (*Ma-gkrood*)

has dried up and become too thick. Season to taste with fish sauce and palm sugar. Continue to cook until the potatoes and onions are tender. Stir in the tamarind water and make final flavor adjustments to your liking as necessary during the last couple of minutes of cooking. Serve with hot steamed rice or a Muslim fried bread.

NOTES AND POINTERS

Lamb or goat meat should be precooked before stewing in the curry sauce because the length of time needed to cook meat until it is tender would likely cause a breakdown in the coconut cream, making the curry oily and causing the cream to form curds. More coconut milk would have to be added later on to reconstitute the sauce to its rich, smooth texture, thereby making the curry unnecessarily high in calories.

Curry Paste Ingredients:

10–15 large dried red chillies, roasted, seeded and finely ground

¼ tsp. white peppercorns, ground finely

1 Tbs. coriander seeds, roasted, then ground finely

1 tsp. cumin, roasted, then ground finely

4 whole cloves, roasted, then ground finely

4 Thai cardamoms, shelled and roasted, then ground finely

¼ tsp. freshly ground nutmeg

¼ tsp. ground mace

½ tsp. coarse salt, or sea salt

2 Tbs. chopped lemon grass (use the bottom part of stalk, sliced thinly in rounds before chopping)

1 tsp. chopped Thai galanga

1 tsp. grated zest of fresh kaffir lime; or substitute with finely chopped reconstituted dried kaffir lime peel

2 tsp. chopped cilantro roots, or substitute with 1 Tbs. chopped stems

3–4 shallots, roasted until soft

10 cloves garlic, roasted until soft

1 tsp. gkapi shrimp paste, wrapped in banana leaf and roasted

CRISPY FRIED CATFISH COATED WITH RED CURRY SAUCE

(Pad Ped Bplah Doog Tod Gkrawp)

Two whole catfish, 1–1½ lbs. each, or substitute with 2 lbs. of catfish fillets

½ tsp. sea salt

3–4 cups peanut oil for deep frying

Unbleached white flour for coating fish pieces for frying

1½ cups coconut cream, or cream from the top of a large can of coconut milk

Homemade curry paste (see facing page)

2–3 Tbs. fish sauce (näm bplah), or to taste

1–2 tsp. palm sugar, or to taste

8 medium-size kaffir lime leaves, finely slivered

1 cup fresh Thai basil leaves and flowers (bai horapa)

½ cup young green peppercorns

Prepare the curry paste ingredients. If using dried kaffir lime peel, soak first to soften for about 10–15 minutes. For galanga, use the fuller-flavored, reddish tan root grown in Thailand, available in frozen form. Grind the dry spices finely in a dry stone mortar or spice grinder. Set aside. Pound the chopped herbs a little at a time and reduce each to a paste, starting with the dryer, hardier ones. Then, combine the pounded herbs, powdered spices and *gkapi* shrimp paste and pound together to form a smooth, well-blended paste. If the dried and fresh chillies do not impart sufficient redness to the paste, use some paprika to add a richer red color. Set aside.

Chop the fish through the bone into ½-inch steaks; if substituting with boneless fillets, cut into 1½-inch chunks. Sprinkle about half a teaspoon of sea salt over the fish pieces to coat them evenly.

Heat oil in a wok over high heat until it starts to smoke. There should be enough volume to submerge all the fish pieces. Coat the fish pieces lightly with a thin coating of flour and deep-fry in the hot oil until they are crispy and dry; they should be a rich brown color, not just golden brown—this may take 12–15 minutes. If you have a very hot stove, reduce the heat so that the fish pieces do not burn before they turn crispy. When ready, remove from oil and let the fish pieces drain and air-cool on a wire strainer balanced over a bowl. This will help them stay crispy longer. Do the frying in two separate batches if you do not have a hot burner so that the wok does not get overloaded.

After all the fish pieces are fried, remove the oil from the wok. Strain it after it has cooled and store for future use. Clean the wok and reheat until the entire surface is hot. Spoon in about a cup of thick cream from the top of a can of coconut milk (or use rich milk from the first pressing of coconut pulp) and heat over medium to high heat. Reduce until oil begins to separate, or until it is thick and bubbly. Add the curry paste and fry in the cream for several minutes. When the mixture is aromatic and the flavors released, add another

Young Peppercorns (*Priktai Awn*)

Kaffir Lime Leaf (*Bai Ma-gkrood*)

half cup of coconut cream, the fish sauce and palm sugar. Reduce to make a thick reddish sauce, sufficient in quantity to coat the fish pieces. Taste and adjust flavors to the desired saltiness and sweetness with fish sauce and palm sugar.

Toss the fried fish pieces, kaffir lime leaf slivers, basil and young green peppercorns with the thick curry sauce in the wok until the fish pieces are evenly coated with the spices and the basil is wilted. Transfer to a serving platter and serve with lots of plain steamed rice.

NOTES AND POINTERS

In Thailand, we normally use cut-up whole catfish for this dish. The small, thin steaks, with skin attached, fry up to a crispiness that holds well when they are later cooked with curry. Skinned fillets will not stay crispy for long.

Red Curry Paste:

8 large dried red chillies, seeded and soaked to soften, then chopped

10–15 fresh red Thai chillies (prik kee noo), finely chopped

1/4 tsp. white peppercorns, freshly ground

1/2 tsp. cumin, ground finely

1 tsp. coriander seeds, ground finely

1/4 tsp. ground mace

3 Thai cardamoms, removed from strawlike hull and ground finely

1/2 tsp. ground nutmeg

1/2 tsp. course salt, or sea salt

1 stalk lemon grass, thinly sliced in rounds, then chopped

1 Tbs. chopped Thai galanga

1 Tbs. grated zest of fresh kaffir lime, or substitute with chopped reconstituted dried kaffir lime peel

1 Tbs. chopped cilantro roots, or substitute with 2 Tbs. chopped stems

2 Tbs. chopped gkra-chai root (lesser ginger)

8 cloves garlic, chopped

1 tsp. gkapi shrimp paste

Paprika as needed for a richer red color

The hot spells of summer in the Bay Area remind me of carefree afternoons spent along the southwestern coast of Thailand. Following a day of swimming and snorkeling in the warm waters, it's a delight to relax in the shade of swaying palms by the sandy beach, sipping on ice-cold *näm manao* (fresh limeade) and nibbling on spicy cashews and a refreshing *yäm talay* (hot-and-sour seafood salad). The contrast of the hotness of the chillies and gingers with the cool freshness of mint leaves and lemon grass in the salad parallels the hot tropical climate, punctuated by cooling sea breezes.

Most of my life I have lived near the coast, and some of my most vivid memories from childhood center around the countless weekends and vacations on the beaches of the eastern gulf. During the 1950s, beaches like Pattaya—which today is an overdeveloped and touted tourist mecca—were tranquil and almost deserted. My parents share a deep love for the sea, which I inherited, and they took us children to the secluded shores as frequently as their schedules would permit.

We used to stay in a homey wooden house on stilts during our visits, only a stone's throw from the beach. Early each morning, I accompanied my mother to the nearby fishing village just as the fishermen were pulling in with their morning's catch. I always loved looking through the colorful fishes still flopping around in the huge woven baskets. Mother would bargain for her selections of the day, and soon we would return home to cook up a big pot of seafood rice soup for breakfast in the open-air kitchen. Later in the day, I would help Mother make other seafood dishes, including one of her special *yäm talay*.

On those hot "Thai weather" days where you live, there's nothing like a good Thai seafood salad to invite a cooling sea breeze into your home. I have included two recipes at the end of this chapter for you to try. One is a simple, light and refreshing squid salad, which also works well with shrimps, scallops and white-flesh fish, or a combination of these. The other is more complex and contains a richer blending, which works better with heavier-tasting seafoods, such as mussels, oysters and salmon, or a mixture of different shellfish.

"SEA BREEZES" COOL HOT SUMMER DAYS

CREATING A BREEZY HARMONY: BLENDING FLAVORS AND INGREDIENTS

Most Thai seafood salads are characteristically hot and sour, although they actually are composed of a delicate blending of the four main flavor groupings—hot, sour, sweet and salty—with aromatic herbs. By varying the degree and sources of each of these flavors, the kinds and combinations of herbs and the methods of preparation, a creative cook can come up with an amazing array of different-tasting salads. Play around with the two recipes given and you'll see how varying the proportions and preparation methods of very similar ingredients, or just adding a new ingredient to the same formula, can surprise you with new and exciting results.

The contrast as well as the harmonious blending of various fresh and exotic herbs in Thai seafood salads distinguish them from their Western counterparts. Along with adding their distinctive flavors, most herbs also impart nutritional and medicinal qualities, making the salad a wholesome food. Those most commonly used are aromatic lemon grass, pungent galanga root, refreshing mint, fragrant cilantro, piquant kaffir lime leaves and, of course, the indispensable garlic and shallots common to most Thai dishes.

The favorite source of hotness for seafood salads is the little *prik kee noo*, commonly known as Thai chillies, but other sources of heat may also be used. Sourness comes primarily from fresh lime juice, and saltiness from no other than Thailand's prized elixir itself: fish sauce (*näm bplah*). A small amount of sugar is added, not to make the salad taste sweet but as an essential balancing agent to pull together and intensify the other three flavors and help them blend in with the aromatic herbs.

Depending on the salad and what is desired, the sauce ingredients can be blended and adjusted according to taste. Experiment with the balancing flavors taste test (see page 64) when you make your sauce.

CALLING UP THE SEA BREEZE: ASSEMBLING THE SALAD

Besides the use of fresh ingredients, the key to a succulent, fresh-tasting seafood salad is to not overcook the seafood. In hot boiling water, squid, medium-size shrimps, raw shucked mussels and oysters are usually ready in a mere thirty seconds (there is no need to wait for the water to return to a boil after you have dumped in the seafood). Fish pieces will take a little longer, depending on the type of fish and the size of the pieces.

Most fine restaurants in Thailand make seafood salads to order rather than in big batches ahead of time because the fresh flavors of herbs, as well as the fresh tastes and succulent textures of seafood, dissipate over time. Also, a freshly made salad will tend to be dryer and more robust. The longer the seafood and herbs sit in the sauce, the more its saltiness and sourness will draw out their juices, thus diluting the flavors in the salad.

In restaurants in Thailand, fresh seafood is cooked to order in a small wire basket with a long bamboo handle and a holding capacity of about two cups. Just enough seafood for one order is placed in the basket, which is dipped in a large pot of boiling water or broth that is always ready at hand. A chopstick or long-handled implement is used to stir the seafood quickly so that it cooks evenly. In half a minute or less, the basket is lifted out of the hot water and shaken a few times to drain the seafood. (This process of blanching is called to *luak* in Thai.) While still hot, the seafood is tossed with the spicy dressing and fresh herbs, wilting them a little and allowing their flavors to coat the seafood pieces. The mixture is then served—still warm—on a platter lined on one side with lettuce leaves and tomato slices and garnished with cilantro or mint sprigs.

The pot of broth in which the seafood is blanched becomes richer over time, as more seafood is cooked in it through the day in the restaurant. This rich broth, sweet and full of flavor, is then used as stock for seafood soups.

If you want to make a seafood salad ahead of time, it will taste just fine, cold or at room temperature, but remember that the flavors will change as they are diluted by the juices of the seafood. In fact, seafood such as squid becomes more tender as it sits in the limy sauce, and the salad picks up an overall character more like ceviche. The color will change as the herbs will lose some of their fresh greenness, and eventually the seafood will look pickled. If you must make the salad ahead of time, make sure the seafood is

Wire Mesh Basket with Handle

drained well after blanching—especially squid, as water can get trapped in its round, tubelike pieces. Any extra water will dilute the intensity of the hot, sour, sweet and salty flavors in the sauce. Occasionally I have had squid and mussel salads left over from my cooking classes, and they taste marvelous straight out of the refrigerator the next day or even up to a week later (the spicy sauce preserves the seafood). Seafood salads are delicious especially on hot days, served as first-course salads or even as main luncheon dishes, with rice or some good sourdough bread.

A SOUTHERN SEA BREEZE

The final recipe in this chapter is for a spicy cashew salad, one of the all-time, easy-to-make favorites among my advanced cooking students. Simple but packed with a punch, these spicy cashews are a Thai equivalent to "beer nuts," but instead of beer they are more likely to accompany *Maekong*, the popular local liquor distilled from rice, similar to a smooth rum. Because cashews are a major crop of southern Thailand, this salad frequently reminds me of blissful days spent along the beautiful southwestern coast and on enchanting offshore islands, where I have nibbled on countless plates of spicy cashews while watching the day end in a dazzling glow.

The southern province of Ranong is particularly known for its large, sweet cashews, which people of the area call *gka-yoo*, a name sounding very similar to the English "cashew." In other southern provinces, the nut is called *gka-yee*, while the remainder of the country knows it as *med mamuang himapahn*, or *med mamuang* ("mango seed") for short, because of its shape. Himapahn is the name of the mythical forest near the legendary mountain abode of the gods, so its inclusion in the nut's name could suggest a divine quality. Ranong grows such an abundance of cashews that every March, following the harvest, the provincial capital hosts a "Sweet Cashew Fair," complete with all forms of merriment. The province has also adopted the cashew fruit and nut as its symbol.

Cashews are unusual nuts. They are seeds that develop before the fruits and are attached outside the fruits. In Thailand, cashew trees start flowering in January, and by February, fleshy green, crescent-shaped beans form on the stems where the blossoms used to be. As the beans develop and grow, sections of the stems above the beans begin to swell and eventually ripen into bright red or yellow fruits about the size and shape of rose apples (*chompoo*). By then the cashews have matured beneath the fruits, developed hard shells and turned dark brown. Removing the shells is a painstaking task because they not only are very hard but also contain a caustic substance that can sting and cause injury to sensitive skin. Commercially, a special piece of equipment is used to crack the nuts, one at a time, with an operator setting the nuts precisely in place so that the precious insides come out whole. This labor-intensive process explains why cashews command a high price, especially the ones that are whole. Though edible and sweet, the fruits do not have a distinctive flavor and are usually tossed into a hot-and-sour salad or eaten with chillies and salt. Tender cashew leaves are also edible and frequently served raw with pungent dipping sauces and southern curries.

Cashew (*Med Mamuang*)

Hot-and-Sour Squid Salad

(Yäm Bplah Meuk)

3 lbs. whole squid

1 stalk lemon grass

1-inch section fresh galanga (or substitute with fresh ginger)

4 shallots

½ cup cilantro leaves

½ cup fresh mint leaves

2 qts. water

½ cup white vinegar

4 lettuce leaves

Hot-and-Sour Sauce or Dressing:

10–15 fresh Thai chillies, or 3–4 fresh red jalapeño or fresno peppers

6 cloves garlic

3–4 Tbs. fish sauce (näm bplah), to taste

Juice of 2–3 fresh limes, to taste

2–4 tsp. sugar, to taste

First make the sauce or salad dressing so that the ingredients have a chance to sit together and their flavors can blend and integrate. Chop the chillies and garlic. If you have a mortar and pestle, pound them to a paste, or mash well with a spoon. This helps distribute their heat and flavor more evenly when tossed with the squid. Transfer to a sauce bowl and add fish sauce, lime juice and sugar. Mix well and adjust the flavors to the desired combination, keeping in mind that the intensity will be reduced when the sauce is tossed in with the bulk of the other ingredients. The sauce should be equally sour and salty, with sugar as the balancing agent to harmonize the flavors.

Clean and skin the squid and cut each tube section into 3–4 rounds, about an inch apart, depending on the size of the squid. Split the larger tentacles into two segments. Rinse and store in water until ready to cook.

Cut and discard the bottom ¼- to ½-inch section of the lemon grass and remove the loose outer layer(s). Slice the stalk in very thin rounds up to just below where the grass blade starts. Place in a large mixing bowl. Cut the galanga in thin slices, then stack a few slices at a time and cut into very fine slivers to yield about ¼ cup. (The galanga does not need to be peeled if it is very fresh and white and does not have any brown spots. If substituting with ginger, peel before using.) Add the slivers to the bowl, along with 4 thinly sliced shallots, cilantro and mint leaves. (Leave small mint leaves whole and tear the large ones into smaller pieces.)

Bring 2 quarts of water to a rolling boil, add ½ cup of vinegar and return to a boil. Drain the squid and add to the boiling water. Stir and after 30 seconds, remove from heat. Drain well. While still warm, toss with the fresh ingredients in the mixing bowl and the hot-and-sour sauce.

Spoon the tossed squid onto a serving plate lined with lettuce leaves along the edges. Serve warm or at room temperature.

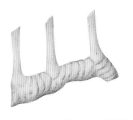

Galanga (Kah)

NOTES AND POINTERS

If you have never cleaned squid before or are curious about learning new techniques, read the following chapter for a quick and easy method.

If you think you do not like squid, or if you have never tasted it, read the next chapter and give this recipe a try. You may not yet have tasted squid that has been cooked correctly, and you certainly have the potential to turn into a squid lover!

Vinegar added to the boiling water will help the squid cook cleaner, whiter and more tender. The squid pieces will also pick up a subtle vinegary taste.

The hot-and-sour sauce can be made in advance. Like many Thai hot sauces, it ages well and increases in intensity over time until it reaches its limit and loses freshness. If you make the sauce a day or more ahead of time, store it in an airtight jar in the refrigerator.

Lemon Grass (*Dta-krai*)

SPICY MUSSEL SALAD

(Yäm Hoi Malaeng Poo)

1 stalk lemon grass

4–6 medium-size kaffir lime leaves

1 to 1 ½-inch section fresh galanga (or substitute with fresh ginger)

½ to 1 cup cilantro leaves

½ to 1 cup mint leaves

6–8 cloves garlic

3–4 shallots

½ cup peanut oil

2 qts. water

1 ½ lbs. raw shucked mussels

6 lettuce leaves

Spicy Sauce or Salad Dressing:

10–20 Thai chillies, to desired hotness

3–4 Tbs. fish sauce (näm bplah), to taste

2 Tbs. vinegar

Juice of ½–1 lime, to taste

1 Tbs. thick tamarind water

1–2 Tbs. sugar, to taste

Kaffir Lime Leaf (*Bai Ma-gkrood*)

Make the sauce or salad dressing first, allowing the ingredients to sit together so that their flavors blend and integrate. Chop the chillies finely; if you have a mortar and pestle, pound them to a paste. Place in a sauce bowl. Add fish sauce, vinegar, lime juice, tamarind water and sugar. Set aside.

Next, prepare the herbs. Slice the lemon grass into very thin rounds, discarding the loose outer layer(s) of the stalk and the ¼- to ½-inch bottom section that is very woody. Use most of the stalk, from the more fibrous lower end to the greener upper stalk, just below where the grass blade starts. Place the thin, sliced pieces in a large mixing bowl.

Layer the kaffir lime leaves and using a sharp knife, cut them into very fine slivers. Trim off the eyes and brown spots on the galanga and slice into thin rounds; then layer the rounds a few at a time and shred into fine slivers to yield about ¼ cup. (If using ginger, peel first before slivering.) Add both to the mixing bowl, along with cilantro and mint leaves. (Leave the small mint leaves whole and tear the large ones into smaller pieces.)

Chop the garlic and slice the shallots in ⅛-inch-thick rounds. Heat the peanut oil in a small saucepan and fry the shallots in it over low to medium heat, stirring frequently until evenly browned. Remove from oil and drain. Using the remaining oil in the saucepan (there should be enough to submerge the chopped garlic), fry the garlic over medium heat until golden and crispy. Remove from heat and set aside.

Bring 2 quarts of water to a boil. Blanch the mussels about 15 seconds. Drain well before tossing with the fresh ingredients in the mixing bowl. When ready to serve, add the fried shallots, fried garlic pieces with a little of the oil, and the sauce or dressing. Toss well and serve on a plate lined along the sides with lettuce leaves. Garnish with a few cilantro leaves or mint sprigs.

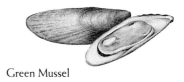

Green Mussel

NOTES AND POINTERS

If you are unable to buy fresh shelled mussels and it is too much of a task to shuck raw ones yourself, you may wish to steam fresh whole mussels on a steamer rack until the shells begin to open. Remove from heat and pry them open; the flesh inside should slide off the shell easily.

If fresh mussels are unavailable or prohibitively expensive—and you live near a well-stocked Asian market—you may wish to try the large green mussels imported from New Zealand. They come frozen, on the half shell in 1-kg boxes (about 2.2 lbs.), or already removed from the shells in 1-lb. bags. Sweet and flavorful, these mussels are larger, firmer and more meaty than the variety found in California coastal waters. They are reasonably priced in Bay Area Asian markets that carry them, costing around five dollars for the kilogram box or three dollars for the 1-lb. package.

Because they are very large, I usually cut these mussels in half before blanching and tossing with the herbs and sauce. This allows more surface area to coat with the sauce.

If your mussel salad tastes bitter, it may be because you browned the garlic or shallots too much, or the galanga was old and you used too much of it.

This recipe is also great for scallops, oysters and shrimps, or a combination of these with mussels for a mixed shellfish salad.

$\mathcal{S}$PICY CASHEW SALAD

(Yäm Med Mamuang)

2 cups peanut oil

1 cup raw cashews

1 tsp. sea salt

1 green onion, cut in thin rounds

2 shallots, thinly sliced

1 red jalapeño pepper, or 2 red serrano peppers, cut in half lengthwise, then sliced thinly crosswise

6–8 Thai chillies, cut in thin rounds

½ a fresh lime

Heat the oil in a wok and fry the cashew nuts over low to medium heat, stirring frequently so that the nuts brown slowly and evenly. When they are an even golden brown, remove from oil with a slotted spoon. Allow to drain and air-cool on a wire-mesh strainer balanced over a bowl, or use a large, Asian wire strainer-spatula used for deep frying.

When the nuts have partially cooled, place them in a small, clean, brown paper sack and shake lightly to blot out the excess oil on the surface. Then transfer to a mixing bowl and sprinkle with salt. Stir to coat nuts evenly.

While the cashews are still slightly warm to the touch, toss with the prepared green onion, shallots, jalapeño or serrano peppers and Thai chillies. Just before serving, squeeze a little lime juice over the cashews.

Serve as an appetizer or as a snack with your favorite drinks.

NOTES AND POINTERS

Cashews should not be eaten raw, as they contain a substance that is hard to digest until it is transformed by cooking. Slow frying allows the heat to penetrate and cook the dense nuts through to the core while making them crunchy all the way through.

Foods other than nuts are fried in very hot oil that sears but does not penetrate them. Nuts have a high oil content in themselves, so as they fry in lower heat, the surrounding oil penetrates, dissolves and draws out some of the fatty oils inside. The process is similar to rendering animal fat. If done correctly, this "roasting" of the nuts sometimes ends with more oil in the pan than was there at the start of the procedure.

When nuts are hot, they are somewhat soft but will gradually harden as they cool. If any moisture is added while they are hot, it will penetrate and turn them soggy. As they cool and harden, they become more

Shallots

resistant to moisture. Therefore, allow the cashews to cool some before tossing with the herbs, or they won't develop a good crunch. For the same reason, avoid adding lime juice until you are ready to serve. I toss the cashews with the herbs while they are still slightly warm to the touch; the warm surfaces pick up the herb flavors but are not hot enough to wilt and draw out their juices.

Air cooling as described, rather than draining immediately on paper towels, keeps the nuts crunchier for a longer time. Also, bleached paper products can contain residues of dioxin, a carcinogen that is both oil and water soluble. Foods that contact bleached paper products stand the chance of absorbing this toxic substance, so if you do drain the nuts on paper towels, make sure they are unbleached, or use brown paper bags instead.

Try this recipe with peanuts, almonds or other favorite nuts. Start out with raw nuts rather than the preroasted varieties; they make for a fresher and more delightful flavor. (Whole raw cashews and peanuts are usually available at reasonable prices in Chinatown grocery stores.) Enjoy them with your favorite drinks on a hot afternoon or as an appetizer before your evening meal, and feel the cooling sea breezes gently blowing on your face.

Wire Mesh Spatula

Squid is a strange animal that evokes an emotional response in people. Some rave about it, regarding it as one of the world's greatest foods. Restaurants have been named after it, specializing in serving this seafood in as many different ways as they can. An entire cookbook has been devoted to it. From the evidence, it would seem there is a love affair going on with this shy creature of the sea.

On the other hand, there are people who have opposite opinions about this same animal. They don't understand why others rave about it. They think it tastes rubbery and has absolutely no flavor. They think the eyes and tentacles are disgusting and wouldn't care if they ever saw one again.

Most squid lovers would argue that people who don't like squid have never had it cooked right before. There can be truth to this assertion. Squid will turn tough if it is overcooked; it will cook in hot water in a mere thirty seconds and in one to two minutes when fried or stir-fried. Overcooking causes a rubbery texture that is more often than not the reason why so many people have developed a misconception and dislike of this succulent fish. So if your past experiences with squid have not been favorable and you have formed the opinion that it is a tough, rubbery creature, maybe you will consider giving it a second chance. Maybe on this next try, you will find it to be quite different from your first encounters. Squid is really very tender and tasty if it is fresh and cooked just right.

The Thai word for squid is *bplah meuk*—*bplah* meaning fish, and *meuk*, ink. A squid has ink sacs around its eyes, the ink being its main natural defense against predators. When a squid senses danger, it squirts ink to muddy up the water and disorient its predator. This gives the creature time to make its quick escape via jet propulsion made possible with its many-armed tentacles. It literally swims backwards.

All the way up and down the two coasts of Thailand, small wooden squid boats can be seen with their long poles dangling dozens of large, powerful light bulbs. At night the poles are stretched out over the surrounding water, and thousands of volts of electric current are turned on to attract the squid. These boats take to the open sea late in the day, when the sun is low and beginning to make its descent below the horizon.

There have been many nights when I have sat alongside the southern beaches after dark, watching the squid boats switch on their lights. Out amid the darkness of the night, short strings of light sparkle and dazzle here and there. Sometimes there are so many of them that together they look like the glittering lights of some great distant city. Like moths drawn to a flame, the otherwise shy, quiet creatures of the sea are pulled toward the bright lights, surfacing from the hidden depths below. Suddenly, without warning, the nets are pulled. The swarm of squid, realizing something has gone amiss, squirts in a frenzy, turning the sea around them into a dark soup. By then, it's too late. (When you clean squid, just imagine how much ink they originally must have held in their sacs. The ink that remains is only a fraction of what they had before they were caught.)

The squid boats return before dawn, and their catch is sold and transported to markets before most city folk awaken from their sleep. They will eat them that day, perhaps in a salad at lunch or stir-fried with garlic and spices for dinner.

Squid tales and cleaning tips

"SOLAR" SQUID

Not all squid are consumed fresh. In fact, it seems much more of them are dried, especially if you've ever made a stop in one of the numerous squid fishing villages along the gulf coast. On the "homemade" tours I lead to Thailand, we usually make a lunch stop at the quaint, small-town marina of Pranburi. All along the beach on both sides of the marina, up and down numerous alleyways and outside shopfronts and fisherfolk's homes are wire-mesh racks of various proportions. They display squid drying; squid of all sizes and a few different colors—small purple ones, medium pink ones, larger white ones, and so on.

The children of the village help their parents, aunts and uncles clean and arrange the squid on the racks, spreading them out flat with heads still attached in attractive, symmetrical designs. The large-size squid and cuttlefish, which fetch a better price, usually are hung on lines much like laundry but with hooks instead of clothespins. Their translucent bodies and willowy tentacles pick up a glow from the afternoon sun as they sway ever so gently to the rhythm of the soft sea breeze.

The restaurant we dine in on Pranburi marina is a small, unpretentious, family-owned operation. Tables are set on the open verandah just a few meters from the sandy beach, on which a good surf pounds a large part of each day. While we lunch, the sight, sound and smell of the sea transport us far away from the congestion of traffic and worries of the city. Sunee, the woman who owns and runs the place, also cooks the delicious feast we have every time we stop there. She's a very sweet woman, always tidy in appearance with hair neatly combed and bright red lipstick, and always warm and friendly, welcoming us with a winner of a smile each time. After we order all the very best foods of the house, she fires up the charcoal stoves in her kitchen and starts cooking the fresh seafood, which is being cleaned by family members not far from our chosen table.

One of the specialties of the house is *bplah meuk daed dio*, literally meaning "single sun ink fish." The squid is dried in the hot sun for one day, then fried and served with a spicy dipping sauce—"solar" squid, you might say. The sun adds a delightful depth of flavor to the squid. Though firmer and chewier in texture, each chew releases a wonderfully full-bodied, fragrant taste that is lacking in fresh squid. Every time I order and devour "solar" squid, I am convinced once again that surely this must be the best squid I've ever eaten! The recipe is not included here as drying squid in the sun for a day in your backyard would probably not endear you to your neighbors (but their cats would love you!).

Dried squid is easy to store and transport and is exported to other parts of the world. They can be reconstituted and used in stir-fried dishes or seafood soups, the crisp texture and flavor much different from the fresh variety. Or, they are left dried, to be roasted over charcoal until fragrant (they pick up an irresistible wonderful aroma), then run through a press for tenderizing and eaten as chewy jerky. Sometimes the pressed, roasted squid is coated with flavorings, such as chillies, salt (or fish sauce) and sugar; other times it is left plain to be dipped in a hot-sweet-and-sour sauce. If you've been to Thailand, you probably have seen push-cart vendors with small charcoal stoves and hand-cranked presses, their carts decorated with dried squid strung neatly in rows.

MORE SQUID TALES

Besides being captured at night with nets, squid are also caught by traps, much like fish traps and crab traps. These are usually used by small "mom-and-pop" fisherfolk in the south of Thailand, who practically do all their fishing off of small, roofless, "long-tail" boats (*reua hahng yao*).

A long-tail boat is a shallow wooden boat whose name is derived from the long moveable shaft attached to the engine that is mounted on a swivel at the stern. A propeller at the end of the shaft serves as a rudder to steer the vessel. This moveable "tail" makes it possible to traverse very shallow waters without danger of damaging the rudder and engine. When nearing shore or entering reefy areas, a long-tail driver lifts the tail, sometimes such that the propeller spins partially out of the water; when the water becomes too shallow, shaft and propeller are simply suspended or pulled aboard, and the boat can float its way ashore.

On boating trips in the beautiful Andaman Sea, one often sees these small, long-tail fishing boats trolling around. Sometimes whole families are aboard, throwing lines, gathering traps, mending nets or spending lazy afternoons resting from the scorching tropical sun. You see them in the shelter of numerous craggy coves beneath towering limestone karsts that dot the coastline, or parked along stunning beaches of secluded islets, their owners napping in the quiet shade of trees. Nowadays, many of the more enterprising fishermen have all but abandoned their traditional occupation. Instead, they are making an increasingly lucrative living by using their boats to haul tourists around from island to island, or to take them fishing—which earns much more money more easily than catching and selling fish themselves.

Several years ago along the southwest coast of Thailand, I had the good fortune of observing how squid is trapped. The occasion was neither expected nor planned. A few tour members, my assistants and I had just spent an invigorating afternoon snorkeling along the lively reef of a favorite island off the Krabi coast. While heading back to our beachside resort on the mainland, the boat we hired for the day came to an abrupt stop, after making some worrisome chugging noises. The radio on board wasn't working either. There we sat in the middle of the lovely sea, longing to return to a refreshing shower and some good food to replenish our energies.

The captain and his assistant fiddled with the engine a long while but couldn't get it working again. Seeing how their efforts had failed to produce any results, we decided to wave a boat down and hitch a ride back to shore. That proved to be a difficult task that afternoon because it happened to be the day of the big annual Pee-Pee-Island-to-Krabi fishing competition. All the boats passing by were in a hurry to make it to the main pier in town before five o'clock for the official weigh-in of their catch. It was around half past four. We managed to make enough noise to slow down a couple of boats but gained only a promise from one of them to return in about two hours if we happened to still be there.

Another half hour passed. We were about to give up hope when a handsome long-tail boat approached us. It was indeed a gorgeous boat, hand crafted of high-quality wood, unlike a lot of older, funkier long-tails we had seen before in the area. To add to the pleasing aesthetics, the boat had a pretty, woven bamboo mat covering the floor. But most interesting of all were the two dark, handsome Muslim men aboard, one sporting an attractive moustache and both with *pah kao-mah* smartly tied around their foreheads for protection from the afternoon sun. (*Pah kao-mah* is the versatile, all-purpose, striped cotton cloth that is an indispensable possession of most Thai men, particularly in the country.)

The two men were curious (and we were curious about them, too!). After a cursory look at the engine, they chuckled and probably told our two boatmen the boat should be overhauled. They spoke a fast and choppy dialect of the south that was very difficult to understand. Fortunately, we were able to communicate to them our need of transport back to shore. They looked at each other, and after a few moments' pause—placing us in great suspense—they nodded, but indicated that there were a few traps they needed to check along the way back to our beach. So we precariously transferred ourselves from our taller, larger boat onto the beautiful little boat, and off we went, gliding over the water, our hair blowing in the wind again.

Fish traps in Thailand are marked by chunks of styrofoam with flags attached, floating here and there over the surface of the sea. The flags identify to whom the floats belong. We stopped at a few of these and watched our fishermen pull up their traps. In them were gigantic squid, which the fishermen emptied into large, recycled plastic jugs with their tops cut off. I had never seen such squid before. They were different from the varieties I had known, with firm thick flesh, a radiant luster and a refreshing smell of the sea that evidenced their freshness. Each was about a foot long, from the tip of the tentacles to the pointed rear end, and must have weighed close to a pound.

My tour assistant, who is as much a gourmet as I am, excitedly informed us that this type of squid is especially delicious and often does not make it to the marketplace. My mouth was already starting to water just thinking how good they would be if we could cook them up for dinner that evening. We wasted no time asking our the fishermen if they would sell us some, and, of course, they obliged. We filled a big bag full of the plumpest, most delicious-looking ones and that night gorged ourselves with some of the most delectable squid I've ever had on the southwestern coast. They were fried very quickly in hot oil with lots of garlic and white pepper (see recipe on page 168) and were delectably succulent, sweet and full of flavor. I never cease to be amazed at how fresh-caught-same-day seafood tastes so good.

After feasting on the absolutely divine squid, we couldn't help but dream of more for the next meal. Dominating the post-dinner conversation were ruminations of how good the squid would have been prepared a dozen other ways, including two favorite and easy stand-bys: stir-fried with lots of fresh chillies, garlic and fragrant holy basil (*pad gka-prow*) and stir-fried with roasted chilli paste (*pad prik pow*). (See recipes on pages 100 and 67 for ideas.)

Another memorable experience on the southwest coast involved my younger "brother" Mohng (not a true blood relative but a good friend). He loves fishing, and he talked me into going with him one day while I was vacationing in Krabi. I am not much of a fisher, but I love any excuse to tag along on boat rides around the charming Andaman Sea. Mohng convinced me that in order to catch the "big one," we had to leave before daybreak. I managed to get myself out of bed while it was still dark out, and we were off by the first light of dawn in his fishing partner's long-tail boat.

We trolled all around for hours, circling this islet and that limestone outcropping, this bay and that cove and into the open sea, but no "big one" was

biting. This was puzzling for Mohng because he is always so sure of his calculations of the tide tables, figuring exactly when certain fish will be biting, and he swore he had never been out fishing before without catching some big fish.

By noon no big fish had yet appeared. Mohng decided we should go to Koh Daeng, a red rock promontory surrounded by a teeming reef, and drop lines to catch smaller fish. But he had not brought any bait with him, confident as he was that we would catch the "big one" by trolling with our rubber squid lures. He suggested we stop by a beautiful island along the way to buy fresh squid to use as bait from fishermen who might be hiding from the midday sun in a protected cove. I knew I would enjoy a swim in the lovely cove, so we headed for the island. Sure enough, there were several long-tails parked along the gorgeous white-sand beach.

While I was delighting myself with a swim in the refreshing, crystal-clear waters, Mohng went searching for fishermen behind the shelter of tall trees that lined the beach. Soon he returned with a few large squid in his hand. I swam back to shore and was ready to get back on our boat to take off fishing again when I noticed an unusual expression on Mohng's face. When I asked him what was wrong, he replied, "Don't these squid look good! How can we use them for bait?" With that, we gathered some wood, built a small fire and roasted the squid on sticks right there on the beach. The squid were delicious, the company good and the ambiance most delightful.

After eating up our bait, we were too embarrassed to ask for more from the kindhearted fisherman who had given us the squid free of charge, so we decided to chance trolling again. Soon after we headed out from the island, as if guided by the spirits of the very fresh squid we had just eaten in ritualistic style, Mohng reeled in a winner: a five-kilogram (eleven-pound) yellowtail tuna. That evening, we feasted on fresh sashimi, followed by grilled tuna with spicy chilli sauce (see the next chapter for ideas), accompanied with rice and hot-and-sour tuna soup. This, we concluded, was indeed the good life!

OTHER THOUGHTS ON SQUID AND CLEANING SQUID

Commercial squid fishing in developed Western countries uses large fleets of specialty ships with refrigeration facilities that go out to sea usually for several days at a time. The squid are frozen on board soon after they are caught to keep them fresh. Squid freeze comparatively well, and most of what you buy at the supermarket and fresh fish market have been frozen and then defrosted the day they are sold ("fresh-frozen"). Because squid go bad quickly, the fresh-frozen ones sometimes look better than those purported to be "fresh" (never frozen).

Squid are plentiful in the various seas and oceans around the world, and therefore they are a rather inexpensive seafood. In the San Francisco Bay Area, you can buy them for under a dollar a pound. They cost much more if purchased already cleaned. Cleaned squid usually do not come with tentacles—the part most squid enthusiasts love—and they may not be as clean as they look. When you buy precleaned squid, check inside the body cavities to see how clean they really are.

I prefer to buy squid before they are cleaned, not only because I like the tentacles but also because the luster and coloration on their skin indicates how fresh they are (the same is true for all fish). Besides, cleaning squid is easy and fun and can be a therapeutic activity much like meditation. Once you get the hang of it, you develop a certain rhythm that soon takes you away from the stresses of the working day.

There is much distaste in the West for having to clean squid and fish. Some people abhor the thought of having to deal with the head and eyes, but I feel that when we work with the whole animal, we learn to respect it for what it is—for the "whole" of what it is. Fish are not headless or heartless; they are not sticks packaged together in printed boxes in the frozen compartments of supermarkets.

Most indigenous cultures of the world hold a deep respect for the spirit of the animal that is slaughtered for food. They observe that humans do not exist on their own accord without the existence of everything else, and because all living things must eat to live, something must die in order that life can be sustained. Life and death are inextricably intertwined and inseparable. Death, as such, is never final as the spirit of the food that has sacrificed its life continues to live on in the body of another form of life. The slaughtering of animals for food, therefore, becomes a ritualistic act, done with much reverence and a depth of understanding of the interrelationship between life and death.

In midday meal ceremonies held in some Thai monasteries, the meal is prefaced with a prayer, inviting the spirits of the life forms that have been sacrificed for food, to live on and bless the people who partake of them. The monks pray to be worthy of the food, to become healthy and strong and to use the vitality gained for the benefit of all sentient beings.

There is a story about one of the Buddha's many past lives, in which he was a hunter who went into the forest in search of food. He came across a hungry female tiger with baby cubs. The mother tiger looked emaciated and in dire need of nourishment to maintain her strength, so that she could properly care for and feed her young cubs. Instead of killing the tiger, the hunter felt much compassion for her and her young ones. He lay down in front of her, offering himself as food for her to devour to regain her strength. He thus lived on in the tiger and her young ones, and this noble act of sacrifice brought great merit in the evolution of his soul.

CLEANING SQUID: A QUICK AND EASY METHOD

There are several different ways to clean squid, depending on the type and size of the squid. For the small, thinner squid we commonly get from temperate, Pacific coastal waters (e.g., Monterey squid), I have found the following method, which leaves the body in its tubelike shape to be cut into rounds, to be the easiest. (In the tropical waters of Thailand, the same-size squid generally has thicker flesh; therefore, they are usually cut open lengthwise across the belly and spread out into flat steaks. The steaks are then scored diagonally in a criss-cross pattern and cut in rectangular pieces. When cooked, the pieces curl up to reveal a lovely design. Scoring helps thicker squid cook more evenly and more tender, but the squid from California coastal waters are a bit thin for scoring and are better kept in tubes to be cut into rounds. Also, although scoring is fun and yields pretty pieces of cooked squid, it is time-consuming.)

To start cleaning your squid, hold the body loosely with one hand, and with the other, gently pull off the head with the tentacles. It helps to give a little bit of a yanking motion. If you are squeezing down too tightly on the body, it will be harder to pull. Avoid using a knife to cut off the head instead, as pulling loosens and removes most of the insides, making it easier to do the other steps.

Cut between the eyes and tentacles and discard the eyes with the ink sacs. Try not to break the ink sacs as this would leave an inky mess, but also be careful not to cut too closely to the tentacles, lest they break apart into strings. You may find a small, firm ball between the eyes and tentacles; discard this along with the eyes. It is the beak of the squid, through which it feeds (I like to refer to it as "squid lips"). Split the large tentacles in half lengthwise; leave the smaller ones whole.

Next, lay the body on its back on a cutting board. The back is usually darker than the belly side, from darker ink spots on the skin. You will notice that the top edge of the back is pointed at its center. This is the tip of the squid "bone" or "quill," which runs the full length of the body. The flippers or fins are also attached to the back, toward the bottom end of the tubelike body. Lay the squid with the finside down, with the fins spread out flat on the cutting board and the whiter belly facing up. If you are right-handed, position the squid horizontally, so that its top points to the right (vice versa for left-handed cooks). Using a fairly large, sharp knife with some weight for leverage, scrape and make a break in the skin on the bottom tip of the belly. Then, angle the knife at least forty-five degrees (or sharper) to your right (if right-handed), and using a stroking motion, run the knife across the surface of the squid from left to right (or right to left if left-handed). Apply enough pressure to push out any remaining contents from the inside, while you scrape off the skin at the same time. Angling the knife prevents you from cutting into the squid as you push and scrape. At the end of your stroke, hold down on the tip of the squid quill with the knife as you pull the body back with your other hand to dislodge and remove it.

The above may sound confusing, but after you try it a few times you may find it really isn't as difficult as it may seem. In one quick stroke the squid is both skinned and cleaned from the inside out, including the plastic-like quill. It's quite easy to do—after you have developed a sense of how to angle your knife and how firmly to apply pressure to push out the insides. Practice makes perfect.

Sometimes you will come across egg sacs, and sometimes these take up half or more of the squid. You can tell which squid have them by how much bulge appears in the belly. When you clean a squid, make sure you start pushing and scraping from the very bottom tip of the tube as the egg sac is usually lodged low in the body. If you start applying the pressure midway up, you will mush and break the egg sac, which can get messy. The egg sac is firm and almost transparent, with a shiny luster. If you hold it up to a light and look closely, you will see that it is made up of hundreds of tiny round eggs stuck together in a mass. Attached to the transparent sac is a white oval piece of meat that together with the sac is edible and delicious if cooked right.

Squid "caviar" does not taste like caviar or fish roe at all; in fact, it doesn't even taste like fish but more like some kind of meat. It is great sautéed with garlic, roasted chilli paste (*näm prik pow*), fish sauce and sweet basil (so is the flesh of squid itself; see the recipe on page 67 for ideas). So don't throw away the sac; it is a good source of protein and a large part of the squid's weight. In Thailand, the egg sacs are sometimes sold separately as a delicacy; they are also dried and preserved with the rest of the squid in coastal fishing villages.

After the quill and all the insides are removed, it is easy to pull off the skin on the back side with your fingers, or you can scrape it off with the knife. Make sure you don't pull the fins off. When you have a clean, white squid body, cut it crosswise into three or four pieces, an inch or so apart. Now that squid is ready to cook. With practice, you will find squid cleaning to be easier and faster than cleaning shrimp (squid is a cleaner animal than shrimp). Once you develop a rhythm, you will be able to clean three pounds of squid in no time at all.

Cleaned squid should be stored in water until you are ready to cook them. Drain well before cooking. If you will not be using the squid for a few hours or until the next day, add salt (preferably sea salt) to the water and keep covered in the refrigerator. Squid should be cleaned the day it is defrosted or bought fresh, as the ink in the spots on the skin will quickly seep in and dis-color the flesh, giving the squid an old taste. If you absolutely have no time to get to them that day, the least you should do is store them in salt water. Uncleaned squid do not refreeze well; cleaned ones refreeze a little better, but the best solution is to eat them soon after they are cleaned.

Squid (*Bplah Meuk*)

GARLIC-PEPPERED SQUID

(Bplah Meuk Tod Gkra-tiem Priktai)

2 lbs. fresh squid

2–3 Tbs. fish sauce (näm bplah)

1–2 Tbs. white peppercorns,
coarsely ground

10 large cloves garlic, chopped

1 Tbs. tapioca or corn starch

2 Tbs. unbleached white flour

3–4 cups peanut oil for deep frying

Lettuce leaves to line serving platter

2 small tomatoes, sliced in rounds

Clean and skin the squid, cutting each body tube into 3–4 segments, about 1 inch apart. Leave the tentacles whole. Rinse and drain well. With your hand, gently squeeze the squid to remove any remaining pockets of water. Place in a bowl and sprinkle with fish sauce to coat evenly. Set aside. The squid should be at room temperature before frying.

Grind peppercorns in a spice mill or clean coffee grinder and chop the garlic evenly. When ready to cook, heat the oil in a wok. Drain squid of any excess fish sauce, squeezing lightly with your hand until the pieces are no longer dripping with liquid. Toss with the coarsely ground pepper, chopped garlic, tapioca or corn starch and flour. Use your hand to mix so that you can feel and make sure all the pieces are evenly coated with the flours, white pepper and garlic. The tapioca starch helps some of the garlic and pepper to stick to the squid during frying.

Test to make sure the oil is hot enough by dropping a small piece of garlic in it. It should sizzle and not sink to the bottom before surfacing. It also should not burn in a matter of seconds; reduce heat if it does. Fry half of the squid pieces at a time. They should sizzle loudly, and the garlic pieces should turn golden in a minute or so. Use a fork or a pair of chopsticks to separate those pieces that are sticking together because of the flour.

Fry only 30–60 seconds. Remove from oil with a slotted spoon or wire spatula and allow to air drain on a wire basket balanced over a bowl. Use a fine wire-mesh spatula to remove loose garlic pieces from the oil; allow the oil to reheat before frying the next batch. Cool the fried squid 1–2 minutes and serve while warm—topped with the loose garlic pieces—on a platter lined with lettuce and encircled by tomato slices. Good as an appetizer, or serve with other courses family-style with a hot-and-sour or sweet-and sour sauce.

Garlic (*Gkratiem*)

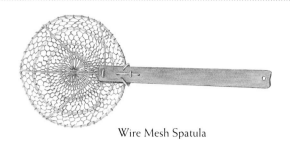
Wire Mesh Spatula

Allow oil to cool in the wok, then strain and store in a tight jar for future use. Refrigerate to keep fresh if you will not be using it again for a while. Because the oil picks up a garlicky and peppery flavor, it can be used with good results for stir-frying vegetables or seafood.

NOTES AND POINTERS

Squid fried quickly this way is not crispy and chewy like batter-fried squid you may have had elsewhere. Instead, it is succulent and tender, with a lot of garlic and pepper flavor.

This recipe is also good with a variety of other seafood and meats. See the recipe for garlic-peppered shrimps on page 80.

FISH AND MORE FISH

Since inaugurating my "homemade" tours in 1986, I spend three to four months every fall and winter in Southeast Asia, showing people around to my favorite places, exploring new territories on my own and visiting with family and friends. On my return to California each spring to start another joyful season of cooking classes, long-time students and friends in the Bay Area are eager to hear my stories of the road. And every year, there is one exciting adventure or another to share with them.

Being a lover of the sea, many of my fondest stories are of unforgettable times spent along both the eastern and western coasts of my country, and some of the more vivid of my memories are of days gone fishing with friends in the enchanting Andaman Sea, off the provincial coast of Krabi. Not that I am an avid fisher—I wouldn't know where to begin to string a pole, much less how to reel in a fish should one bite the line—I go along for the ride. The timeless hours spent over the wide open sea, far away from the cares and demands of everyday life, are very nurturing. The soulful company of wonderful friends; the songs and laughter; the silence and contemplative moments; the excitement of dolphin sightings and fish biting on lines; and the expansive views of an azure sea, dramatically decorated with limestone karsts jutting here and there out of the water—all these things are priceless rewards of fishing trips following intensive weeks leading tour groups.

Particularly satisfying were the fishing trips during my earlier years of leading tours, when I had the pleasure of the company of my brother Mohng, indisputably an old hand at fishing, though less than half my age. He's the one who has reeled in all the fish "I" have ever caught. As I mentioned before, Mohng is not a real blood brother, but I love him just the same as if he were. The custom in Thailand is to address those younger than we are as our younger brothers and sisters (Nong) and those older than us as our older brothers and sisters (Pee), aunts (Bpah) and uncles (Loong), mothers (Mae) and fathers (Paw) or grandmas (Yaiy) and grandpas (Dtah). Such customary use of language ties us to those around us as if we were all related—and we *are* related in the larger picture, as citizens of the same country and, even more so, as members of the human family.

I have watched Mohng grow from a bright-eyed sixteen-year-old, training to be a waiter at the then quaint, rustic Krabi Resort (in those days there were no other accommodations on lovely Ao Nang Bay), to a handsome, young headwaiter par excellence in his prime twenties. He is warm and personable, very charming and likable, with a sweet naiveté that can melt hearts. Mohng and my playful tour assistant, Ong, provide me with endless hours of entertainment, singing and dancing with childlike glee, teasing and laughing in unceasing spontaneity, with arms around each other's shoulders like the closest of buddies. But whenever the thrilling sounds of dragging lines suddenly intrude, they take to their posts like serious grown men, reeling in the catch with such genteel strength, all the while feeling out the fish on the other end of the line with such finesse that I swear the fish don't even know they are being caught! The two of them keep me continually amused, as I soak in the fresh sea air and the rejuvenating ambiance of the lovely surroundings.

We have usually gone trolling for the "big one," a fast-swimming tuna or maybe a giant mackerel. Mohng's friend Bangluen has accompanied us with his long-tail boat; he knows the sea well, having grown up as a fisherman in the area. Bangluen would feel out the wind and note the changing tides, guiding his boat skillfully along the open sea, circling deserted islets far and near, some lined with dazzling white-sand beaches, others with alluring coves. Some days, after long hours of trolling without any takers for our plastic lures, we would head for the red rocks, where there are deep reefs and underwater caverns. There, we dropped lines—using fresh squid as bait—to catch smaller fish, like the good-eating, flat *mong* fish, a variety particular to these parts. We always returned to shore with dinner fresh in our hands.

A MOST UNFORGETTABLE FISHING TRIP

If I were to name the most beautiful and most unforgettable day from my past ten years of travel, it would have to be the day many years ago when we were caught in a storm during one of our fishing excursions. The evening before, Mohng excitedly informed us that the tide would be perfect for trolling early the next morning. So we woke ourselves up before daybreak, collected our breakfast and lunch boxes from the friendly kitchen staff (who were so kind to get up early to fix our meals) and headed out to Bangluen's waiting boat. Four other people came along: two tour members, a friend and another tour assistant.

The sky was overcast, but we didn't think much about it. Our breakfast of spicy seafood noodles (the recipe follows on page 178) warmed us as we headed northwest. The air was delightfully crisp and refreshing, and there was a soft breeze playing in my hair. Humming and singing softly, Ong and Mohng lulled us with a lovely melody. The light was beautiful as the day dawned—what a gorgeous morning! I felt so content to be out over the glistening sea at that quiet morning hour.

One of the lines rattled and Mohng reeled it in, but it was only a small mackerel—nothing exciting. Still, we thought it must be a good sign to catch something so soon. Our boat continued to chug along. We were barely half an hour out to sea when we noticed dark clouds forming on the western horizon. A deepening gray began to color the distant skies. But in the midst of the dark gray skies, there glowed a mysterious circle of golden light. Such a feeling of peace and calm radiated out from it that I couldn't stop gazing into that circle of warmth—it was so comforting and hypnotizing! I had never seen or felt anything like it before and wondered if it was the "eye" of the storm.

The breeze soon blew stronger, but it was still gentle and embracing. We watched as the dark clouds painted streaking, vertical gray lines of what had to be downpours of rain onto the now blurred horizon. We could no longer tell where the sky ended and where the sea began. The storm grew and seemed to be moving in our direction. With great interest, we watched the islands, rocks and limestone karsts off to our left as they were gobbled up one by one. All the while the golden glow kept shining through, surrounded by enveloping darkness.

Before long, the wind came upon us in a sudden fury. The waves swelled and our boat rocked about. Pelting rain beat down on us—giant, cold raindrops. We quickly huddled close together on the bottom of the boat, trying to cover ourselves with the two plastic ponchos we had brought with us. A few of us shrieked, others roared with excitement, but no one seemed particularly fearful—in fact, most of us seemed to be enjoying the ride. As we hung on to each other screeching and screaming, visions of the tranquil circle of light glowed in my mind's eye. I felt calmed and protected by it. The wind howled, and I could hear the ponchos flapping wildly; one soon ripped, causing more shrieks and outbursts of laughter.

Drenched with cold rain and blown about by raging winds, Bangluen fearlessly held his ground on the back of the boat, firmly grasping on to the long shaft and guiding the boat toward the island straight ahead. We were amazed at how well the little long-tail boat took to the swelling waves. Though we rocked back and forth, the motion was not terribly rough, and it never crossed our minds that the boat might be in danger of capsizing. Of course, we had much confidence in our captain, who skillfully maneuvered his vessel.

In less than half an hour, the boat pulled into a sheltered cove fringed by an incredibly beautiful beach that curved around in a near semicircle. There were no big waves crashing on the shore, just a gentle lapping of crystal clear waters. Beyond the sparkling, white sandy beach lush rain-forest vegetation led up to enormous vertical cliffs. We gasped. Was this all real, or were we in a dream? Breaking the spell, Mohng pointed toward some big trees to our right, saying something about an abandoned shelter where we could keep dry until the storm passed. We quickly jumped over the sides of the boat.

The sand was so soft and fine that my feet gave way and I splashed into the water. In contrast with the cold rain, it was surprisingly warm and comforting and felt so good that I didn't want to get out. As I sat there soaking in the prettiest aqua blue water, my eyes were greeted by a scintillating spectacle of sparkling jewels all around me, as pearly raindrops caught the morning light and rippled over the surface of the water. I was so enraptured by the breathtaking surroundings, I couldn't help but laugh with joy. As many times as I have gone fishing and boating in these parts, each time has always been a completely new experience, filled with surprises and unsuspected treasures to nourish the soul.

A few others in our entourage were just as captivated as I was by this paradise. We bobbed about in the water, staying warm and soaking in the beauty and serenity of this pristine, hidden bay. We felt like Robinson Crusoes, shipwrecked on a deserted island, so idyllic and enchanting!

Some time had passed when we noticed smoke rising from behind the trees. A few minutes later, Mohng ran down toward us and enticed us out of the water with news of a warm fire where we could dry ourselves before an early lunch of grilled, fresh-caught fish. Hungry and with skin wrinkled from the long soak, we swam to shore and walked dreamily up the gorgeous powdery beach to the shelter. As we warmed ourselves in front of the fire, surrounded by a thick canopy of greenery, Mohng roasted the fish caught earlier in the morning on a stick while Ong readied a large leaf from a nearby tree to use as a serving platter. The two of them sang back and forth to each other with spontaneously made-up rhymes about life's many adventures, enough to make us beam and chuckle. Later, as we indulged ourselves on the delicious fresh fish and the tasty fried rice in our lunch boxes, Mohng and Ong continued to entertain us with their silly antics and heartwarming jesting and singing.

The storm eventually passed. Sunshine peeped through the clouds, here and there. We took one more walk down the lovely beach, collecting colorful shells and coral pieces along our path. Then, we took one more swim in the inviting waters before bidding farewell to our tropical island paradise. It was

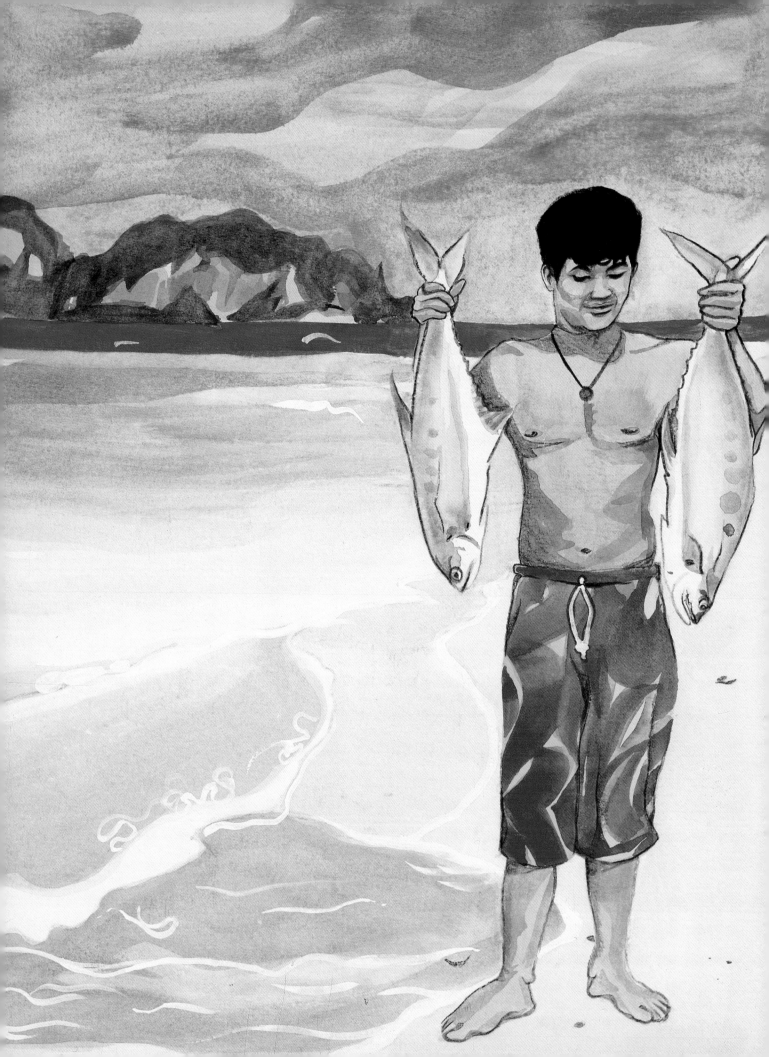

time to head back out to the open sea in search of fish. The clearing skies gradually brightened, welcoming the cheery colors of rainbows. This was truly a most beautiful day, absolutely magical and unparalleled by any other! Of course, we had fish to show off when we returned to the resort—two handsome yellow-fin tuna, about fifteen pounds each—and tales galore to tell those who thought they had been smart not venturing off to sea on that stormy day. They knew not the splendor of nature they had missed!

Years have passed since that very special day. I still recall vividly all the magical moments as if they took place only yesterday. Since then, Mohng has taken jobs in other resorts on distant shores, as far as Koh Samui and Phuket. He has not strayed far from the sea he loves. His friends at Krabi Resort told me recently that he now works as the manager of the restaurant at a plush new resort not far up the coast and frequently comes to visit his sweetheart in Krabi on his days off. Perhaps one of these days we may find ourselves on Bangluen's boat again, heading out in the sunrise for yet another adventurous day. In the meantime, wherever he is, I hope my brother is happy.

A FEW FAVORITE WAYS TO FIX FISH

On the seacoast, there are a few favorite ways to prepare fresh catch, depending on the type of fish and the type of meal. Flat fishes like *mong* fish and pompano and certain meaty, firm-flesh varieties like grouper and barracuda are usually fried to a crisp, either with lots of pepper and garlic (*tod gkra-tiem priktai*; see recipe on page 80 for ideas) or smothered with a chilli sauce (*rahd prik*). Both are very popular ways to serve just about any kind of fish and can be ordered in every seafood restaurant in Thailand, whether or not they are listed on the menu.

If something lighter and more delicate is called for, steaming with chillies and lime juice is a good alternative (recipe follows on page 185). For fish to taste good steamed, it has to be very fresh, and the softer-flesh varieties, such as red snapper, perch, cod and seabass, steam with the best results. Firmer, more meaty fish, like grouper or tuna, do not taste as good steamed as they do fried or grilled. Instead of steamed over a stove, sometimes fish is cooked wrapped in banana leaves or foil over a charcoal brazier. Although fish prepared this way is referred to as "roasted" (*bplah pow*), the fish actually steams in its own juices and picks up the flavors of the herbs with which it is stuffed and marinated (see recipe on page 180). Fish can also be barbecued unwrapped directly over coals and served with a spicy dipping sauce on the side. Fish prepared this way is also called *bplah pow* ("roasted fish"). Depending on where you order *bplah pow*, it can come in either of these two forms, the first soft and wet with herbs and the other dried and slightly charred. Both are served with a special dipping sauce.

Thai people love fried fish and probably eat more fish fried than steamed or grilled. Fried fish does not have to be greasy and heavy-tasting, and fried foods do not have to be high in calories and unhealthy. In fact, many people who have traveled with me in Thailand are surprised at the lightness of the fried fish and other fried foods. The secret lies in the kind of oil used. I prefer to use peanut oil for any kind of deep frying because it can be heated to very high temperatures without burning and breaking down,

Garlic (*Gkratiem*)

and the hot oil sears the outside of foods quickly without penetrating them. When I fry with peanut oil, I often have almost as much oil left in the pan when I'm done as when I started. In contrast, oils that cannot be heated to high temperatures will seep inside and be retained in the foods, making them heavy and greasy. These oils usually break down when exposed to high heat, imparting a strange flavor and causing havoc in the digestive system. Besides peanut oil, sunflower and safflower oils are relatively good for deep frying.

Thai people like to fry their fish longer than Westerners are used to, so that they are not just cooked through and still moist with juices, but until they are dried and crispy all around. We like to crunch on the crispy fins, heads and tails, the best parts of the fish! We usually like to fry smaller fishes, so that we can crunch and chew up most parts of them, save for the center skeletons. The wonderful crispy fins, tails and heads have a rich and fragrant taste we describe as *mân*, and they provide good sources of natural calcium. Try fried fish the Thai way, and you may soon find yourself fighting a Thai for that crispy fin or that crispy head. (Ong hated it when on one of my tours, several people knew to go for the head, tail and fins. For years he had teased that *farangs* didn't know how to eat fish, always leaving him the best parts. Now, feeling his gastronomic experiences threatened, he has requested that I screen future tour groups to make sure no one knows how to eat those best parts of the fish.)

Besides serving with a hot-and-limy dipping sauce, another favorite way to serve crisp-fried fish is to top them with a tangy and slightly sweet chilli sauce, a dish we call *bplah rahd prik* (*bplah* is fish; *rahd*, pour over; *prik*, chilli). There are numerous ways to make the chilli sauce, and fine chefs add their own special touches to the old familiar recipes. Some versions taste very different from those made in other restaurants, so much so that you may think the dishes ought to have different names. The commonality is that the spicy sauce is always made with fresh chillies of some kind and usually has a tang coming from some sour ingredient, be it lime juice, tamarind or vinegar. It is not a runny sauce, but has just enough juice to coat the outside of the fish without making it soggy. In more touristed areas on the seacoast, tomato sauce or ketchup may be one of the ingredients used. Usually, such versions have a sweeter and heavier reddish sauce.

One of the best *bplah rahd prik* I've had was a creation of a cook at Krabi Resort during the first few years I started making annual pilgrimages there. He inspired me to develop the recipe I teach in my cooking classes, using fresh jalapeño, fresno or serrano peppers, lots of garlic and shallots, some galanga and cilantro roots and a tanginess from fruity tamarind, balanced by sweetness from palm sugar (see recipe on page 182). For different emphases, I sometimes do without the galanga, or use lime juice in the place of tamarind; for friends with an extra-spicy palate, I make a version using Thailand's favorite chilli, *prik kee noo*, instead of the milder jalapeño, fresno or serrano. After trying out the recipe, play around with the ingredients, substituting different sources of hot, sour, sweet and salty, or varying the herb flavors to create your own special sauces to fit varying moods.

Another fabulous fried fish—with fresh turmeric—reminds me of Krabi. I highly recommend this dish if you ever dine in the fine, homey restaurant called Reuan Mai ("Wooden House") in town, a favorite haunt of local Krabiites. Frying fish with turmeric is common in the southern part of Thailand,

Tamarind (*Ma-kahm*)

and whenever I dine at Reuan Mai, I am partial to ordering catfish fried this way. I have included the recipe to close this chapter (see page 186). For other fish recipes in this book, check the listings of recipes in the table of contents.

Red Snapper

$\mathscr{S}$PICY SEAFOOD NOODLES—
"DRUNKEN" NOODLES

(Gkuay Dtiow Pad Kee Mao)

1 lb. fresh wide rice noodles (gkuay dtiow sen yai)

A few bite-size pieces each of several different kinds of seafood, about ½–¾ lb. total (firm-flesh fish, shrimps, scallops, shelled mussels, squid)

3–4 Tbs. peanut oil for stir-frying

8–10 cloves garlic, chopped

½ cup sliced onion

10–15 Thai chillies (prik kee noo), cut into small pieces and crushed with a heavy mortar and pestle

2–3 cups bite-size pieces of Chinese broccoli (ka-nah), or substitute with cabbage

2–3 Tbs. Thai oyster sauce

2–3 tsp. black soy sauce (the semi-sweet kind; see page 63)

2–3 Tbs. fish sauce (näm bplah), to taste

1 tsp. sugar, to taste

¼ tsp. ground white pepper

½ to 1 cup fresh holy basil leaves and flowers (bai gka-prow); or if unavailable, substitute with Thai sweet basil (bai horapa)

1 small tomato, cut into small wedges

Holy Basil (*Bai Gka-prow*)

Separate the block of fresh noodles into individual strands. Do not rinse. Keep the different kinds of seafood separate. Make sure they are well drained and brought to room temperature before stir-frying. Prepare the remaining ingredients as indicated.

Heat a well-seasoned wok over a high flame until it is hot and smoking. Swirl the oil in to coat the surface. Allow the oil to heat up before adding the chopped garlic, followed shortly by the sliced onion. Sauté 10–15 seconds or so. Toss in the fish pieces, stir a few seconds, then add the shrimps, scallops and mussels. Stir-fry together about 10–15 seconds before throwing in the squid. Sauté a few seconds more. Add the crushed Thai chillies and stir again to mix. Try to keep the wok surface as hot as possible over a high setting during the entire stir-fry.

Next, toss in the noodles and broccoli pieces (or cabbage). Stir to mix all the ingredients together well. Sprinkle in the oyster sauce; stir and toss to distribute evenly. Follow with black soy sauce. Stir and toss some more. Spread the noodles up along the heated sides of the wok so that the strands get even contact with the hot metal. Let them pan-fry a short while before stirring again and respreading the strands over the hot wok surface. Then, sprinkle in the fish sauce, a little sugar and white pepper. Stir and toss well. Taste and adjust flavors to desired saltiness and sweetness. Add the holy basil and tomato wedges. Continue to stir-fry until the basil is wilted. Serve while still warm.

NOTES AND POINTERS

Gkuay dtiow, Thailand's favorite noodle, is the same rice noodle used for "chow fun" in Chinese restaurants. It usually comes in 2-lb. packages in Chinese grocery stores.

If you are not yet experienced in stir-frying and are afraid of overcooking the seafoods, you may wish to stir-fry them separately from the noodles. Sauté the various seafoods until they are just cooked with some of the

Thai Chillies (*Prik Kee Noo*)

oil, garlic, chillies, seasonings and basil. Add the various kinds according to required cooking times; avoid overcooking squid by adding it last. Remove from wok. Then stir-fry the noodles and vegetables with the remaining oil, herbs and seasonings until they are cooked and evenly browned. Always let the wok and oil heat up before adding any of the ingredients. Combine the cooked seafoods, noodles and vegetables, toss well and serve.

I call this noodle dish "drunken noodles" because the Thai word *pad* means "stir-fry" and *kee mao* refers to someone who likes to get drunk. *Pad kee mao* is very spicy and a great accompaniment to alcoholic beverages—hence its name. Of course, you don't have to drink or be a drunk to enjoy this dish. This recipe is a *pad kee mao* with rice noodles (*gkuay dtiow*). You can also make a straight stir-fry with seafood to make a *pad kee mao talay* ("drunken seafood"), or with beef for a *pad kee mao neua* ("drunken beef"). Serve both with lots of plain, steamed rice.

Several of my long-time cooking students on one of my earlier tours delighted in spicy Thai food, any time of day. When we stayed at Krabi Resort, the kitchen staff whipped up an absolutely heavenly version of this noodle dish for our breakfast one morning. It was so good I decided to make it a tradition for all future tours, but years later the resort went upscale and began providing a Western-style buffet breakfast. One of the cooks remembers our preference, however, and from time to time, if he is on duty, Dtaem cooks us a batch of these noodles for lunch, for old time's sake.

ROASTED FISH IN BANANA LEAF
(Bplah Pow)

1 whole fish (sea bass, perch, red snapper or cod), weighing approximately 1½ lbs.

½ tsp. white peppercorns

6–8 cloves garlic

1 Tbs. chopped cilantro roots plus 1 Tbs. chopped cilantro stems; or if roots are not available, use 2–3 Tbs. chopped stems

1 Tbs. Thai oyster sauce

2 Tbs. light soy sauce, or fish sauce (näm bplah)

Banana leaf, large enough to wrap around fish once or twice

1–2 Tbs. cooking oil

Aluminum foil

Tomato, cucumber and/or pineapple for garnish

Hot-and Sour-Dipping Sauce:

3–4 red serrano or 1–2 jalapeño/fresno chilli peppers, chopped

4–6 cloves garlic, chopped

1 shallot, finely chopped

2–3 Tbs. fish sauce (näm bplah), to taste

Juice of 1–2 limes (about 3–4 Tbs.)

2–3 tsp. granulated sugar, to taste

Clean the fish, removing the scales, guts and gills. Cut two to three diagonal gashes to bone level on both sides of the fish, spacing them about two inches apart. Rinse and drain well. Set aside.

Pulverize the white peppercorns in a heavy stone mortar. Add the garlic and cilantro roots and pound together to form a paste. Mix with the oyster sauce and light soy sauce (or fish sauce). Rub the peppery mixture evenly over the fish and inside the gashes and body cavity. Allow to marinate for about half an hour.

Make the hot-and-sour dipping sauce. Pound the chopped chillies and garlic together until pasty. Transfer to a sauce dish and add the chopped shallot, fish sauce, lime juice and sugar. Stir well to mix. Adjust the flavors so that the sauce is equally salty and sour with a light touch of sweetness. Allow the sauce to sit at least 15 minutes before using to allow the flavors to pull together.

Clean the surface of a banana leaf and brush oil to liberally coat one side. Place the fish and marinade on the leaf and wrap it around once or twice. Then wrap in aluminum foil, sealing the edges.

Roast over medium-hot coals, turning the fish from time to time until it is cooked through, about 15–20 minutes. Remove the foil and most of the banana leaf, except for the small section on which the fish rests. Place on a serving platter and garnish with slices of tomato, cucumber and/or pineapple. Serve with the hot-and-sour dipping sauce.

NOTES AND POINTERS

Most fresh fish markets in American Chinatowns will clean the fish for you. If you must do it yourself, you may find scaling the fish to be less of a messy job if you do it while it is submerged in a basin of water. Use a sharp knife or a scraping implement. The water will catch the loosened scales so you won't have them flying all over your kitchen. To clean the insides, use a sharp knife and cut along the edge of the belly. Pull out all the guts; also pull out the gills.

Banana leaves are available packaged in 1-lb. plastic bags in the frozen foods compartment of Southeast Asian markets. Instead of foil, the fish can be wrapped in additional layers of banana leaf, the ends sealed with toothpicks or bamboo skewers. The outer layers of leaf may dry up and char; be careful not to allow them to burn through, as this may cause the fish to dry out and stick to the leaf. Turning the leaf packet frequently and sprinkling the outside with water can help.

Cilantro (*Pak Chee*)

CRISPY FRIED RED SNAPPER OR GROUPER WITH CHILLI-TAMARIND SAUCE

(Bplah Rahd Prik)

1 whole red snapper or grouper, weighing approximately 1½ lbs.

¼–½ tsp. sea salt

8–10 cloves garlic, minced

4–6 fresh red jalapeño or fresno peppers, minced

2 shallots, minced

A 1-inch section fresh galanga root (or substitute with peeled fresh ginger), yielding about 1 Tbs. minced

1 Tbs. minced cilantro roots (or substitute with stem sections)

10 white peppercorns

3–4 cups peanut oil for frying fish

¼ cup tapioca starch or unbleached white flour for coating fish before frying (optional)

2–3 Tbs. fish sauce (näm bplah), to taste

About 1 Tbs. palm sugar, to taste

¼–½ cup tamarind water, to taste

A few sprigs of cilantro or Thai sweet basil (bai horapa) for garnishing

Clean the fish, removing the scales, guts and gills. Rinse and drain. Cut diagonal gashes to bone level about 1½ inches apart on both sides of the fish. Rub a little salt evenly over the fish and inside the gashes and body cavity. Set aside. If it has been refrigerated, the fish should be brought to room temperature before frying.

Mince the garlic, red chilli peppers, shallots, galanga and cilantro roots/stems. Do not deseed the chillies. If you wish a milder dish, remove seeds from half the chillies but leave one or two with seeds. Using a clean mortar and pestle, pulverize the peppercorns. Then toss in the five minced roots and herbs and pound for a few minutes to a coarse paste.

Heat the oil in a wok to deep-fry the fish. There should be sufficient volume so that the fish will be at least half-submerged in the oil. Drain the fish from its juices which the salt may have drawn out. If you wish, coat with a thin layer of tapioca starch or white flour, including the body cavity. Besides adding a texture to the crispiness, this will help reduce splattering during frying. Make sure the oil is sizzling hot (test with a piece of garlic) before sliding the fish gently into it head first while holding on to the tail end.

Fry the fish, tilting the wok occasionally from side to side while holding on to the side handle(s) so that the hot oil can evenly brown the fish, from the top of its head to the tip of the tail. Maintain the heat at an even level—about medium-high to high, depending on your stove—so that the fish continues to sizzle as it fries, without browning or burning too quickly. Fry about 10 minutes. Then, nudging the wok spatula under the middle of the fish from its top edge, gently flip it over its belly to the other side. Avoid lifting the fish above the oil to flip as this may cause splattering. It is usually easier to flip the fish over its belly because there is a large pointed fin on its other edge.

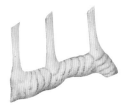

Galanga (Kah)

Red Fresno and Green Jalapeño Peppers

Fry the second side about 8–10 minutes, or until the fish is golden brown and crispy on the outside, along the edges and on the head and the tail. Again, slide the wok spatula under the fish from its top edge, tilt it up on its belly along one side of the wok above the oil, and allow the trapped oil to drain from the body cavity before lifting it over the top of the wok onto a serving platter. Set aside. Do not put inside a warm oven as this will cause the fish to sweat and lose its crispiness.

Remove the remaining oil from the wok, except for 2–3 tablespoons, reserving the rest for future use in frying fish. Add the chilli mixture and sauté until the flavors and aromas are released—about 3 minutes. Season the mixture with fish sauce, palm sugar and tamarind water to the desired balance. The sauce should be equally sweet and tangy, with saltiness in the lead. The consistency should be thick, but if it appears too dry, add 1–2 tablespoons of water. Let the sauce ingredients cook another minute or two to pull their flavors together. Then spoon sauce evenly over the top of the fish, spreading some along the side of the platter as well so that servings from the second side will include some sauce, too. Garnish with sprigs of cilantro or Thai basil. Serve immediately with plain steamed rice.

NOTES AND POINTERS

Certain types of fish fry up better with a thin coating of flour; others do not need it. Often it depends on the thickness of the skin and its oil content, as well as the degree of freshness. If you haven't been having good success doing it one way, try it the other way next time. See which you like better, for the type of fish you like to eat. Tapioca starch sticks better to the fish and fries up to a lighter crisp than regular wheat flour. It is available from most Chinese and Southeast Asian markets.

A good, deep wok is one of the best and safest utensils for deep-frying, especially when cooking a whole fish, which fits inside a wok more easily than in a flat skillet. The rounded sides make turning the fish over much easier, too, and because of the wok's shape, oil seldom splatters outside of its confines and is kept farther away from direct contact with the flames. The likelihood of a grease fire is minimal, as long as the wok is not filled more than two-thirds with oil. The standard-size wok sold is 14 inches wide, but I recommend a larger, more practical 16-inch size, particularly good for frying whole fish. It can be used to cook large or small quantities of food. Cookware shops in Chinatowns offer a range of sizes and depths for very reasonable prices. Select a deep, rounded one.

For this recipe, fry the fish longer than normally recommended in American or Chinese cooking. You want the fish not just cooked through and still moist with its juices, but dried up most of the way through and crispy all around. Coat its surface lightly with the spicy sauce, as if you were glazing it. This way, the fish does not quickly lose its crispiness. Don't forget that the crispy fins, tail and head are the best parts and provide a natural source of calcium.

For a change, make the spicy sauce to go over grilled or poached fish; or use the chilli paste to stir-fry with various kinds of fresh seafoods.

Red Snapper

STEAMED STRIPED BASS WITH CHILLI-LIME SAUCE

(Bplah Neung Manao)

1–1½ lb. very fresh whole striped
    bass, scaled and cleaned

8–10 cloves garlic, chopped

8–10 green and red Thai chillies,
    cut in very thin rounds

2 tsp. chopped cilantro roots,
    or 1 Tbs. chopped stems

¼ cup unsalted chicken or
    vegetable broth

2–3 Tbs. fish sauce (näm bplah),
    or light soy sauce

3–4 Tbs. lime juice
    (about 1½–2 limes)

2 green onions, cut in thin rounds

Rinse the cleaned fish and drain well. Cut diagonal gashes on both sides of the fish to bone level about 1½–2 inches apart. Place on a heat-proof serving platter large enough to hold the fish for steaming that will fit on a steamer rack. The platter should have some depth to hold the juices from the steamed fish.

Mix the chopped garlic, chillies and cilantro roots or stems with the chicken broth. Add fish sauce and lime juice to make a hot, salty and limy sauce. Spoon sauce and spread evenly over the fish. Top with green onions and steam over medium-high heat for about 15 minutes. Serve while fish is still hot.

NOTES AND POINTERS

See notes on page 181 about cleaning fish.

Asian Steamer Set

SOUTHERN FRIED TURMERIC CATFISH

(Bplah Doog Tod Kamin)

1 fresh whole catfish, weighing approximately 1½ lbs.

2 fingers fresh turmeric, or about 1½–2 Tbs. chopped

8 cloves garlic, chopped

1 tsp. sea salt

1 tsp. white peppercorns, freshly ground

4 cups peanut oil for frying

About ¼–½ cup tapioca starch or white flour to coat fish for frying

Cucumber, tomato, pineapple and/or orange slices for garnish

Hot-and-Sour Sauce:

8–10 Thai chillies (prik kee noo), thinly sliced in rounds

2 shallots, halved and sliced thinly

¼ cup white vinegar

3–4 Tbs. fish sauce (näm bplah), to taste

2–3 tsp. granulated sugar, to taste

Clean the catfish and leave whole, with the skin on and head still attached. Remove any oil sacs there may be from the body cavity. Rinse and drain. Cut slanted diagonal gashes to bone level, about an inch apart, on both sides of the fish, from behind the head all the way down to the tail. Set aside on a platter.

Peel the turmeric and chop finely. Place in a mortar along with the chopped garlic, sea salt and freshly ground white pepper. Pound to mix and blend the ingredients into a coarse paste. Rub the paste evenly over the catfish, including the body cavity, head, tail and inside the gashes. Set aside to marinate for at least half an hour. Fish should be brought to room temperature before frying.

Make the hot-and-sour sauce. Mix the sauce ingredients and allow to sit at least half an hour before serving.

In a large wok, heat about 4 cups of peanut oil, or enough to submerge at least two-thirds of the fish during frying. Allow the oil to heat until it is smoking hot. Just before sliding the fish into the hot oil, brush the chopped garlic and turmeric pieces off the fish and coat with a thin layer of flour, including the inside of the body cavity and the gashes, the head and tail. This will help reduce splattering during frying and also adds a texture to the crispiness of the fried fish. Tapioca starch sticks better to the fish and fries up to a lighter crisp. Reserve the marinade for frying later.

Fry the fish 10–12 minutes on each side, or until the fish is dry and crispy. If you have a very hot stove, fry at medium heat; otherwise, use high heat. While frying, tilt the wok occasionally from side to side, allowing the head and tail to be submerged from time to time in the hot oil. When the fish is browned and crispy all around, from head to tail, add the marinade to the oil and fry with the fish until the chopped pieces of garlic and turmeric are also brown and crispy.

Garlic (Gkratiem)

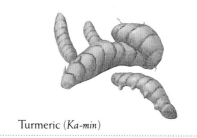

Turmeric (*Ka-min*)

Holding the wok spatula under the fish from its top edge, tilt it up on one side of the wok above the oil. Allow excess oil to drain out of the body cavity before sliding the fish gently out of the wok onto a serving platter. Using a fine wire-mesh strainer spoon, remove the crispy bits of fried marinade from the oil. Spread over the fish.

Serve while still warm and crispy with the hot-and-sour sauce, and, if you wish, sliced cucumbers, tomatoes, pineapples and/or oranges arranged on the side of the serving platter. Strain and refrigerate oil for future use in frying fish.

NOTES AND POINTERS

It is imperative to coat the catfish with flour before frying. Once I forgot to and ended up with a string of mini-explosions, as tiny oil sacs near the top of the skin and juice oozing out from inside the fish reacted violently with the hot oil. The coating of flour dries and seals the fish, making frying a pleasant and easy experience. You do not want to remove the skin of the catfish, because it fries to a nice crisp, makes the fish look good and adds great flavor.

The catfish can be fried ahead of time and refried with the marinade to recrisp it a few minutes before serving.

THE FLYING MORNING GLORY

Thai people are very fond of a vegetable they call *pak boong*. This viny crawler with hollow stems and long triangular leaves is also a favorite among other Southeast Asians. I've heard Vietnamese people refer to it as the "Vietnamese vegetable," and Laotians claim it as the "Laotian vegetable." The Chinese eat plenty of it, too, and in American Chinatowns, Cantonese shopkeepers will tell you its name is "ong choi." But ask an Indonesian and you'll be told it is none other than their delicious "kang kung."

Whatever it is called and no matter who lays claim to it as "their vegetable," *pak boong* is a prolific grower and can be found in profusion throughout the wet Asian countryside. It is practically a free source of food for rural folk and dirt-cheap in marketplaces for town folk, and rich and poor alike eat it with a passion.

Various food writers in the West have referred to this very likable vegetable by different names, trying to capture what they feel best describes its essence. "Water spinach" is one popular given name because the vine loves water and, like spinach, wilts quite a bit when stir-fried. But *pak boong* is not at all related to spinach, and its taste and texture are nothing like those of its cooler climate friend. "Swamp spinach" and "swamp cabbage," names reflecting the natural habitat of the plant, are used in botanical writings, but they are not especially favorable descriptions likely to entice gastronomes.

"Water morning glory," or simply "morning glory," is another English name used in many Asian markets in the West and the one I prefer because of its more charming appeal. Also, morning glory comes much closer to describing one of the delightful features of this herbaceous plant, for its flowers are none other than the delicate, bell-shaped morning glories that herald in the morning sun and fade away before the day is out. But instead of the radiant deep blues, purples and bright pinks characteristic of its distant climbing cousins, the edible morning glory of Thai waterways bears blossoms of innocent pinkish white with soft violet centers.

The extent of similarity, however, ends with the flowers. The leaves of the *pak boong* are a lighter green than the non-edible garden variety and are long, narrow and pointed, spaced two to three inches apart along fleshy hollow stems. The vines creep and crawl over wet ground or float over water, sending out roots from nodes along the stems to lay claim to their territorial spread.

Pak boong loves water and needs lots of it to thrive. As such, you will see it in abundance, wild as much as cultivated, alongside Thailand's numerous canals, rivers and wetlands, such as swamps and boggy fields. If left unchecked, it can choke out lily ponds, spreading so profusely over the surface of the water that you wouldn't know there's a pond beneath. Fortunately, people love to eat it, and if you visit Thailand's countryside, you will frequently see people wading through boggy fields to pick the young shoots for their lunch or dinner, or perhaps to sell at the local market. The tender leaves and stems are very tasty, either quickly stir-fried with garlic, little hot Thai chillies, fish sauce or fermented soy bean sauce. They are also good boiled in curries or served raw with spicy salads and various hot *näm prik* dipping sauces.

Besides tasting good, morning glory is very nutritious and has medicinal qualities as well. High in calcium and iron, it is also a rich source of vitamins A and C. In Thai folk medicine, an infusion made from boiling the plant is said to be a good detoxifier to remedy the overconsumption of alcohol or drugs or the accidental ingestion of poisons. Moreover, there are some herb books that identify its value in treating fevers and dehydration in children, as well as cer-

Morning Glory (*Pak Boong*)

tain kinds of nerve disorders. Rubbed over the skin, the fresh leaves are also used as a folk remedy against insect bites.

Because it grows easily where there is adequate water, sun and warmth, morning glory is now available during the warmer months of the year in most Chinese and Asian produce markets across California and other states with sizable Chinese and Southeast Asian populations. Next time you visit such a market, look for a vegetable that fits the description, or ask for it by its various names. It is usually bundled in bunches larger than spinach, and its long stems are noticeably hollow. Because morning glory wilts easily when exposed to warm, dry conditions, do not leave the vegetable sitting in a hot car for very long. Also, make sure to wrap it well in a plastic bag before storing it in the refrigerator. It is best to cook morning glory the same day you buy it. Once wilted, it cannot be revived by sticking the cut stems in water because the hollow stems are not able to draw in water. Try submerging the whole bunch in a basin of cold tap water instead, and allow it to soak until freshness is regained.

WOKKING OVER RED HOT FLAMES

A favorite way to cook morning glory is to stir-fry it in a very hot wok, with red flames leaping up the sides of the wok. Thai people call it *pak boong fai daeng* (*fai* means fire or flame, and *daeng* is red).

For the foreign traveler, it is exciting to watch a cook in a small rice shop with an open cooking area fire up a wok and toss the vegetable in a frenzy while flames leap up in all directions. Some outdoor, night-market food vendors are even more dramatic, inviting flames into the wok for just a few seconds, then dousing them out with a splash of broth. Morning glory cooks quickly, wilting down to a third of its raw mass in just a few short minutes. Fumes rising from the wok fill the air with aromas, making hungry mouths water in anticipation. Watching this live performance—while sitting on an old rickety stool in front of a discolored rickety table in the midst of a bustling crowd of casual diners—can make one wonder how the cook can take the heat of the flames for so many hours each night in such hot tropical weather.

"Red-flamed" morning glory uses lots of garlic, bruised Thai chillies (*prik kee noo*) for those who like it spicy and either fish sauce or fermented soy bean sauce, or both. Most rice shops in Thailand stir-fry the vegetable more often than not with the chillies unless a customer specifies otherwise. However, Thai people usually take pity on the pale-skinned *farang* who seems to get burned so easily inside out and often serve watered-down versions of anything spicy to Western visitors. So if you like your food hot and spicy, learn a few essential words before you visit Thailand, like *chawb* (like), *ped* (spicy hot) and *ped mahk* (very spicy), and ask for *prik kee noo* ("mouse shit chillies") in your *pak boong fai daeng*. But remember that those little chillies do like to hide under the wilted leaves and hit you when you least expect them to, in full fire. Then you wonder why the cooks always seem to use the dark green ones that camouflage themselves so easily among the green stems and leaves, rather than the red ones that would have been easier to spot. Well, the truth of the matter is, the "red flames" in the name refers to the fire of the stove and not the fire of the chillies! Don't curse too soon, for in a few minutes, while you are swimming in a pool of sweat and tears, endorphins will be released in your brain and you may experience an aliveness within that may make up for all the painfully burning sensations. After a few of these hits, you may perhaps fall in love with these little *prik kee noo* and welcome them in any *pak boong fai daeng*; indeed, to me, any morning glory stir-fry tastes incomplete without them.

Stir-frying over hot, leaping red flames adds a special smoky flavor to morning glory. However, if you do not have a gas stove with big flames, you can still stir-fry morning glory with good success as long as your wok is pre-heated as much as possible—until it is smoking hot—before you begin your stir-fry. The vegetable should hit the oil in the wok with a loud splash and maintain a good sizzling sound throughout the cooking process. Morning glory stir-fried in a cooler wok will not taste good and will seem greasy.

FLYING INTO THE NIGHT

As if the act of stir-frying morning glory over red, hot flames is not dramatic enough, several open-air restaurants across the country have added showman-ship to their cooking skills by making their morning glory "fly"—from wok to serving plate—at heights of more than ten feet and over distances twice that far. I believe the trend was started by the eccentric cooks of a small rice shop in the central region. Not only was their *pak boong fai daeng* fabulous, but their incredi-ble tossing and catching abilities were so entertaining to packed dinner crowds that others elsewhere started to add the drama to their cooking routines.

Through the grapevine, the tale was told of two brothers who worked as mechanics by day and cooks at night, setting out tables and chairs on the sidewalk outside their shop. Their powerful portable burners were propped up nearby, alongside carts filled with fresh meats and fish over ice and hanging vegetables. They were great cooks, and people came from the surrounding areas in throngs nightly to dine. On occasion, well-dressed patrons from far-away cities would drive great distances in their fancy cars to seek out this humble joint and mingle with local crowds in enjoying the delicious home-cooked food.

Their "red-flamed" morning glory soon became particularly famous when it started to fly. While one cook dramatically tossed a batch of the vegetable in a large wok surrounded by leaping flames, another took position with an empty plate across the street. Then, suddenly, the mass of morning glory was thrown out of the wok and up in the air, flying across the street where it was caught by the other cook, sauce and all. The flying morning glory was born!

Although I have not been to the original rice shop that started this crazy trend, I have come across another small-town restaurant that serves the flying morning glory. I have watched the two men there perform time and again with great precision. The cook is very dramatic, wildly waving his spatula and tossing the vegetable in his flaming wok with great intensity. On the other end, the catcher is cool and calm, waiting quietly in the shadows for the precise moment to perform his part. Cooked morning glory is dark in color; it is thrown steam-ing hot from the flaming wok across the street in the darkness of the night and is caught with ease, not a drop of sauce lost in the flight. The vegetable is then brought to the table for serving, still hot and delicious. I've heard that elsewhere in Thailand, the act has grown even more spectacular as experienced catchers climb atop high platforms or parked busses to do their catching.

Thai Chillies (*Prik Kee Noo*)

One time the catcher persuaded one of my American tour members to give it a try. David was a good sport; on his first attempt he lost half the vegetables—an excellent first effort! He would have caught the entire batch had he not pulled his arm back a bit too far in fear of being hit by the steaming vegetables. (I am sure it would have been painful both physically and emotionally to be splattered with piping hot morning glory and *prik kee noo* in front of a cheering audience.) A second try missed all together. I asked the resident catcher whether he had ever missed. "Oh yes!" he replied, "there are off nights not good for the business!"

These theatrics are beginning to lose some of their novel appeal among people who have seen morning glory fly time and again. Some do not care to watch the drama any more, although they claim *pak boong* does taste better after it has flown. Maybe the excitement of its unexpected flight peps up its flavor; perhaps it catches magical, unseen ingredients en route.

If you wish to see this unusual drama when you visit Thailand, morning glory is still flying in the town of Pitsunulohk. There is also an open-air restaurant in the food section of Chiang Mai's extensive Night Bazaar that has been giving flying lessons to its morning glory. The drama is staged almost nightly for foreign tourists, many of whom are bussed in for the show. If you are caught unawares as you walk through the Night Bazaar by drops of liquid falling on you, remember that they may not be rain or water dripping from a gutter, but could very likely be garlicky sauce from the flying vegetables. Watch out!

"RED-FLAMED" MORNING GLORY
(Pak Boong Fai Daeng)

8–10 cups morning glory (pak boong)

8 cloves chopped garlic

6–8 Thai chillies (prik kee noo)

About 3 Tbs. peanut oil

About 1 Tbs. salted soy bean (or yellow bean) sauce, plus 1 Tbs. fish sauce (näm bplah), to taste; or 2–3 Tbs. fish sauce (näm bplah), to taste

½–1 tsp. sugar (if using salted soy or yellow bean sauce), to taste

Pinch or snap the morning glory about 2 inches apart down the stem, such that you have pieces of stem with a leaf atttached. Young tender stems can be used most of the way down the stalk. Discard the lower half of fibrous larger stems, save for the leaves. As a general rule, use the stems down to about an inch below the last good leaf. An average bunch yields about 8–12 cups, which cook down to a third or less of the raw mass. Rinse and drain well.

Chop the garlic. Remove the stems from the chillies; cut the chillies in half and bruise with the flat side of a cleaver or heavy knife.

Heat a wok until the entire surface is very hot. Swirl in the oil to coat the wok surface and allow to heat up until it is smoking hot. Add the garlic (it should sizzle loudly) and the bruised Thai chillies, followed a few seconds later with the salted soy or yellow bean sauce (if using), fish sauce and sugar. Stir, then toss in the morning glory. Stir-fry vigorously until the vegetable starts to wilt. Add more fish sauce as necessary to the desired saltiness. Toss and continue to stir-fry until the vegetable is well wilted. Test for doneness. Serve while still hot with steamed rice.

NOTES AND POINTERS

If you are not able to find water morning glory, *do not* substitute with the broader-leafed garden variety which is *not* edible. Regular spinach and other crisp leafy greens work well prepared in this same manner, as do firmer, deep green vegetables like broccoli and Chinese kale (known as *ka-nah* in Thailand). The water mimosa (*pak gkra-chehd*), another well-loved Thai vegetable, is excellent "red-flamed," too; it is, however, even more difficult to find in Western markets than *pak boong*.

Remember that it is essential for the wok to stay very hot throughout the entire stir-fry. If not, the vegetable may pick up a greasy taste. If you do not have a very hot stove, it would help to stir-fry in smaller batches.

Garlic (*Gkratiem*)

When purchasing morning glory, select the bunch with small, young stems. Bunches with bigger stems yield less because large parts of the stems are tough and too fibrous.

Refer to page 55 for information on fermented soybean or yellow bean sauce. Do not use too much as it is quite salty. Sugar helps counterbalance. The darker sauces, such as the Dragon Fly brand, are more strongly flavored and saltier than the lighter-color ones, such as the Healthy Boy brand. If using the former, you may need to add more sugar to round out its strong flavor; the latter already has a faint touch of sweetness in it.

For those who like hot and spicy dishes, eat the Thai chillies along with the vegetables with mouthfuls of steamed rice. Some of the heat in the chillies will have cooked into the vegetables, making them less hot in themselves. For those who prefer a less spicy meal, watch out for the chillies; use red ones and keep them in larger pieces to make them easier to spot.

Morning Glory (*Pak Boong*)

One of the greatest joys of Thai people is our love of good food and the sharing of food. We like to nibble—a little here, a little there—around three light meals. We like variety, too, preferring not to eat a lot of one thing, but a little bit of a lot of different things throughout the day. In Thailand, these eating habits are easily satisfied by the countless varieties of tantalizing "street food" that are sold each day along the sidewalks near shopping areas and marketplaces, bus stations and business offices and busy neighborhood centers.

Enterprising food vendors set up clusters of stalls, transforming major street corners, empty lots and alleys into lively food bazaars. Many are mobile, peddling from one area to another on tricycles and motorcycles with fixtures attached, or pushing mini-kitchens around on wooden carts. More modest are hawkers on foot, bearing filled baskets balanced on a wooden yoke upon one shoulder. Along the *klong* (canals) and waterways, sellers paddle their mini-shops from home to home, offering "boat noodles," curries over rice and an assortment of *kanom* (sweetmeats and snack foods).

Whenever I think of street food, a profusion of images comes to mind. It is difficult to separate the experience of street food from the context in which it is made and sold: the people, their imaginative personal touches, the on-the-spot cooking demonstrations, the elaborate displays and set-ups, the often festive environment, and the enveloping sounds, colors and aromas. It is the gray-haired grandma in well-worn *pasin* (sarong) squatting all day long, patiently making crispy golden crêpes. It is the chirpy woman in the bustling morning market turning out little round coconut hotcakes as fast as she can sell them. It is the boat noodle man whipping up one bowl after another of steaming hot-and-sour soup noodles for a hungry crowd sitting on low stools along the landing. It is the sharp cry of the hefty woman announcing her presence as she huffs and puffs down the street, carrying woven baskets neatly arranged with goodies. It is the aroma of chicken, pork and satays barbecuing on charcoal stoves under bright, colorful tarps, the sizzling sound of fishcakes frying, the deep yellow of peeled jackfruit and the neatly shaped packets of banana leaves filled with delicate sweet treats. It is the noonday crowds in fancy work clothes eagerly searching from stall to stall for the delicacies that tempt them most that day. . . .

Nibbling on street food is an inexpensive way to dine out in Thailand. You can fill yourself with a soulful lunch for a dollar or less—not much more will buy a hearty, well-balanced supper of several courses—and spend maybe a quarter here and a quarter there for a refreshing mid-morning or mid-afternoon snack. But the low price does not necessarily bespeak the quality of food. In fact, a lot of street cuisine is very good and rivals some of the more refined gourmet restaurants. The variety to choose from is immense and includes many wonderful treats rarely seen on restaurant menus. Among these are traditional delicacies that are complicated to make and labor intensive, requiring constant care and attention during cooking, which many street vendors are able to give owing to their specialization in only one or a few items. And they get quite good at what they make, after having done it every day for years, often becoming well known and patronized in their area of the city.

Mobile Bangkokians are known to travel great distances in horrible traffic to particular corners of the city, where so-and-so "aunt" or "uncle," "grandma" or "grandpa" makes the best of this or that. Sitting on shaky stools around well-worn tables, or mingling with the crowds, might be seen some of the city's affluent citizens, well groomed and well dressed, next to laborers in tattered clothes. The vendors need no advertising other than their products, as news of good food spreads like wildfire in a culture with a highly cultivated sense of taste. I am reminded of one autumn when a group of my cooking students traveled with me around Thailand for twenty-five days. Seventy-five meals and innumerable snacks later, several of them were convinced that some of the best eats we'd had were along the streets and canals, in parking lots and at truck stops along highways. They wondered how I found out about these places.

There are many independent, undiscovered great chefs along the sidewalks of Bangkok. Give yourself a treat the next time you are in Thailand and walk the streets, allowing your eyes and nose to guide you. Don't stick to what looks familiar; try out the more exotic delights that have yet to see their day in Thai food places in the Western world. Do not worry too much about getting sick; use your discretion and common sense. Today's cosmopolitan Bangkok is not the same as twenty or thirty years ago; the cleanliness standards are remarkably high. But if you are not courageous, seek out restaurants that provide refined "street food" in settings that may be more appealing to you. Silom Village is one such restaurant, offering a demonstration area where pretty ladies neatly dressed in traditional Thai costume turn out some of the favorites from the streets to order.

My mother once jokingly told me that if she ever ran low on her savings, she would set up a portable stove outside her front gate and make my favorite street food, *kanom krok*, a sweet and savory coconut-rice pancake. Because she is such a good cook, she probably would not have much trouble building up patronage among the neighbors on her street. That's what street cooking is all about—a way of life and equal opportunity employment for city folk who take advantage of it. It is little wonder, therefore, that the small, unpretentious stalls serve food as good as homemake—because it *is* homemade.

This way of life, however, is threatened by a move in recent years to ban sidewalk vendors from selected areas around Bangkok. The contention is that the vendors contribute to the horrendous traffic problems for which the over-populated capital city has become famous. Perhaps a compromise can be reached, for street vendors provide an essential service by making inexpensive food readily available to busy working-class people with meager salaries, long working hours and limited mealtime breaks. They also provide an unceasing source of the colors, smells, textures and tastes that make the city culture of Bangkok unique. Many foreign visitors recall with great enthusiasm the magnificent array of exquisite sweetmeats and other fabulous treats along the sidewalks of the city. Perhaps these lively images, coupled with recollections of all the mouth-watering smells and friendly smiles of people serving and enjoying food, make them forget the terrible traffic, which is likely the least favorite of their experiences in the crowded city.

A SAMPLING OF STREET CUISINE

The ready-to-eat delicacies along the sidewalks and open-air marketplaces of Thailand range from meal-type items—such as barbecued meats, curries, salads and noodles of all kinds—to sweet-and-salty snacks, dainty sweet-

meats, cooked fruit and sweet soupy concoctions with crushed ice. There is so much variety that I can only present here a small nibbling of well-known and well-liked snacks.

As already mentioned, my personal favorite (and that of many Thais) is the irresistible treat *kanom krok*, sweet and savory, custardy pancakes made of coconut milk and ground rice, cooked in griddles similar to Ebelskiver Danish pancake pans, but larger in size and with smaller, shallower indentations. The round, bite-size hotcakes are a great breakfast food and are churned out in large quantities early each morning by push-cart vendors in marketplaces all over the country. During my childhood, Mother frequently came home from the market with a batch of these cakes, still warm and so satisfying they never had the chance to get cold.

Afternoon and evening vendors also proffer these yummy nibbles in various neighborhoods. The hotcakes sometimes have fillings, such as green onion, pumpkin, taro, corn and cilantro. If you happen to be on Sukumvit Road in the vicinity of Tonglaw some evening, join the crowd in the festive night food bazaar and look for the stall near the intersection with Soi 55 for its sensational *kanom krok* with extra-crispy edges. (Don't go on a Wednesday; many street vendors take that weekday off, apparently in accordance with a city ordinance on street cleaning.)

Kanom krok has also become a favorite among many of my cooking students. I have simplified the recipe (see page 200) so that you can make it easily with a minimum of effort and with ingredients readily available from Asian food stores. Some of these markets also carry the big round griddles or Ebelskiver pans at much lower prices than at gourmet cookware shops.

Another common street food I loved as a child and indulged in throughout my growing up is fried bananas. There are several kinds of good cooking bananas in Thailand, and used for frying are the firm varieties that sizzle to a golden, crisp and chewy texture. The recipe that follows on page 201 is adapted for the common banana available in American supermarkets, though this softer fruit is seldom used for cooking in Thailand as it gets mushy and falls apart easily.

A third example of street food, *miang käm*, is a delightful snack that involves wrapping little tidbits of several items in a leaf along with a sweet-and-salty sauce. Chewing all the ingredients together gives taste receptacles on the tongue and mouth a thrilling experience—from the rich, roasted flavors of coconut and peanut to the tanginess of lime with zest and the pungent bursts of diced ginger and chillies.

While in Bangkok, look for street hawkers whose baskets are neatly arranged with prepackaged plastic bags containing leaves and various tidbits separately wrapped in individual pouches. Usually the lime is left in a large wedge to be cut up when the snacker is ready to indulge. Prepackaged *miang käm* sets can also be purchased from snack stands in marketplaces throughout the country. These days, to encourage consumption, street hawkers are making it easier for busy people to have their *miang käm* with a minimum of fuss. They prewrap each individual mouthful in a leaf and skewer it onto a bamboo stick; five bites per stick cost five *baht* (one *baht* is equivalent to four U.S. pennies). Watching them assemble the packets skillfully in an aesthetically pleasing, pyramidal shape is very entertaining. Several such hawkers squat along the sidewalks of the enormous Chatuchak Market every weekend, offering their delicious *miang käm* on a stick—don't miss them!

The last two recipes that I have selected to present are noodle dishes. Noodle carts along the streets are common everyday sightings, as noodles rank among the most popular of fast-food lunches. They are also consumed throughout the day whenever hunger strikes. Though bowl-by-bowl statistics would probably award soup noodles the highest market share in Thailand, the undisputed leader in the Western world seems to be *pad thai*, perhaps because its rich and sweet character appeals to Western palates. I have read reviews of Bay Area Thai restaurants that rate them by the quality of their *pad thai*; this is amusing to me because it is like judging fine American restaurants by the quality of their hamburgers. In Thailand, I seldom go to a fine restaurant to eat *pad thai*, as some of the best is made on the streets and in no-frills noodle shops. One of my friends told me that the best he has had is in a small, open-air noodle shop next to a Caltex gas station just a few kilometers south of Chiang Mai along the super-highway.

Lastly, I have included a recipe for a hot-and-sour noodle dish, largely because it reminds me of countless wonderful breakfasts along Damneun Saduak canal. Not only does the boat noodle man I visit there make terrific noodles in a dramatic fashion, the ambiance of sitting along the edge of the water in the cool of the morning, while wooden boats filled with colorful seasonal produce and mini floating cafes paddle by, is something more than words can describe. A woman on one of my tours, who adamantly claimed to dislike noodles, changed her mind after sampling these delicious hot-and-sour noodles and downed two bowls one morning much to everyone's surprise. Ong, in the meantime, had slurped up his usual four!

GRILLED COCONUT-RICE PANCAKES
(Kanom Krok)

3 14-oz. cans coconut milk, or 1¾ cups coconut cream with 3½ cups lighter coconut milk

¼ cup plus 1 Tbs. sugar

2½ Tbs. tapioca or arrowroot flour

3 Tbs. uncooked white rice

⅓ cup finely shredded fresh coconut, or ¼ cup dried, unsweetened shredded coconut

2 cups rice flour

2 tsp. sea salt

2–3 Tbs. peanut or corn oil

Optional filling ingredients:

¼ cup green onions, cut in thin rounds

¼ cup fresh corn kernels

2 Tbs. cilantro leaves

If using canned coconut milk, spoon into a small saucepan 1¾ cup of the creamiest part from the top of three cans of coconut milk. Heat just enough to melt and smooth out the lumps. Add sugar and stir to dissolve. Allow to cool before mixing in 2½ Tbs. of tapioca or arrowroot flour. Stir until smooth. Set aside.

Combine the remaining coconut milk from the cans and stir until smooth, heating if necessary to melt the coagulated parts. Allow to cool. Grind the uncooked white rice in a food mill or clean coffee grinder as finely as possible. Do the same with the shredded coconut. Combine the two with the rice flour, salt and coconut milk. Stir and mix until well blended and smooth.

Heat a well-seasoned *kanom krok* griddle (or substitute with an Ebelskiver pancake griddle) on the stove, in a hot oven or over a small round barbecue kettle with medium-hot charcoals. When the griddle is hot, brush the surface indentations with peanut or corn oil. Wait a few seconds before spooning the salty rice mixture into each indentation to about two-thirds full. The batter should sizzle when it hits the hot metal. (If you have a tea kettle with a spout, you may find it helpful as a container from which to pour the rice batter onto the griddle.)

Immediately add a dab of the sweet coconut cream mixture over the top to fill and sprinkle the center of each cake with a little bit of one of the toppings, or leave plain. Cover with a round lid and allow to cook for a few minutes, or until the pancakes are firm and crispy brown on the bottom. Remove gently with a rounded spoon. Regrease the griddle before making the next batch. Because rice flour tends to settle, stir the coconut mixture well before pouring onto the griddle.

Serve warm.

Rice Stalk (*Kao*)

FRIED BANANAS

(Gkluey Tod)

½ cup unbleached white flour

½ cup rice flour

½ tsp. salt

2 tsp. baking powder

½ cup sugar

½ cup red limestone water
    (see notes below)

⅓ cup lightly toasted sesame seeds
    (optional)

1 cup shredded fresh coconut meat;
    or substitute with ⅔ cup
    dried unsweetened
    shredded coconut with
    ¼ cup hot water added

4 firm bananas

3–4 cups peanut oil for deep frying

Sift the two kinds of flour, salt and baking powder together into a large bowl. Add sugar and limestone water. Stir to make a smooth, thick batter. Then add the sesame seeds and shredded coconut. Mix well.

Cut the bananas in half lengthwise, then in sections about 2½ inches long. Heat 3–4 cups of peanut oil in a wok until hot. Coat the banana pieces with the batter; spoon a piece at a time with some of the batter and drop gently into the hot oil. Fry until golden brown and crispy on the outside. Remove from oil and drain on a wire strainer balanced over a bowl, or on a cookie rack. Allow to cool a few minutes before serving. Air cooling will allow the bananas to stay crisper for longer than draining on paper towels on a plate.

NOTES AND POINTERS

Limestone water is widely used in making Thai pastries and fried foods as a key ingredient that promotes crispness. It is also used for pickling or to crisp up vegetables for salads. To make limestone water, start out with limestone paste, available in small plastic containers from Thai and Southeast Asian markets. It is red or white in color and smells just like the mineral limestone; use the red for this recipe. Empty the contents of a small container into a two-quart jar. Fill with water, cover tightly with a lid and shake to dissolve the limestone. Allow to stand about 1–1½ hours, or until the water has almost cleared, before using. Store the limestone unrefrigerated in the jar for future use, each time adding more water and shaking the jar about an hour or so before using. A package will last you a very long time and keeps indefinitely.

Matured Coconut (Ma-prao)

MIANG KÄM

(Mouthful of Tidbits Wrapped in a Leaf)

Large leaves from 1–2 bunches of spinach; or 1 head of leafy lettuce, with leaves torn into 3- to 4-inch pieces

Filling Ingredients:

½ cup unsalted roasted peanuts

½ cup roasted, unsweetened, shredded coconut

¼ cup small dried shrimps

⅓ cup diced ginger, with pieces about the size of a pea

⅓ cup diced shallots or onion

1 lime, cut into small peanut-size pieces including the peel

4 heads pickled garlic, stem removed and bulb cut into peanut-size pieces

4 serrano peppers, cut into thin half circles; or use Thai chillies (prik kee noo), cut into thin rounds

⅓ cup cilantro leaves

Sauce Ingredients:

¼ cup finely ground dried shrimps

¼ cup roasted, unsweetened, shredded coconut

2 Tbs. unsalted roasted peanuts

1 tsp. gkapi shrimp paste

¼ cup palm sugar, to taste

2 Tbs. fish sauce (näm bplah), to taste

½ cup water

Arrange the spinach or lettuce leaves and filling ingredients on a large serving platter, piling each separately and aesthetically for a pleasing presentation.

To make the sauce, grind the dried shrimp, roasted coconut and peanuts separately and as finely as possible in a clean coffee grinder. Wrap the *gkapi* shrimp paste in a piece of banana leaf or aluminum foil and roast over a direct flame for several minutes. You may do this by using a pair of tongs to hold the leaf packet directly in the flame of a gas burner. Turn the packet frequently and allow the banana leaf to char and burn. Unwrap and place in a small saucepan together with the three ground ingredients.

Add palm sugar, fish sauce and water. Bring to a boil, then lower heat and simmer, stirring occasionally to make sure all the ingredients are well blended and the sauce is as smooth as possible. Cook about 10 minutes, or until the mixture has thickened to the consistency of light batter. Adjust the flavors so that it is almost as sweet as it is salty. Transfer to a sauce bowl and allow to cool to room temperature before using. The sauce will thicken more as it cools.

To eat, take a spinach or lettuce leaf, fill with a little bit of everything, top with a dab of sauce, roll or wrap up, stuff into your mouth and chew everything all at once. Enjoy the explosion of flavors!

NOTES AND POINTERS

There are numerous kinds of *miang*, which refers to a snack or appetizer composed of tidbits of various items wrapped in some kind of leaf or tossed together in a salad. *Miang käm* is the most common, *käm* meaning "mouthful." As the name suggests, the leaf-wrapped packets should be made no larger than can be taken in a mouthful. The little tidbits of the ingredients chewed together all at once make *miang käm* extraordinarily delightful. You may find the result to be much more delectable than what you had expected from the individual ingredients.

Matured Coconut (*Ma-prao*)

Thai people use a round, deep-green leaf called *bai cha-ploo* for their *miang käm*. The leaf is thick and shiny, does not tear easily and has a distinct flavor of its own. Because it is not yet available in markets here, I have substituted with spinach. Select a bunch with large leaves.

Although *miang käm* is eaten primarily as an in-between-meals snack, it also makes a great party food, allowing your guests to participate in assembling their own nibbles. For a sit-down dinner, you may wish to prearrange the leaves on a large platter around the sauce dish with the various ingredients already on top of the leaves, making it easy for your guests to simply apply the sauce, roll up their packets and enjoy with a minimum of fuss.

To make roasted coconut, either start with a fresh whole coconut or buy dried, unsweetened, shredded coconut from a Southeast Asian market. If you use the former, pry the flesh from the shell and cut into small, thin "sticks." Place in a dry pan on a burner and roast over medium heat, stirring frequently until the coconut shreds are evenly browned and fragrant.

Sometimes I like to add crispy fried rice pieces to the list of filling ingredients as they add a wonderful crunch. Dried rice squares can be purchased from some Asian grocery stores. Simply fry them in hot oil. They will puff up into crispy rice crackers. Break into small chunks and add to the *miang käm* platter. You can make the rice squares yourself by drying cooked rice in a low oven (about 200°) for several hours. Spread freshly cooked rice about $1/2$-inch thick on a greased cookie sheet. When dried, break into chunks and deep-fry to make the rice crisps.

If you are grinding your own dried shrimp rather than using prepackaged shrimp powder, keep in mind that whole shrimp will fluff up quite a bit after grinding. Use 2–3 Tbs. of whole dried shrimps to yield the $1/4$ cup of ground powder needed for the sauce.

The sauce recipe makes a concoction that is strongly shrimp-flavored. By itself, it may seem too shrimpy, but when eaten together with the pungent fillings, it harmonizes and adds lots of flavor. So try it as it is described first. Then, if you decide you wish a less shrimpy sauce, next time you make it omit the *gkapi* shrimp paste and cut down on the amount of ground dried shrimp. Add more ground roasted peanuts and/or coconut for a richer sauce. For a tangy sauce, add some tamarind water, but usually the fresh lime pieces in the filling already impart enough of a sharp bite. Cut the lime so that each piece has both some of the sour and juicy flesh and a little of the peel.

If you have little bits and pieces of filling ingredients and some sauce leftover after a party, they can be put to good use the next day in making a delicious *miang käm* fried rice.

Shallots

HOT-AND-SOUR DRY RICE NOODLES

(Sen Lek Dtom Yäm Haeng)

1 tsp. ground dried red chillies

6–10 chopped fresh Thai chillies
   (prik kee noo)

Juice of 2 fresh limes

1 Tbs. vinegar

2 Tbs. roasted chilli paste
   (näm prik pow)

2–3 Tbs. fish sauce (näm bplah),
   to taste

½ cup ground pork

½ lb. fresh thin rice noodles
   (gkuay dtiow sen lek)

3 cups bite-size lettuce leaf pieces

½ cup thinly sliced boiled pork, or
   barbecued pork

¼ cup thinly sliced cooked
   pork liver

½ cup chopped unsalted roasted
   peanuts

1 stalk green onion, cut in thin
   rounds (use both white
   and green parts)

2 Tbs. chopped cilantro

Mix the two kinds of chillies, lime juice, vinegar, roasted chilli paste and fish sauce together. Set aside.

Spread the ground pork loosely over a wire-mesh strainer with handle and dip in hot boiling water until cooked through, stirring to break into bits. Drain and set aside.

Cook the noodles quickly by blanching in hot water for a few seconds. Drain and toss with the hot-and-sour sauce. Dish into individual serving bowls lined on the bottom with lettuce pieces. Arrange the sliced pork, pork liver slices and ground pork over the top of each serving. Sprinkle with chopped peanuts and garnish with green onions and cilantro. As a breakfast food or for lunch, this recipe serves two to four.

NOTES AND POINTERS

This "dry" noodle dish can easily be converted into soup noodles by adding a broth made by simmering pork bones with some crushed garlic, cilantro roots and ground white pepper, and lightly salted with light soy sauce, sea salt or fish sauce. For added flavor and sweetness, cook the pork meat, liver and ground pork in this broth. Adjustment in the amount of fish sauce, lime juice, vinegar and *näm prik pow* in the chilli sauce may be needed as the broth will likely dilute the intensity of the sauce.

If you are not able to find fresh, thin rice noodles, substitute with a ¼ lb. of dried rice noodles. Soak first to soften, then cook in boiling water to the firmness you like. This may take a few minutes.

This recipe makes a very spicy batch of noodles. For milder palates, simply cut back on the amount of both dried and fresh chillies, or strain out the chillies and use only the liquid part of the sauce.

For a change, use chicken, shrimp or a combination of seafoods in the place of pork.

Thai Chillies (*Prik Kee Noo*)

$\mathcal{P}$AD THAI NOODLES
(Thai-Style Stir-Fried Noodles)

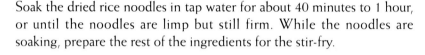

¼ lb. dried ¼-inch-wide gkuay dtiow or rice noodles (also known as ban pho to the Vietnamese)

2–3 Tbs. peanut oil for stir-frying

3–4 cloves garlic, finely chopped

2 shallots, thinly sliced (or substitute with half a small onion)

¼ lb. fresh small shrimps, shelled and butterflied; or use a combination of half shrimp and half pork meat, cut into thin matchstick strips

½ cup firm pressed tofu, cut into strips about 1–1½ inches long, ½ inch wide and ¼ inch thick

2–3 Tbs. small dried shrimps

2–3 Tbs. sweetened-salted radish (see page 57), chopped

1–2 tsp. dried red hot pepper flakes, to taste

2 eggs

2 Tbs. fish sauce (näm bplah), to taste

2–3 Tbs. granulated sugar, to taste

1 Tbs. white vinegar

¼ cup chopped unsalted roasted peanuts

1 cup fresh bean sprouts

½ cup garlic chives, cut in 1½-inch-long segments (optional)

Shrimp (Gkung)

Soak the dried rice noodles in tap water for about 40 minutes to 1 hour, or until the noodles are limp but still firm. While the noodles are soaking, prepare the rest of the ingredients for the stir-fry.

When ready to make your *pad thai*, drain the soaked noodles and heat a wok over high heat until it begins to smoke. Add the oil and swirl to coat the wok surface. Allow the oil to heat up. When hot, toss in the chopped garlic and sliced shallots (or onion) and sauté 10–15 seconds. Add the pork (if using), stir, cook a few seconds, then add the tofu. Sauté another 10–15 seconds and follow with the shrimps. Stir. Then add the dried shrimps, chopped sweetened-salted radish and hot pepper flakes. Stir and mix well.

Toss in the noodles and stir-fry with the ingredients already in the wok. After one to two minutes, or when the noodles begin to change texture and soften, push the mass up along the side of the wok, add a teaspoon of oil to the cleared area and allow to heat up a few seconds. Crack the eggs into the oiled area, using the edge of the spatula to break the yolks. Allow the eggs to set, turning them over as needed until they are cooked. Avoid scrambling. When the eggs are set, cut with the spatula into small chunks and toss in with the noodles.

Sprinkle fish sauce and sugar over the noodles. Mix well, then add the vinegar and continue to stir-fry. If the noodles feel dry and still too firm to your liking, sprinkle a tablespoon or two of water over them. Add the chopped roasted peanuts, stir, then toss in the bean sprouts and chives. Stir well and cook until the vegetables are partially wilted. Taste and adjust flavors to the desired salty-sweet combination.

Transfer noodles onto a serving platter, or dish onto individual dinner plates. Serve with raw bean sprouts, lime wedges, extra chopped peanuts, cilantro and green onions. Before eating, squeeze lime juice over each serving. Serve while still warm.

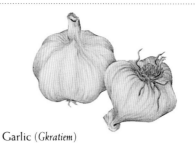

Garlic (*Gkratiem*)

Garnish:

½ to 1 cup fresh bean sprouts

1 lime, cut into 6 wedges

*¼ cup coarsely chopped unsalted
roasted peanuts*

A few cilantro sprigs

*2 stems green onions, cut into
3-inch segments*

NOTES AND POINTERS

As a one-dish meal for breakfast or lunch, this recipe makes enough for two to four.

If you prefer softer noodles, soak dried noodles in hot water. However, with some brands of noodles, this may result in soggy *pad thai*. If you prefer your noodles al dente, it is preferable to soak in cool tap water, adding liquid to the stir-fry as needed to cook to the desired texture.

The *pad thai* served in many American Thai restaurants is liberally flavored with ketchup. Use this ingredient if you wish as some cookbooks advise, though it is the exception rather than the rule in Thailand. Some noodle shops use black soy (the semi-sweet kind) in their *pad thai*; others use the orange chilli sauce called *prik Sriracha*. Add your own touches to create your own version.

The language of a people reveals a lot about their culture. I was reminded of this when a tour member on one of my trips asked me one day what the word *jai* meant. He had been hearing it repeatedly in the lyrics of Thai contemporary and folk music.

Jai means "heart." The word appears prevalently in the Thai language, not only by itself but more so as part of numerous compound words and phrases. In Thailand the heart and states of emotions—rather than the mind and reason—are foremost in the way we relate with the world. In fact, heart and mind are inseparable in our language, as shown in the word *jit-jai*, which means both heart and mind, soul and spirit. The state of the mind reflects the condition of the heart, and vice versa. The two are not split and do not function in isolation.

While cultures in the West subscribe to the philosophy "I think, therefore, I am," Thai people are more aptly characterized by the statement "we feel, therefore, we are." Not only are we concerned about our own feelings, we are even more so concerned about the feelings of others, for we do not exist in isolation but in relationship to all those around us. Each individual is an integral part of his or her environment and not separate from it. Therefore, maintaining social harmony and a heartfelt state of peaceful coexistence are very important values in our society.

The following commonly used compound words and phrases exemplify how we Thai people comprehend the world with our hearts. To "understand" someone or something we use *kao-jai*, which means to "enter the heart," and when we misunderstand, we *kao-jai-pit*, or "enter the heart wrongly." These terms apply whether the understanding pertains to a human relationship and an emotional expression or to the intellect, such as understanding technical information and business instructions.

When we make a decision to take a certain course of action, we "fall into our heart" (*dtoklohng-jai*), and when we change our mind, we "change our heart" (*bplien-jai*). When we approach our work with interest, we "take our heart and put it into" that work (*ow-jai-sai*), but when we can't concentrate and get distracted, we are "not putting our heart" where it should be (*mai-ow-jai-sai*). When we see eye-to-eye with a friend, we share the "same heart" (*jai-diow-gkan*), and when we trust someone, we can "place our heart" with that person (*wahng-jai*). When we try to uplift and give encouragement, we give "strength and energy to the heart" (*gkämlâng-jai*), and when we allow our children to make their own choices, we say to them "*Dtahm-jai*," or "Follow your heart." When we are generous and kind to others, we have a "good heart" (*jai-dee*), but when we are selfish, our heart is "narrow" (*jai-kaep*). When we feel let down or disappointed, our heart is "heavy" (*nak-jai*), but when we are joyful, our heart feels "cheerful and refreshing" (*cheun-jai*).

There are hundreds of other heart expressions in common usage, and new combinations continually emerge as people spontaneously attempt to express their inner states and processes. *Jai* is tangible; it can be felt. The heart that beats in our chest is none other than *hua-jai* ("head of the heart"). It keeps us alive and is the place where our soul and spirit reside.

HEART CULTURE, "SOUL FOOD"

SOME IMPORTANT HEART VALUES

Of the many heart values important in Thai culture, there are three on the top of the list that are difficult to explain, for there are no close English equivalents. The first is *näm-jai*, "water that flows from the heart." This refers to the genuine, unconditional generosity that comes straight from the heart, without agenda, without ulterior motivation for gain or expectation of return. Through my years of travel, I have been deeply moved by the warmth and overwhelming flowingness of *näm-jai* from rural folk.

The second heart value of great importance in Thai society is *gkrehng-jai*. *Gkrehng* can be translated as "to be in awe of" or "to fear." This "fear" is not so much the feeling of being afraid of someone as it is a quality of reverence, respect and high regard and an implication of social boundaries. When you *gkrehng-jai*, you have consideration for someone, and this is shown in considerate behavior toward that person. You may, for instance, be reluctant to impose on someone by asking for a favor, or you may refrain from doing something that you feel may overextend your boundary or cause someone embarrassment or to "lose face." This person for whom you have high regard may in turn reciprocate with considerate behavior toward you. *Gkrehng-jai* is a very important value in maintaining harmonious social relationships and one that has a protective quality among the people involved. It accounts for the high degree of politeness and civility you see in exchanges among Thai people everywhere.

A third heart value is that of maintaining a "cool heart" (*jai-yen*) as opposed to a "hot heart" (*jai-ron*). A person who is *jai-yen* is patient, forgiving, accepting of the circumstances that life brings, easy-going and can stay calm and collected even in the face of provocation or distress. A hot-hearted person, on the other hand, is impatient, hot-tempered, easily provoked and prone to emotional upsets over seemingly small matters. Having a cool heart is often regarded as a sign of emotional maturity. In a culture that places great importance on social harmony, relationships and feelings, cultivating *jai-yen* is highly valued. In modern ways of conducting business, however, a person who has a hot heart is gaining favor because he or she has the temperament to demand quick responses from others and to get things done faster. A person with too cool a heart may not function well in such high-stress jobs.

Possessing *jai-yen* goes hand in hand with the easy-going attitude of *mai bpen rai*, which universally permeates the Thai culture. *Mai pen rai* means "it doesn't matter," "it's all right," "it's fine and okay," "never mind," and so on, reflecting a penchant to go with the flow of things and not to hold on to expectations and disappointments. Thai people brush aside things that don't turn out well with a "*mai bpen rai*," saying it with a smile and moving on to something else that may provide just as much satisfaction. If there is little one can do to change things, saying "*mai bpen rai*" may be preferable to pursuing the matter, especially if the change may impose on someone else's feelings. If you visit Thailand, be sure to practice a *mai bpen rai* attitude along with a big smile, and you will endear yourself to the gentle and easy-going people. Give your linear, analytical mind a vacation and experience this "Land of Smiles" with your heart. Keep your heart cool, too; the weather and food are hot enough so that you won't need any extra heat to spoil your days there.

FOOD FOR SOUL AND SPIRIT

Because Thai people value social harmony and relationships so highly, we delight in spending time with friends and loved ones, coworkers and acquaintances. We like company; we enjoy sharing. Because we enjoy good food, there is no better way to spend time with friends than sharing a good meal or snack. There are lots of dining opportunities available, as noodle shops, sidewalk cafes, rice shops, street hawkers and fine neighborhood restaurants can be found on just about every block. As we nibble and dine away, the food nourishes not only our bodies but our souls as well; it is "soul food" when shared in a heart culture.

Food has always held a central place in the many celebrations and festivals that are woven into the tapestry of Thai culture. Special dishes are prepared to mark these events, and many of them have symbolic significance related to the meanings of the occasions. Rites of passage and important milestones in life from birth to death are always occasions to feast. Even after death the feasting continues, as relatives send off food offerings to the departed souls of loved ones.

One festival in the south pays homage to the departed souls of ancestors and friends who have yet to find their way to a peaceful incarnation. During the fifteen-day period of the festival, all the *bprehd* (ancestors who have been damned to hell) are permitted to return to visit the world. Relatives prepare food offerings to make merit so that their suffering may be eased. Among the special foods is *kanom lah*, a sweet treat comprised of fine threads of batter, woven like a thin mat in the wok. This food is made so that the ancestors can have something they can eat. The *bprehd* are "hungry ghosts" with very tiny mouths like needles, and although they are very big—some as tall as palm trees—they can only suck in very small things a little at a time.

Kanom lah is a special treat for the living, too. There are always a few food stalls at temple fairs in the south where one can watch the sweet treat made by sprinkling batter quickly over the surface of a heated wok through the many tiny holes etched into the bottom of a metal cup. The big sheet of cooked woven threads is than removed from the wok skillfully with the aid of a stick and folded. Vendors making and selling *kanom lah* can also be seen daily outside Wat Mahataht in the old city of Nakon Si Tammarahj, the south's most sacred temple and an important pilgrimage point for people from all over the country. It is believed to be the ancient site from which Buddhism spread to other parts of the country.

Thai people also take care to respect, feed and coexist peacefully with other spirits in the unseen realm, including guardian spirits of the land and nature spirits. We perceive our physical existence and the material world as representing only a small dimension of the vast universe; greater still is the ethereal world where spirits and the vital essences of things dwell. These entities have occupied our living and working spaces long before us, so it is important when we move to a new home or place of business that we acknowledge their presence by setting up a spirit house for them in an auspicious location and invite them to bless and protect us. Should there be malevolent energies lurking about, we hope our acknowledgment and goodwill offerings will appease them. Just as we would not want intruders to trespass on our land, we make sure that we do not trespass on the space of our spirit homemates.

Every day, all around Thailand, people light incense and candles and take a moment of silent prayer before the spirit shrine. Flowers, food and drink are offered on a regular basis. On special days on the lunar calendar, more elaborate offerings are presented; on some occasions, feasts of many courses are religiously prepared and placed on tables in front of the spirit house. This food is later gathered to feed the family of human residents. Blessed by the essence of the spirits, it is believed to provide spiritual as well as physical nourishment.

Spirit houses grace the land everywhere, from the gardens of elegant mansions to crowded shop houses in the inner city. Some of these shrines are simple structures of wood, miniatures of the humble dwellings of country folk. Others are beautifully detailed and built like temples. Places of business usually have larger shrines that house the omniscient, many-armed Brahmin deity. Fresh flower garlands are draped over him daily along with offerings of fruit and other food. He likes coconut, so fresh young coconuts with their tops already chopped open and straws inserted are usually included. He likes elephants, too, and is most often surrounded by carved wooden pachyderms of varying sizes. Brahma grants favors, and people whose wishes have been fulfilled return with more food to keep their part of the bargain. When big fortunes have been granted, scrumptious feasts, complete with dancing girls in glittering costumes, are laid out before him in joyous celebration.

Every town and city also has a spirit shrine to house her guardian spirit. There is always a flurry of activities around these shrines as residents of the town or city come to make offerings and ask for favors. The city shrine in Bangkok is very festive almost every day; it's a great place to catch a free show of classical dancing. Among the offerings may be piles of boiled eggs, whole cooked pig's head, whole cooked chickens and big slabs of meat.

I witnessed a ceremony early one morning many years ago by the Bping River in Chiang Mai. A Brahmin priest was performing the opening ceremony for the boat-racing competition, a major event of the city's very colorful Loy Gkratong Festival during the full moon in November. A long table with all sorts of food offerings stood in front of him. While the athletes gathered behind him with heads bowed, incense sticks protruding from the folded palms of their hands and a single cord of unspun cotton encircling them in unity, the priest invoked a multitude of spirits, inviting them to come and bless the event. He chanted almost a half hour's worth of names, spirits from time immemorial through recorded history up to the present. What a feast that must have been for all the unseen attendees!

Another soul-nourishing practice of giving food can be witnessed early every morning throughout the kingdom. Saffron-robed monks, barefoot and with shaven heads, quietly leave the temples with their alms bowls to "beg" for their daily sustenance. They have taken vows not to own material possessions so that they may discover that peace and happiness come from within rather than without. Food is considered such a possession, so they are at the mercy of lay people to feed them. In turn, villagers gain an opportunity to practice generosity and to make merit to improve the quality of their lives. Every day as they rise with the dawn, the first thing many devout Buddhists do is prepare food—prayerfully and reverently—to fill the alms bowls of the monks who wander by. The young monks they feed could be their own sons or their neighbors' sons, who have taken their vows to learn humility and the values of human relationships, and as an act of merit-making to better the lives of their parents.

Young Coconut (*Ma-prao Awn*)

This heartwarming exchange early every morning demonstrates the closely-knit interrelationships among the people of Thailand's Buddhist society. The Buddha's wise teachings tell us that we do not exist in isolation but in relationship with everything and everyone around us. We all belong to one great unity. By giving, by practicing generosity and loving kindness, our souls are nourished, for what we selflessly put out into the world will eventually recycle and come back to us. When *näm-jai* is universally embraced, everyone is fed and nourished and our collective energies work to make the world a more wholesome place.

AN
EXPLANATION
OF PHONETICAL
SPELLINGS

The Thai language is tonal and has its own script. Because it has many sounds not found in the English language, the task of representing Thai words with English letters is very challenging. The official system now in use in most publications has many flaws, which have led to the mispronunciation of many Thai words. For instance, the island of *Phuket* (pronounced Poo-ghet), a renowned tourist destination, has become the subject of much joking for tourists who unknowingly pronounce it like an obscenity.

In this book, I have attempted to spell Thai words as phonetically as possible, according to common American pronunciation. (One notable exception is the spelling of the name of the country and her people. *Thai* is correctly pronounced as one would the English word "tie" and not "thigh," but I have kept the accepted English spelling.) My spelling, therefore, may be very different from that of other cookbooks, travel books and newspapers, but I hope it will will help you to pronounce many Thai words in a way easier for Thai people to understand. The following clarifies some of the sounds as they are represented in this book:

k   hard sound as used in the English language. In the official system, this is represented with *kh* and called an "articulated k."

gk   neither a *g* nor a *k* sound but somewhere in between. This is represented with *k* in the official system and called "an unarticulated k."

p   as used in the English language. In the official system, this is represented with *ph* and called an "articulated p." (*Never* use the "f" sound to pronounce Thai words beginning with *ph*.)

bp   neither a *b* nor a *p* sound but somewhere in between. This is represented with *p* in the official system and called an "unarticulated p."

t   as used in the English language. In the official system, this is represented with *th* and called an "articulated t." (*Never* use the soft "th" sound to pronounce Thai words beginning with *th*.)

ä   the vowel sound as in "sum," "numb," "come"

a, â   the vowel sound as in sun, fun, run. *Man* would be pronounced as in the first syllable in "Monday;" *lak* would be pronounced the same way as "luck," *pak* as "puck," *pad* as in the first syllable in "puddle," etc.

ae   the "a" sound as in such words as "mad," "pad," "dad" in common American pronunciation, or the vowel sound as in "care" without articulating the "r"

ah   as in the interjection "ah;" or the vowel sound in "calm" without articulating the "l;" represented with *aa* under the official system

ai   as in "I" or "eye"

ao   as in "now," "how," "cow"

ow   same as *ao* but shorter

eh   as in "hey," "gray," "say"

eu   as in "her" or "occur" without articulating the "r" at the end

u   short *oo* sound

METRIC CONVERSION TABLE

LIQUID MEASURES

U.S. Measures	Fluid Ounces	Imperial Measures	Milliliters
1 teaspoon	$\frac{1}{8}$	1 teaspoon	5
2 teaspoons	$\frac{1}{4}$	1 dessertspoon	10
1 tablespoon	$\frac{1}{2}$	1 tablespoon	15
2 tablespoons	1	2 tablespoons	30
$\frac{1}{4}$ cup	2	4 tablespoons	56
$\frac{1}{3}$ cup	$2\frac{2}{3}$		80
$\frac{1}{2}$ cup	4		110
$\frac{2}{3}$ cup	5	$\frac{1}{4}$ pint / 1 gill	140
$\frac{3}{4}$ cup	6		170
1 cup / $\frac{1}{2}$ pint	8		225
$1\frac{1}{4}$ cups	10	$\frac{1}{2}$ pint	280
$1\frac{1}{2}$ cups	12		420
2 cups / 1 pint	16	generous $\frac{3}{4}$ pint	450
$2\frac{1}{2}$ cups	20	1 pint	560
3 cups / $1\frac{1}{2}$ pints	24		675
$3\frac{1}{2}$ cups	27		750
$3\frac{3}{4}$ cups	30	$1\frac{1}{2}$ pints	840
4 cups / 2 pints / 1 quart	32		900
$4\frac{1}{2}$ cups	36		1000/1 liter
5 cups	40		1120
6 cups / 3 pints	48	scant $2\frac{1}{2}$ pints	1350
7 cups	56	$2\frac{3}{4}$ pints	1600
8 cups / 2 quarts	64	$3\frac{1}{4}$ pints	1800
9 cups	72	$3\frac{1}{2}$ pints	2000/2 liters
10 cups / 5 pints	80	4 pints	2250

SOLID MEASURES

U.S. and Imperial	Metric Equivalent	U.S. and Imperial	Metric Equivalent
1 oz.	25 g.	12 oz. / $\frac{3}{4}$ lb.	350 g.
$1\frac{1}{2}$ oz.	40 g.	16 oz. / 1 lb.	450 g.
2 oz.	50 g.	$1\frac{1}{4}$ lb.	575 g.
3 oz.	60 g.	$1\frac{1}{2}$ lb.	675 g.
$3\frac{1}{2}$ oz.	100 g.	$1\frac{3}{4}$ lb.	800 g.
4 oz. / $\frac{1}{4}$ lb.	110 g.	2 lb.	900 g.
5 oz.	150 g.	$2\frac{1}{4}$ lb.	1000/1 kg.
6 oz.	175 g.	3 lb.	1 kg. 350 g.
7 oz.	200 g.	4 lb.	1 kg. 800 g.
8 oz. / $\frac{1}{2}$ lb.	225 g.	$4\frac{1}{2}$ lb.	2 kg.
9 oz.	250 g.	5 lb.	2 kg. 250 g.
10 oz.	275 g.	6 lb.	2 kg. 750 g.

OVEN TEMPERATURE EQUIVALENTS

Fahrenheit	Celsius	Gas Mark	Heat of Oven
225°	110°	$\frac{1}{4}$	Very cool
250°	120°	$\frac{1}{2}$	Very cool
275°	140°	1	Cool
300°	150°	2	Cool
325°	160°	3	Moderate
350°	180°	4	Moderate
375°	190°	5	Moderately hot
400°	200°	6	Moderately hot
425°	220°	7	Hot
450°	230°	8	Hot
475°	240°	9	Very Hot

$\mathcal{I}$NDEX

Recipe titles are noted in bold type.